HELP!
WHAT'S THE SECRET TO
LEADING ENGINEERS?

7 insights for leading smart people in the real-world

TREVOR MANNING

CONTENTS

PROLOGUE

My motivation for writing this book is to help others become better leaders. The approach I have used is to share my insights and mistakes and my overall goal is to help my readers ensure that their success at work contributes to their success in life.

This is the first book I am publishing on leadership. I plan to write many more but I need your help. Without the marketing resources of an international publisher, your review and feedback is the primary means that will make a difference. Please do review the book and provide me with feedback once you have read it.

Mark Twain said, "*The man who does not read good books has no advantage over the man who cannot read them.*" I am a believer in lifelong learning and think that reading books opens up a world of ideas, thoughts and insights, that helps us navigate our way through life.

ACKNOWLEDGEMENTS

I would like to thank my wife Berry, who has spent countless hours listening to my ideas, reviewing my material, editing the book and providing me with the help, support and encouragement I needed to persevere with writing this book series.

I would also like to thank all my work colleagues and many training delegates, who over the years have provided the real-world, university-of-life stories and testing ground for the material in these books.

INSIGHT 1

LEADERSHIP STARTS IN THE MIND

Leadership effectiveness starts in your head. *Undoing 200 years of management thinking is the key to leading smart people.*

*The field of management started in the industrial revolution, where managers eliminated the **thinking** element from work, in order to improve efficiencies. In today's workplace, technology is advancing incredibly fast, and manufacturing itself is largely done by machines. Workers are not just obeying instructions or following step-by-step guides - they often know more about the job itself than their managers do. Workers are also expected to innovate, to show initiative, to please customers and add business value. These functions are historically the responsibility of management. The thinking element has been added back to work - everyone knows it, but the way the workplace is set up can seem to contradict it. Team members end up wondering why their management don't address the things that they can see are so obvious to improve and managers wonder why team members don't show more accountability in getting the desired results - whatever it takes!*

*Leadership is now required at all levels in the company. Management guru, the late Peter Drucker, called these skilled, thinking workers **knowledge workers**.*

Knowledge-workers add most of their value through working smarter. They usually know how to do the task aspect of their job. Where they need help is in understanding what the ultimate purpose of those outputs are, so they can apply their smart thinking to get a better business outcome. Knowledge-workers often find it demotivating to have a supervisory boss who tells them what to do, how to do it and even when to do it. Knowledge-workers work best when they are encouraged to think! Knowledge-workers do not want a supervisory boss, but interestingly knowledge-workers actually do still want a manager. They want someone that can help guide them to apply their skills and knowledge to maximise business value. They also want someone who shows an interest in their career development, so that the skills they are learning are actually useful to their growth and development.

Businesses still do need managers too, as Google found out the hard way. In 2002 the founders experimented with a totally flat structure and they found it too hard to manage. Managers are required to ensure that at least the minimum standards and outputs are achieved.

So the challenge we face in a modern organisation is that fully empowered, cross functional teams operate simultaneously with a hierarchical, functionally-based organisational structure. The role of the manager has changed and so we need to adapt our view of leadership to this complex reality.

Leading knowledge-workers requires a different mindset - a mindset where you are not the boss.

1.1 When did bosses go extinct?

The black rhino is now officially extinct - was the headline in one of my recent social media news feeds. Having grown up in South Africa, living near fantastic game parks where I had close contact with the sister species, the white rhino, it is sad to think these mighty creatures have been hunted to extinction for their horn, which is no more than mattered hair! Not that it makes it any less sad, but it turns out this is the third time the announcement has gone global. The first official announcement was in 2011, when after no sightings in a decade, the International Union for Conservation of Nature officially announced them extinct. In November 2013, CNN ran the two-year old story, and it was assumed it had only just happened, and the story went viral. In November 2015, this story hit the headlines, once again.

The reality in the workplace is that for most skilled workers they no longer have a boss! The supervisory manager is officially extinct! All the facts around them indicate that this is true but the lack of an authoritative official announcement, and misunderstandings about what the organisational chart means, makes it hard to accept. In my consulting business, I constantly hear cries from engineers that their bosses know less than they do. They complain that their bosses do not understand their workload. They complain that all the problems that they escalate do not get resolved! They seem constantly surprised that their boss is not acting as a supervisor.

Skilled staff need to realise they are their own boss, for the task element of their role. Usually they have the skills and expertise to complete their work and they understand the operational problems better than anyone else in the business. Who better, therefore, to solve them? Bosses are there to own the outcomes of a specific functional area of the business. Their role is to support, encourage and drive the right business results. The team usually knows how to do their job. They want direction or support to produce the right plans and ensure the right outcomes.

Today's leaders are similar to the coach on a sports team. Coaches do not play the game but they are responsible for the game plan (strategic plan), the tactics (operational plans), putting the right players in the game (hiring and developing the team members) and running up the side of field shouting encouragement and direction to win the game (leading the team to business outcomes).

Because the traditional supervisory boss has gone extinct, many businesses suffer from lack of leadership, rather than too much of it. Confused managers abdicate their role as a leader for fear of micro-managing. They develop self-doubt as they reflect on how little they know about the actual work their team does, and so they stay out the way, but then vacillate to command-and-control when things don't go as they expect. Confused managers often claim that their teams are fully empowered and blindly trust them to do what is necessary, with no evidence that this is actually the case. To make matters worse, some knowledge workers do not understand the role of their bosses and so wait for their managers to lead everything. It can end up with no-one leading, and the business becoming a victim of its problems.

Leadership is needed at all levels! A company where leadership has gone extinct is likely to have staff who are extremely busy, extremely disorganised, having no operational discipline, and no doubt producing few actual outputs that can drive up company profits or increase customer satisfaction.

1.2 Footprints in the sand

I went for an early morning beach run today.

When I turned around to make my return journey, I could clearly see the path I had taken, as no-one else was on the beach. Without me knowing it, my footsteps had left a clear demarcation of my journey in the hard, wet sand.

Three observations came to mind:

As we go through our day we leave footprints behind, without even being aware of it. I committed to making sure that my footprints, left with whoever I met today, would be positive ones. Leadership is all about making a positive difference. In fact, management guru, the late Peter Drucker said, *"Our mission in life should be to make a positive difference, not to prove how smart or right we are."*

I also noticed that my footprints were washed away in some places. Obviously, I had misjudged the maximum tide line that I needed to run in order to keep my Nike shoes dry! Yet because the tide didn't rush up that far, at the specific time I had passed that point, I was blissfully unaware of my error. I wondered how often we are actually making errors in judgement without being aware of it. We might be wrong more often than we realise, as associated consequences do not always show up simultaneously to warn us. Getting comfortable with being wrong is a key element to maturing as a leader.

Lastly, and related to the observation above, it also occurred to me that the main benefit in observing my error in judgement was to adjust my path higher up the beach for the return journey. I could do nothing about the steps I had already taken. The opportunity from learning from my mistakes was not to dwell on my error and scold myself for being wrong. The opportunity was to apply my new learning to the future and ensure a better outcome. This *learning*, rather than *judging* mindset, where mistakes are seen as useful feedback, rather than signs of failure, is critical to being an effective leader.

As I ran home I challenged myself to live the lessons of the footprints in the sand!

1.3 What can a zebra teach us about leadership?

What colour is a zebra - black with white stripes or white with black stripes?

In November 2016 I was running two leadership courses at Wisconsin University. I left on the day Donald J Trump was declared the 45th President of the United States. Many of the American people I met were in shock. They were convinced he would not have won, based on polling predictions, as well as the common view expressed in their social media feeds or conversations in their social groups. Even stalwart Trump supporters may have felt some personal doubts on his likely success based on media predictions.

So why did the forecasters get it so wrong? The error in our thinking is to frame a complex situation in black and white terms. If we apply logical, but binary thinking, we would conclude that major groups of people would all vote one way or the other based on a specific variable: For example, if the media aired an interview where Trump made negative remarks about women, binary thinking would conclude all women would be unhappy about that and, therefore, all women would not vote for him. The same incorrect assumptions could be made about Hispanics. The situation is far more complex than that. There are many other variables, such as loyalty to a specific party, political or religious issues that may or may not be supported, deep rooted personal belief systems that are addressed more strongly by one candidate than another, or sometimes it may be a protest vote where people are deliberately voting for a candidate that they do not want to actually win! These factors add complexity to decisions made on binary thinking. Similar errors in prediction were made in the United Kingdom with Britain's exit from the European Union - dubbed Brexit. Actual voting invoked many other variables that were not considered in the analysis that incorrectly predicted the outcome.

1. So, what lessons can we learn to apply to our own leadership, to avoid the flawed cognitive reasoning distortion of black and white thinking? Stop looking for right and wrong decisions. In mathematical equations, there is a right answer. In management, complex business problems seldom have a right answer - there are just less-wrong options. A good decision often has more positives, and less negatives when judged in the light of a successful outcome, but it doesn't make the rejected option wrong. The harsh reality is a so-called right decision may have achieved the desired outcome through luck. Decisions can only be judged as right or wrong in hindsight, therefore, at the time they are made, it's more helpful to consider them viable working options, rather than the right decision. Scott McNealy,

co-founder of SUN Microsystems said *"I am less worried about 'making the right decision' and spend much more time and energy ensuring that any decision I make turns out right."*

2. Bosses are not good or bad. They are complex human beings who have strengths and weaknesses and many of these traits impact a far wider audience than just us, or our team. The problem is once we apply black and white filters to people, we selectively pick data points that support our polarised belief. By thinking in shades of grey we can more objectively evaluate our boss's behaviour and work together more effectively towards good business outcomes.

3. If we are not right about something it is really, really OK. In other words, let's stop trying to justify how right we are and welcome insights that we might be wrong. Engineers or other analytical thinkers such as accountants, or lawyers, really struggle with accepting this fact and, therefore, are often very defensive and closed to constructive feedback. It is hard to logically accept you may be wrong, as the moment you do accept your error, you become right about the fact you were previously wrong. A better alternative is to become very comfortable accepting that the current belief and set of opinions you have may well be wrong. This allows you to be open to any new insights or information that may lead to you changing your mind about something. Being more open-minded will make you a more effective leader as you will continually learn and grow.

1.4 Defending my right to annoy myself

I have just got back from a gruelling round-the-world trip from Australia to the US (via the UK) and back, spending over 50 hours just sitting on planes. I have learnt that in order to cope with this trip, it's all about mindset. If you sit down and start counting the hours of how long you have to endure this suffering, you will suffer. If you sit down and think how wonderful it is to have a whole day with nobody demanding anything of you, a whole day to read a book, watch a movie, catch up on a few emails, be waited on hand and foot, somehow it doesn't seem quite so bad.

But controlling your own mind isn't always easy. After two particularly uncomfortable, internal US flights, on old planes with no entertainment and no free food or drinks, my positive mindset about the upcoming 15-hour flight back to Australia was being challenged, especially as I got to sit in front of one of those nightmare passengers. He had barged his way to his seat and kept blocking the aisle as he jumped up and down to retrieve items from his oversized bag, filling the overhead hand luggage tray. To make things worse, he then started banging his TV monitor that was of course located on the back of my chair - because he couldn't get the touch screen technology to work. He shouted loudly to his wife for hours about how annoyed he was with everything and everybody. He marched up the aisles demanding the food arrive quicker. He rang his bell countless times because the technology was failing him and eventually after 5 hours of this, I had had enough. I turned around and scolded him like he was a naughty schoolboy. By then I had really worked myself up emotionally, and was furious that this man had ruined my journey!

Reflecting on this later, it occurred to me that I had allowed this to happen. Apart from a couple of fellow sufferers who shared my frustration and almost applauded me for my outburst, most people had just ignored him and were peacefully sleeping or were deeply enthralled by the movie they were watching. I was the one waiting in angry anticipation for every poke of my chair, every verbal outburst, every push of his attendants' button – and every time, my blood boiled. In my mind, I fully justified my anger, and knew that when I told this story to anyone else who travelled, they would understand my anger too. I had a right to be angry and I was going to indulge it!

Realising it was my mindset that was the real problem, I got up, replaced the flat batteries in my noise cancelling headset, got out my iPhone, selected my favourite playlist from my Spotify music downloads, and drifted off to sleep to the sound of Coldplay's *Fix you...*

At that moment, I realised that actually, it wasn't about fixing him, it was about fixing me!

In management, especially when managing upwards, we often allow ourselves to become victims of our situation too. Instead of calmly working out a plan of how to improve our situation, and learning to accept those parts that we cannot change, we become angry at the situation. We become angry at the company for not hiring enough staff. We become angry at our bosses for not fixing the problems. We even become angry at customers for not being more reasonable. We know what we are doing is not improving the situation, but we are more concerned with justifying our righteous anger, than addressing the problem to create a winning outcome.

So, next time you are feeling annoyed by everyone else, ask yourself if you are just defending your right to annoy yourself....

INSIGHT 2

LEADERSHIP IS ABOUT CHANGE

Leadership is all **about change**. *If things are fine just the way they are, why would anyone need a leader? Leadership starts with identifying and communicating a future state in such a way that others want to get there.*

The more visionary and exciting the future state is portrayed, the more likely it is to get people to want to follow. Good leaders deliberately get people emotionally connected to a better future.

Dissatisfaction with the present is not a bad thing. Constructive discontent creates the desire to change.

When leading teams, people often want to ensure there is no conflict. Yet healthy conflict is needed if high performance is the aim. Have you ever watched a sports game where there is no constructive conflict? Team members demand urgent and intense responses from one another in the pursuit of a common goal. The key word is constructive. Conflict is good if it is done with respect for others and in pursuit of a jointly desired outcome.

Leadership involves inspiring, influencing and driving others to **change the current situation** *and move to a better future state by achieving the mutual goals that have been set.*

2.1 Changing the outcome

Recently I had a fantastic holiday in South Africa. What a beautiful country and what a land of opportunity. *But it seems there is a problem.* Unrest and crime continues; power blackouts are the norm and economic growth is disappointing.

There is no shortage of people who will complain about what is wrong and who are *waiting* for someone to fix it – the government, their company, their managers or even God. Finding blame is easy, especially in a country that has such an appalling political history. And then there are those who are making a difference. They can see what needs to be fixed, they gather a team of people around them, and they do something positive – those people are the true leaders! South Africa could be the most promising of all developing nations, if more people adopted a leadership mindset to drive the changes necessary to improve things, rather than commentating on how bad it all is, and blaming others.

Mother Teresa was asked once how she hoped to help so many millions of people in poverty. Her answer was inspiring: *"Never worry about numbers. Help one person at a time and always start with the person nearest you."*

In business today, leadership training is required at all levels. *Shravanti Chakraborty,* head of HR Operations at *Google,* commented recently that all their staff - even software developers whose primary role is writing code - are interviewed for leadership skills. Why do they need leadership training? Because leadership is about change. Non-leaders may identify that they are not clear on the business outcome of the code they are writing, and complain about it. Leaders will make a concerted effort to find out what business outcome is required and will not allow themselves to be a victim of someone else's poor communication.

When implementing change, there are some things to watch out for:

1. When change occurs, it is like melting an ice cube. It is frightening how quickly an organisation can grind to a halt, even under the rumour of change. Because a lot of work is generated based on thinking about desired outcomes, when the goal posts move people can feel there is no point in continuing playing. Refreeze the ice cube as quickly as possible

2. Communicate why change is necessary. People often focus on how the changes need to be implemented before getting buy-in to why the changes are happening. You are far more likely to get support for change once everyone understands how it could improve things in the future.

3. Be clear about what doesn't change. It is seldom the case that everything needs to change. Some things may be running along really well and you don't want the planned changes to upset what is working well. Make it really clear that certain things need to be kept the way they were.

A leader finds out why the problem exists. A leader makes a plan to sort it out. A leader communicates to everyone that needs to know what is happening to fix the problem. A leader changes the outcome!

2.2 Accountability - is it all my fault?

Unexpected events and accidents happen every day. Machinery breaks down, car accidents occur, unexpected weather events happen and stock markets fall in unpredicted ways. Life is not as predictable as we like to think.

Leadership is about predicting an outcome and getting people to get behind achieving it. So how do we deal with this apparent contradiction?

A key element of leadership is accountability. Some people think this is all about who is to blame. But is it? The Oxford English dictionary suggests being accountable is *being expected to justify actions or decisions*. In business, a firm distinction needs to be made between responsibility and accountability. Unfortunately, business literature contradicts itself, in terms of which of these words is unique and which is shared. For example, project managers often use the RACI model for sign-off of a task. They list those who are Responsible, Accountable, Consulted or Informed. Only one person can be ultimately Accountable in this model. The Responsible persons are those who complete the tasks and therefore, responsibility can be shared. In other literature the definition is the exact opposite - according to this competing view, only one person can be responsible, while everyone is accountable. Whichever definition you agree with, the principle is what is important.

In my view, leadership accountability is really an attitude where you are holding *yourself accountable* to outcomes. It is a mindset, that whatever has happened - whether it is your fault or not – it does indeed have something to do with you, you co-own the outcome, and you are committed to finding solutions to solve it. It is the opposite of the attitude *not my problem*.

Responsibility, in my view, is something an organisation defines that specifies your boundaries of ownership. The job description usually lists things that you, and often you only, are expected to complete. In a sense, it is the things that you are obliged to respond to, because of your job responsibilities. It is ownership as defined by others.

Accountability is broader than responsibility as it is about your mindset that takes ownership for an overall result, even if it lies outside your defined set of responsibilities. Someone who feels accountable to the company will help with any customer problem in the interests of the overall company outcome, whether or not it is within their defined set of responsibilities. Accountability is an attitude that says, *it is not my fault, and I am not to blame, but I am here to help fix it.*

2.3 Shine your mirror and improve your leadership

I am often amazed by how blind we are to our own faults especially when we are busy criticising others. I recently ran a leadership seminar for an international company and during one of the sessions the more senior people in the room started explaining how their bosses on the other side of the Atlantic Ocean were the real problem.

By the senior leaders kicking off the discussion this gave permission for others to wade in and enthusiastically criticise the executives in the company and blame them for all their woes. They explained how the behaviour of these executives made it very difficult for them to motivate their own teams. What they had failed to notice was how their own behaviour was having a negative impact on the less senior people in the room. Watching their own leaders admit that nothing would get better with the current executive leadership in place - something which clearly was not about to change - was very demotivating for them, and it was clear from their body language that they blamed their bosses sitting in front of them, rather than the more senior ones 10,000 miles away.

As leaders, we should focus on the things we *can* change, rather than the things we *can't*.

What we can change is staring right back at us, when we look in the mirror. So, before you start trying to change those around you, shine your mirror and improve your leadership.

2.4 How do I change others?

Leadership is about change and that change starts with ourselves. But how do we get others to change? Joseph Grenny in his excellent book *Influencer*, points out, *"When you understand the forces behind any behaviour along with the strategies to change it, you hold within your grasp the power to change anything."*

We often assume if someone is not changing in the direction we want him or her to, it's because they do not have the personal motivation to change. The authors of *Influencer* point out that it is both *Ability* as well as *Motivation* that play a part.

1. At a personal level, we need to address if the person has the ability to make the change. Our motivation for something often increases if our competence increases. We may first need to validate our assumption that the other person actually knows how to change, before assuming they are not changing because they don't want to change.

2. At a social level, we can help to create lasting change through social influence. Psychologists have studied how children will make better food choices if those foods are linked to their heroes. People will often mimic the behaviours of people they respect, so we need to lead by example and create role models who can endorse the changes required.

3. Lastly, we shouldn't underestimate the power of systems to enforce change. We are learning a lot about the power of propinquity - in other words, how things around us influence our behaviour. Studies have shown that purely moving the location of food at a buffet has a big impact on food selection. Seating arrangements for our staff and the physical environment

and systems we use at work can have a massive impact on enforcing the desired changes.

The authors of this research found that it is the mix of strategies that leads to effective results. It is not a question of deciding whether to lead the changes through personal influence or systematic changes. It is about using a combination of personal, social and system strategies and addressing both ability and motivation in each category, that leads to meaningful and lasting change.

INSIGHT 3

PEOPLE ARE NOT A PROGRAMMABLE RESOURCE

People are not programmable resources *- they are complex emotional creatures that have survived through collaboration. Few people could actually survive if they were totally alone. They certainly would not have the relatively rich lifestyle we enjoy today, without the contribution of others.*

Leading people involves building effective teams. The idea of teamwork sometimes invokes an image of a group of people passively supporting the one person who is actually doing the work. In the knowledge-worker workplace, while the work itself is done alone, its real business contribution is limited without effective collaboration of a team of people. Companies that understand and implement this, find that people are their most valuable asset.

Teamwork is essential in a company to ensure that each functional area does not become siloed and produce outputs that do not contribute to the greater good. People within these teams have different personalities, and are motivated by different things.

There is no software program or mathematical model that can produce the right outcome. To achieve

business success, we need to understand how people
tick! We need to re-humanise the workplace.

3.1 Team building

I read a blog this week by UK-based motivational speaker, Phil Hesketh. In it, he refers to a recent study by Michael Norton of Harvard Business School that indicates that, the old adage *familiarity breeds contempt,* may actually be true. He points out that in the early stages of meeting someone, you look for similarities, and, therefore, the more you interact the more you like them. Later on, you discover the dissimilarities and so start to like them less. Hesketh concludes - "*it all comes down to balance. If you hang around with people for long enough, you'll eventually generate some mutual respect and discover common interests, even if they're not your type.*"

Teamwork is often misunderstood in the workplace. Managers run well-meaning team building exercises to build rapport. While fun on the day, it doesn't always have the desired effect back in the office. A popular team building approach is to go out and build rafts together. In a recent example, I heard the team were literally asked to walk on hot coals so you really get to know, trust and work with your colleagues. I have always been somewhat sceptical of this approach based on a *Team Olympics* team building exercise I did years ago. The goal was to build team rapport between two departments in the company, who were not seeing eye to eye. The day consisted of competing in various sport related activities adapted from Olympic events to be fun. The IT team were full of the stereotypical brilliant but *nerdy* types and the engineering team included some people who actually played sport at a national level. Whoever set the team building exercise up, obviously thought if we all got to know each other better, morale would improve.

It backfired horribly, as whereas previously there was at least mutual respect at a work level for each other's expertise and contributions, on the sports field, the competitive bully behaviour came out in the *jocks* and the *nerds* were ridiculed for having poor hand-eye co-ordination, something which in absolutely no way affected their work performance. Highlighting these differences in fact worsened team spirit back in the workplace. In contrast to this, I have worked on big projects, where the adversity faced by real workplace difficulties, in an environment where the end goal was clearly defined in terms of importance and urgency, actually pulled the team together very well, despite many differences in personality or out of work interests and abilities.

I am not suggesting all team building exercises are bad, but I do think there is sometimes an over emphasis on getting to know each other well outside of work, as a technique for improving team work, rather than building the team spirit in the workplace through clear, common goals and outcomes with a high tolerance for diversity of styles in how the job is done.

Marshall Goldsmith wrote an excellent article called '*Team Building without time-wasting*'. In the introduction, he insightfully summarises the dilemma of many leaders in the real-world. "*Many of today's leaders face a dilemma: as the need to build effective teams is increasing, the time available to build these teams is often decreasing. A common challenge faced by today's leaders is the necessity of building teams in an environment of rapid change with limited resources.*"

He suggests a number of practical steps to this process, summarised below:

1. Establish a baseline. Get the team to rate how well they are working together currently. This establishes buy-in to the need to start the team-building process.

2. Focus on a few key behaviours. Marshall then facilitates each team member to have one-to-one conversations with each other team member, and identify a few key behavioural changes that would improve things.

3. Lastly, follow-up. A repeat survey is done within 6 months to establish if the improvements have actually been made. Discussions are held and lessons learnt. Commitment to continuing the process happens.

Instead of going off site to play games, it is often more effective to learn how to work together effectively in the workplace itself. When teams start operating effectively, the work itself becomes fun, people collaborate better to achieve the desired business results and this is the ultimate goal of team building.

3.2 People are not just resources

It is not uncommon to hear a project manager discussing the progress on a project and making a decision to reallocate resources from one team to another. The resource being referred to has a pulse and will invariably come with a raft of unique attributes including personal ambitions, viewpoints, and attitudes.

There is often an assumption in the workplace that people with a specific set of skills can be easily transferred from one area to another, and produce equal work to the other person with those skills. In terms of the task itself that may well be true, but anyone who has tried this in the real-world soon realises that people cannot be programmed like machines.

In mathematics, a series of logical steps leads you to a right answer.

Some people actually enjoy mathematics, precisely for this reason. It is unambiguous. *There is either a right answer or a wrong answer.* When technical people become managers, they will soon learn that when dealing with people, traditional logic seldom applies.

As managers, we are required to plan (make predictions), and make decisions. Being intelligent human beings we apply our thinking in a logical fashion. Aristotle taught us about syllogisms – or deductive reasoning. An *assertion* is either *affirmed* or *denied*. The 18th century English mathematician George Boole – whose work has subsequently been adapted to create Boolean logic used in computers - introduced us to the idea of deductive reasoning through mathematical equations.

Let us consider the following: IF A=1 AND B=2, THEN A+B=3. It doesn't matter how often we repeat this, or who completes the problem, we always get the same answer. The problem with dealing with people is things are more complex, and they can change.

Deliberately exaggerating my point to the point of absurdity, imagine if we applied logic to see if two staff members would work well together on a project.

IF Jack=Skill 1
AND Jill=Skill 2,
THEN Jack+Jill=Skill (1 +2)

We put them together on the project and it's a disaster! Why? It may be because Jack thinks his abilities in Skill 2 exceeds Jill's and, due to being offended about the choice of help offered, no longer even applies Skill 1. Predicting or modelling this inability of the two parties to work together is hard to do. It is often only after the two have failed to perform well together that we become aware of the motivational complexities. *Hindsight* is an exact science.

The reality is that there is no short cut to working with people. We need to abandon the thought that people are resources who can be programmed to perform repeated tasks in a predicted manner and re-humanise the workplace. Learning how to get the best out of people and creating an environment where people feel motivated to perform well, is a key part of leadership.

3.3 Managing above and below the line

Leaders often face a dilemma. When should they inspire people to greatness and when should they just demand that something is done, to ensure compliance? In broad-brush strokes, the former can be regarded as leadership, whereas the latter is supervisory management.

On the one hand, we know that the best way to get a desired outcome is for the team member to really commit to producing the end result. Getting buy-in and leading through inspiration, allows us to get the best out of people, often exceeding the results we could legitimately demand. An inspirational, supportive style of leadership helps already motivated people become the best that they can be.

On the other hand, we are sometimes dealing with someone who no longer believes in the goals of the business. How do you get buy-in from someone whose attitude stinks? What inspirational motivation can we provide someone who says, "*I just want to do the minimum I can get away with, draw my pay cheque and go home?*" In some cases, the person does not want to produce the end result and, therefore, is not committed to producing the outcome. In this case, the benefit of a directive style of management is that you can *at least* achieve compliance to the minimum standards and norms. To get improved performance, you could try to raise the compliance line, but it is impossible to mandate excellence that you cannot define, so you only ever get as good as you are able to define. The manager's own limited standards become the benchmark. Directive management implies that if you do exactly as you are told, you will meet the standards set by the supervisor. The standard set is what we call *the compliance line.*

It is important for leaders to know where the compliance line is. If someone is below the line, and has been operating below the line despite months of coaching and support, it may be time for more punitive measures. The message needs to be that unless their performance improves to get above the line there will be consequences. When leading people above the line, the message is that as soon as we have mastered this developmental area, we will work on the next area of improvement. It's a continual cycle of improvement – a bit like a golfer perfecting their swing. Nobody would assume that once a beginner was able to hit a 7-iron 150 yards down the fairway that they didn't need coaching anymore. On the other hand, if the person arrived late for their lessons and hadn't even hit a single ball at the driving range between lessons, you would assume that some directive *hard-talk*, rather than performance coaching was needed.

Being adaptive to be able to manage people above and below the line is what makes a manager a good leader!

3.4 Do motivational techniques really work?

My alarm went off and the battle began. *Trevor-the-Manager* had decided that I should go for a run and *Trevor-the-worker* was not having any of it.

"Get out of bed and go for your run as we agreed yesterday," barked the manager.

"No, its cold and dark. I don't want to," the worker replied.

"Listen, we agreed it was good for your health and it's a matter of discipline. Get up and do it now!"

At this point the worker in me realized they would have to come up with a cunning response or I would be pounding the pavement.

*"Now **you** listen! It is still dark and if I trip and fall I won't be able to run for weeks. It's actually a health risk to go running now. I will do it later!"* The manager in me was stumped. The worker had used the ultimate excuse card. How could you argue with health and safety? He was not being defiant, as he did say he would go later. To be reasonable and fair, the manager in me had to compromise.

"OK, but I don't want to hear any excuses later on that you were too busy or that the weather is bad."

Trevor-the-worker tucked back into bed and smiled knowingly;

"We'll see. I have another 8 hours to come up with my next killer excuse."

For anyone trying to achieve a goal there is an internal battle between the planner and the doer. Understanding this manager – worker relationship in ourselves, can teach us a lot about how to manage others. Achieving a goal requires a balance between two motivators: *Extrinsic drivers* that force us to do things we don't want to do; and *intrinsic drivers* that lead us to a new personal best, just because we really want to.

Here is a 3-step approach to consider:

1. Create a plan, which includes both a minimum measurable standard and a vision of the utopia outcome. The minimum standard is not subject to compromises and debates. It is a non-negotiable standard that we must meet. When my worker-self argues that I will run tomorrow, and gets away with it, it's

because I have not set a minimum standard for myself. The utopia goal is something I aspire to because I really want the outcome. Both goals are relevant: the first to at least achieve a minimum standard of compliance, the second to achieve high performance.

2. Create external pressure to meet this minimum standard by sharing it with others and even defining some consequences or rewards. This ensures that you at least get compliance to the basics of the plan through discipline, until it has become a habit - *Skipping my run today is not an option because I promised my partner that I would run at least three times a week, and today is Sunday and I have only run twice.* The worker in me has nowhere to go, as the manager in me is not going to listen to *any* arguments or excuses, come rain or shine. It's a simple question of whether I did it or not and I am too ashamed to admit that I couldn't achieve even the minimum standard set.

3. Visualise the utopia scenario and define some stretch goals that are more about the end result, than the discipline of getting there. What you want is for the motivation to be internalised. Identify what the true internal, personal driver is. External motivators can achieve compliance, but often not more. Internal motivation will encourage innovation, drive and determined commitment to achieve a personal best. While I am running, instead of finding an excuse to settle for mediocrity, I am visualising how fit and healthy I will be and push myself harder.

Motivating staff is a balance between defining the minimum compliance line and sharing the vision for excellence. Define and externally motivate for the minimum *Key Performance Indicators* (KPI's) to be met, and also share the inspirational goals of your team, to get buy-in and commitment to excellence.

Balancing external motivation techniques while nurturing intrinsic motivators is a key leadership skill.

3.5 Are Virtual Teams virtually failing

Sitting at a beachside café this week I was astounded to notice the number of people who were more engaged on their phones, than with the living, breathing people in front of them. No-one was actually talking on their phones – most were engaged in the non-real time world of email, playing games or posting updates on social media. Robots now train our kids to read and we can create an avatar to represent ourselves in virtual reality. Arguably social network sites like Facebook allow us to create a version of ourselves that we want to be, rather than the reality of who we truly are.

In management, few of us have our team members sitting in the same room, yet Lipnack and Stamps, authors of *Virtual Teams*, point to research that shows people stop collaborating if more than 50 foot apart. Without taking active steps to run these teams differently, they are doomed to failure.

Four key steps that will give virtual teams a chance of success are:

1. Communicate a clear and compelling goal, ideally in a face-to-face kick-off meeting. Teams need purpose, and a reason to care; otherwise they will merely comply to the minimum requirements rather than committing to the business outcomes, required by the team.

2. Confirm the desired deliverables required by the customer (internal or external), rather than those defined by the team itself, and measure the results by those standards (Key Performance Indicators or KPI's).

3. Agree when and how to meet in this virtual world, and provide regular progress updates on a shared medium, such as a collaboration website.

4. Be human! Successful teams work well when all team members are treated as unique human beings and not just as project resources. Having fun doing the job and celebrating success are all part of creating a motivating environment for teams to excel.

Virtual teams are here to stay! Being a good leader, requires us to adapt to the environment, not the other way around

INSIGHT 4

LEAD UP AND ACROSS

*Leadership is only 50% about managing your team - the rest is **Leading Up and Across** the organisation. In today's business world, few people have only one functional boss, who directs their day-to-day activities. The days of a traditional boss who was there to manage your priorities and workload, while also paving the way with all your stakeholders, are long gone.*

Most organisations have retained a functional hierarchy of authority, with clear reporting lines which are published in an organisational chart, but its real purpose should not be exaggerated. It certainly is important, and defines the formal reporting lines with pre-defined levels of authority, and functional responsibilities. What it does not define are the informal levels of support and escalation that are required to do anything that happens outside the narrow, core job role. It does not define the levels of influence required up and across the organisation. Knowledge workers are expected to develop those leadership skills themselves, at all levels in the organisation.

With flat structures and complex business structures spread across geographical and functional boundaries, we also end up having multiple bosses. In fact, anyone representing the legitimate needs of the three ultimate stakeholders: the company; the end customer; or the staff, can be considered a boss. Everybody in the chain that delivers something to their boss, is only doing it for that person to pass it onto the subsequent person, until it is delivered to one of these three primary stakeholders.

*A key insight when understanding what your boss wants - both your direct line manager, as well as your many virtual bosses up and across the business - is to reflect on what **their boss** wants. Bosses seldom want things for themselves, they only want them to give to somebody else. This is why a good strategy is to establish influence, two levels up and across the organisation, as a minimum. A key element of being an effective leader is to identify and prioritise the many virtual bosses that exist, and learn to network and influence anyone who can help or hinder your results.*

4.1 Why should I manage my boss?

Managing upwards is a critical skill in being an effective leader in the workplace. The whole idea of a boss is a somewhat old fashioned concept as it implies that somebody knows what you should be doing and is put in charge of making sure you do it. In the knowledge-era workplace, most bosses have no idea about what their employees actually do, so how can they ensure *that it is done properly*? Managers certainly cannot control outputs, as well as they could, when those outputs were tangible. Effective managers will empower their team members to make decisions, let them decide how to do their jobs and play a supportive role in getting the right outputs. This new style of management sometimes leads to the mistaken belief that the manager is no longer responsible for the outputs of the teams. They sit on the sides watching the action and hope it all works out. That is abdication, not empowerment.

There are many reasons why it is important to manage your boss. One key reason is to proactively re-engage a boss that has become an observer. The reality is your boss's boss is 100% clear who owns the outcome – it is your boss, not you. Considering it is not in your best interest that your boss fails, especially if that failure is caused by you, it is important to get your boss engaged in what you are doing and ensure they really understand what outputs to expect. Surprise is an ugly word for senior managers.

Managing your boss does not mean controlling your boss – in the same way that your boss does not control you. What managing upwards is about, is proactively addressing areas that your boss is not addressing. It is about finding out how you can be more effective in delivering to your boss what they need to deliver to their boss.

The question should not be, "*Why should I manage my boss?*", but instead "*Can I afford not to manage my boss?*"

4.2 Can I really manage my boss?

Peter Bregman, in the Harvard Business Review, quotes a story about a colleague, Paul, who got the perfect job but was threatening to quit. When asked why, he said, "*It's my boss – the CEO/founder. He's all over the place, shifting from one vision to the next. He's unfocused, unclear, unrealistic, and, most disturbingly, he's burning bridges with potential investors, as well as colleagues. He even reneged on a commitment he made to me, which I had already extended to other people. He's hurting the business and I'm worried about my reputation by affiliation."*

When running my management seminars, I get this same common objection: *"It's not me, that's the main problem, it's my boss."*

In Peter's blog, he talks about the courage to confront the issue, rather than walking away. Clear, direct communication is key! Generally, the problem stems from each party looking at the same facts from two different perspectives. Many assumptions are made on both sides, often without anyone confronting the real issue. In my coaching role, when I talk to bosses, they complain that their issues are not being prioritised - yet seldom do bosses get to the bottom of why this is so. Unless there is a genuine performance issue, the probability is that the team member genuinely believes that what they are working on, is a higher priority, and that they are working for the good of the business, rather than their boss. In this management era where empowerment is encouraged, clarifying *why* something is important, is the best way to get true commitment to the requested deliverable.

Bosses are human, and don't always get it right. Where we may have misaligned priorities, or feel that the bosses behaviours or demands are impeding progress for the business, we should have the courage to confront the issue, respectfully and openly.

Actively managing your boss and talking openly will at least bring the issues out into the open, and highlight the assumptions made by each party. It is only in extreme cases, that the alignment of purpose is structurally misaligned, in which case it's better for both parties to depart company.

In case you are wondering, the case mentioned in the opening section of this blog had a positive outcome after Paul had an open and frank conversation with the CEO...

4.3 A fishy tale about leadership

The student approached his professor and asked, *"What is the difference between leadership and management?"* The professor smiled broadly and said, *"I am going fishing on Saturday morning – come down to the lake and I will teach you the difference."*

Early the next morning, with the sun yet to break through over the horizon, the student met the professor, but he sat there saying nothing. Confused and bemused, it suddenly occurred to him that the last lecture on leadership had been all about proactivity. Seeing how little success his teacher was having with catching anything, he had a brainwave. Without saying a word, he rushed down to the supermarket and came back with some beautifully shiny, newly cleaned fish fillets - ready to eat. *"Here we go"*, he beamed. *"No need to carry on fishing, I anticipated your needs and solved the problem for you - Isn't that leadership?"*

The professor stretched his arms back in an expansive, relaxed manner and pointed to the surreal setting of water glistening in the early morning sun, and commented. *"Do you really think my primary purpose of coming here is to catch fish? Proactivity in leadership is only helpful if you first understand the real purpose of those you report to."* Catching on fast, and recalling the lesson on asking more than telling, the student responded with a question. *"What can I do to help?"*

"Well my fishing boxes haven't been tidied up in years. I am also getting old and if I do happen to hook a big one, I will need your help to bring it in. But you will have to anticipate that one, as I won't have time to ask for help."

The student immediately got to work, even roping in some passers-by to help with the challenge. Keeping half an eye out in anticipation of his teacher landing the Big One, he busied himself organising 20 years of hooks, line, sinkers and fancy novelty fishing gifts he had been given over the years, all tangled together in the boxes. Encouraging the volunteers to keep going, he suddenly realised he had answered his own question. *"Professor, I think I get it! Leadership is about understanding the purpose and inspiring others to help achieve it. Management is about organising the people and resources you need to achieve it, and then ensuring the work actually gets done. You can't really be successful unless you have both!"*

At that exact moment, the rod bent in half and the student jumped up to help the professor land the biggest catch of the day! No further words were spoken; the lesson was learnt!

4.4 My boss is driving me crazy

While doing some consultancy work this week, I listened with interest as one of the technical support engineers at this company complained about being double booked. The person he was talking to was furious as he had committed to a customer that this engineer would attend a customer meeting, only to find out he was not available anymore. The reason he cited for not being available is he was attending to another customer's problem, which had emerged after he committed to the meeting, and which his boss had said was important. Multiple and sometimes conflicting priorities are the reality of the modern workplace.

"You committed to this meeting a week ago," he barked, *"If only you had told me earlier you were no longer available I could have rescheduled*

this, but now what am I going to do? The customer is expecting you to be there. I am going to speak to your boss."

The engineer involved, stormed off equally aggrieved. *"I wish you would talk to my boss. I have far too much to do and it's not my fault if something else comes up that I have to attend to. I have been saying for ages that we need more staff,"* he complained.

Arguments like this go on in most of the places I have worked, and from what I hear from others, seem to go on in other professions, as diverse as teaching, nursing or even in charities. People struggle with ever increasing demands, linked to ever decreasing staff levels. Usually it is the boss that is blamed. The root cause is seen as being understaffed, and the boss is the person that is blamed for not hiring the extra people. The problem is that the boss is constrained by finances and cannot just hire additional staff. In the past, a supervisory boss would have planned the workload and allocated the staff to the appropriate workload. Today, front line staff are expected to manage their own workload. They are supposed to plan their time and communicate with their multiple internal and external customers what can, and cannot, be done. They also are expected to proactively communicate if their priorities have changed – in essence, they are expected to be their own boss. The problem is no-one tells them the game has changed or, if they are told, they haven't yet learnt how to be a boss!

So, the next time someone tells you their boss is driving them crazy – give them a mirror!

4.5 Who is the boss?

One of my favourite sitcoms when I was growing up was an American sitcom called 'Who's the boss'. It starred Tony Danza (as Tony Micelli) and Judith Light (as Angela Bower) and was about the stereotypical role reversal, where Tony is the housekeeper while Angela heads off to work as a busy executive in advertising. In many of the comedic situations this reciprocal boss relationship was highlighted. At work, in this knowledge era, figuring out who is the real boss is tricky. While we may report to someone on the org chart that normally is our boss, most of us will be acutely aware that many other stakeholders control our priorities.

There is an ongoing debate about which of the three primary stakeholders is most important: the company owners (shareholders); the staff; or the customers. Traditionally the financial owners have been regarded as the primary stakeholder and so in the past few decades it has become popular to highlight the customer as key. More recently companies are arguing that staff are the most critical. The argument goes that if staff are happy they will keep customers happy and if customers are happy they will buy more and keep the shareholders happy.

My view is that it is a *balance between all three*. What I have observed in my career is that if any one becomes more important than the others, the business suffers. Let's take the example of a finance department who have requested critical information for a budget update. If we follow the mantra that the customer always comes first, we would ignore that request until all customer requests have been satisfied. Yet if by ignoring the budget request, it results in lack of funds allocated to our department, this could impact all our customers in the coming months. By prioritising the financial stakeholders, we are indirectly meeting the needs of customers. The key is to understand the impact of delivering or not delivering the request to one stakeholder, compared to the relative merits of meeting the requests from another stakeholder - all three, need to be kept in balance.

Our direct bosses and our virtual bosses up and across the business are just representing one of these three stakeholders. When we end up with conflicting priorities it is helpful to consider which stakeholder this request is ultimately going to, and we can then assess the relative priority.

Developing a strategy for pre-determining the relative importance of our virtual bosses and then learning how to communicate our priorities and negotiate outcomes that meet the overall needs of the business is a critical leadership skill in today's complex organisations.

INSIGHT 5

USE A LEADERSHIP CYCLE

Leadership is about getting the right things done, right. The challenge is that there is no absolute definition of right. If we are not careful we can end up getting nothing finished, as we constantly question our planning decisions or work on constantly improving the outputs through striving for perfection. If we want to actually get something finished that adds true business value, it is necessary to separate the functions of planning, doing and measurement. We need to plan at a time we are not doing, and do at a time we are not planning. These functions require opposite ways of thinking. When we have finished doing, we need to measure the outputs we created to confirm they actually provided the desired business outcomes, and use this learning experience to replan the next steps. This is what I have called **The Leadership Cycle: Plan – Do – Measure - Replan**.

Planning *starts with defining where you are going, who is coming with you and why it's important to get there. Planning is not so much about the planning document itself, but the process the team goes through and assumptions that are made to produce a series of definable milestones* that can help to track progress as things continually change around us. It is almost impossible to get true commitment to results without buy-in to the plan.

Doing is about actually executing the plan, without getting distracted by other priorities. This requires disciplined and effective time management. A key insight is to accept that you cannot manage time - all you can manage is how you prioritise what you do in the time that keeps ticking away, as the earth rotates around its axis. The secret to actually doing what we planned to do, is to learn how to balance and prioritise the virtually infinite demands on our time. Learn to prioritise the most important and most urgent thing and do that first. Getting really good at making decisions, running effective meetings and providing the right feedback and reporting systems is also essential to effective doing.

Lastly, it's about **Measuring** outputs that our stakeholders (customers) really care about and using these results to re-plan. There is a management adage that you get what you measure. Another one states if you can't measure it, you can't manage it. For this reason, measuring the right things is really important. Many companies end up defining Key Performance Indicators (KPI's) based on team activities, not customer outputs, and so end up with meaningless (to the customer) metrics. By measuring the things that the customers (your key stakeholders) care about, you can develop initiatives (internal *projects) that improve the customer measure. This is the power of working to defined objectives.*

5.1 The Leadership Cycle - Plan, Do, Measure

I am sure we have all fallen prey to setting a New Year's Resolution, only to sheepishly admit we failed weeks or even days later. We are often very sincere in stating our goals, but for how long do we actually stick to them? For some people, they are so embarrassed by previous failed resolutions that they no longer want to commit to any new ones. In leadership, executing good plans is a key ingredient to success.

How do we ensure we actually execute the plans we make? To make any dream a reality, the following steps are helpful:

1. **Set the goals linked to a plan**: There must be something important we want to achieve that is different from what we have now. It starts with a level of dissatisfaction with the status quo and a vision of how we would like things to be. Let's say my New Year's Resolution is to *eat better and exercise more.* This desire may be driven by the fact I am not currently feeling as fit or healthy as I would like. I imagine myself feeling more healthy and looking better. This dream of better things to come and dissatisfaction with the present is a good thing, so long as we can actually influence the end result. This is how we learn new things and make progress in our lives. *A dream without a plan is a wish.* Often we are very high on the motivation scale to change, but have not defined any tangible next steps to get us closer to achieving our goals. Our plans may change as we go along, but without a plan we have no reference point around

which to make any changes and so when obstacles happen, we tend to give up, rather than being able to adjust the plans. Plans don't have to be detailed but they should include a very definite first milestone and how you are going to measure it. In the case of an exercise program our resolution may include achieving a particular recovery heart rate or body measurement, by a particular date.

2. **Do something.** *Actions turn plans into reality.* Procrastination is usually the killer for us. Tomorrow we will start exercising… and of course, tomorrow never comes. We often live under this illusion that we will have more time in the future, but the reality is that this perception is only because we can't identify the things that will fill our diaries so far in advance. Life's experiences teach us that those magic demand-free days never come. There is never a better time to do what is important. If it's really important then either do it immediately, or make a commitment in your diary of when you will do it. Putting a specific action into your diary, at a specific time, is a good way to force yourself into action. You may decide to schedule time at 6am on Monday, Wednesday and Friday to go for a run, and you should follow it religiously, for at least a month. After a while, the activity becomes a habit and you can move onto planning your next goal. In the case of a meaningful business objective it may take months or even years to achieve, so it's important to chunk the activity into bite sized chunks that can be completed on a weekly, or even daily basis. Taking the chunked activity off a list and into my diary is the best way I have found, to ensuring what I planned to do, actually gets done.

3. **Measure.** Engaging in any sport, either watching or playing, is not much fun if you don't know the score. Looking at the scoreboard helps to define how you are getting along and what needs to change. It also can be a key part of motivation. If I am running a marathon and want to complete it in a fixed time, I need to work out what pace I need to run each kilometre and then check my time against the plan. That ensures I set the correct pace to achieve my goal. In a business setting, the measure is often hard to actually measure and the first task could be to actually set up the process to measure the output I am monitoring. Measuring the results allows me to see if my plans really achieved the desired outputs and if not, to make new plans.

This cycle of planning, doing and measuring, while deceptively simple is powerful if applied properly. For example, the leadership cycle for working on company objectives may be quarterly. By strategically working in this way it avoids the pitfalls of constantly changing plans before any deliverables are achieved or rushing off to deliver outputs before any definable and measurable benefits have been defined.

5.2 Why Strategy Execution fails

In March 2015, the Harvard Business Review published an article highlighting some fascinating research about why strategy execution fails. A company without a good strategy is like a scavenging hyena that rushes from one carcass to the next, hoping each one will be meatier than the last. Strategy is supposed to focus the company on a game plan and, when well applied, it's what separates the winners from the losers.

In practice, the problem is threefold:

1. Senior management often don't walk the talk. The poster on the wall says customers come first but that only applies when it doesn't cost the company anything. To understand whether the strategy has real teeth, ask yourself what the opposite of the stated strategy is. Many strategies are no more than motherhood statements. For example, claiming to cut costs, expand the business, have world-class customer service, delivered with uncompromising quality – oh and all while maximising profits! If your strategy cannot guide you in making the hard choices, it's not a strategy.

2. There are often far too many goals and objectives, and therefore adequate resources cannot be allocated to the projects. Managers plan their objectives when at an offsite meeting, forgetting the pressures and demands of staff just doing their day jobs. Where companies choose a few critical objectives to pursue in a finite time, they have far more chance of delivering actual business results.

3. There is insufficient alignment of the goals up, down and across the business. Worthwhile goals can seldom be achieved by an individual department. Support is needed from other departments such as operations, sales or from back-office functions. Failure to get buy-in and commitment from all the stakeholders that could affect success leaves the projects aimed at achieving the objectives frustrated and without real progress. Learning how to align goals up, down and across the business is a critical management skill!

5.3 Dolphin watching at work

Recently I went dolphin watching at an idyllic location in Port Stephens, New South Wales, Australia. At one point, we were privileged to have at least THREE pods of dolphins within 50m of the boat we were on. The dolphins had some young ones with them, and so were often disappearing into the depths of the bay, only to resurface some distance from where they had dived in. You only have an instant to see them breach and experience their majestic, shimmering bodies, before they disappear into the depths again. With 30 odd dolphins to choose from, split into three different pods around the boat, the question becomes *"Where should I look?"*

After a while, you perfect the technique of scanning the water surface at all angles around the boat, and then quickly focus, and stop scanning to look at a pod that have started to surface. Once you have enjoyed that moment, and it's unlikely more will surface, you resume scanning again to capture the next event. Scan too slowly and you will miss a pod that already surfaced. Scan too quickly and you miss the enjoyment of the pod that is busy surfacing.

Balancing our work environments is quite similar. We have to balance our attention between the activities in the here-and-now, with the activities required to benefit us in the longer term. We do not want to be so focused on the current task that we miss exciting opportunities in the future. On the other hand, we don't want to be so focused on the long term, that we miss out on what is in front of us.

In my experience, a good technique for balancing this *zoom in – zoom out* requirement is to have quarterly planning sessions where longer-term goals are reviewed. During the three month periods in between, the team should keep measuring results but be in *zoom-in* mode, and just execute the plans set. After three months, another planning session can be held where any changes in the macro environment are evaluated, the results analysed and changes in the plans are approved.

This way, you won't miss out on any dolphins that are about to appear but at the same time will enjoy the experience of the dolphins that have already surfaced.

Happy dolphin watching!

5.4 How to get the really, really important stuff done!

I have just finished designing a new board game, for an upcoming training course on Time Management. Having attended many time-management courses in my working life, I realised most of them miss the point. They all focus on how to be more efficient in cramming more activities into the day. This game highlights that we cannot really manage time - all we can manage is getting better at deciding what we can and cannot do, from the almost infinite list of demands and then prioritising the most important ones balancing the needs of different stakeholders in our lives.

Managers often get into leadership positions because they are hardworking and self-driven. The problem is they do not manage themselves very well. They schedule 60-hour weeks for themselves and then wonder why they are always the last one to leave the office. The trick to effective time management is two-fold: Have less time; and prioritise the most important and most urgent things.

Ironically, when we have less time, we get more done. If we plan our week as though we have 20 hours available, we would end up getting a lot more done, due to the urgency it creates - shorter deadlines. Most of us know what the most important things are we have to do. The trouble is because they are so important, they seldom can be finished in a single session or even by working all day on them. What we end up doing is working on all the less important things that give us a reward from completion, and procrastinate on the big stuff. Many of us will remember the story of the tortoise and the hare, where the tortoise won the race by just plodding along while the hare at first raced ahead, but then got distracted and took long breaks and so lost the race. Getting the really important things done involves daily discipline. It is about planning to do something every day towards that big goal.

I find that by setting aside 15 minutes at the start of each work day to plan my day, I can focus on the most urgent and most important. I then ask myself: "*What key activity will I do today towards achieving my most important goal?*" I then schedule time in my diary to do it, as though it were a dedicated meeting. I can then closet myself away for that time period to work in a focused manner on that next step towards my goal, without interruptions. In isolation, it may appear that little progress is made, depending on the size of the task to finish, but day-by-day and week-by-week, I then notice how my big goal is closer to being achieved. There is an old Chinese proverb that says, "*One step at a time is good walking.*" Jim Collins, in his book *Great By Choice*, talks about the 20-mile march. He compares the polar explorers Roald Amundsen and Robert Falcon Scott, in their efforts to lead their teams to be the first to the South Pole in October 1911. Amundsen had steady, planned progress, day by day and successfully led his team to achieve the mission safely. Scott, who changed progress on the fly as the weather got better or worse was unsuccessful, with his team perishing in the sub-zero temperatures. All great achievements are done by having a clear goal, and then getting on with it, one (aligned and focused) step at a time.

Dreaming big, on its own, will not achieve anything. By setting aside time daily to plan, and then actually doing what we planned, we can achieve great things.

5.5 Are you addicted to email?

Observe people in most businesses these days and you are likely to see them looking very busy tapping away furiously on their laptops or smart phones. Often what they are doing is writing emails to all-and-sundry on any number of unrelated topics. This hard work can often take up a significant percentage of the working day, sometimes extending late into the night.

Yet when I talk to people in my business-coaching role, most confess that this investment in time yields very poor business results. So why do we still do it?

Advances in brain research give us a clue. Scientists tell us that our brains release a feel-good hormone called dopamine, when we achieve something – our self-reward mechanism for encouraging good behaviour! Neuroscientist Charles Gerfen has found that some neurons in the nucleus accumbens produce opioids – so we can literally get a high from thinking! The problem is it is short lived, and so in order to maintain that feel-good feeling we need to keep having these *successes* to continue to feel good. Our brain rewards us with feel-good chemicals when we appear to be busy achieving something – for example, when ticking things off a ToDo list or emptying our email inboxes. The problem is this primitive reward system has no way of knowing if completion of these tasks adds any real business value. To be really effective we have to ignore our own internal reward system, and ask ourselves if what we are currently doing is actually adding true value to the business.

Here are some email tips to stop feeding our drug addiction:

1. Determine set times to read and action emails. Outside those times work on value creating activities. Email is not synchronous,

or real-time, and by stopping acting like it is, we break the cycle and reduce the drug supply.

2. Make decisions based on relative, not absolute, importance and urgency. Everything seems important and urgent in isolation. By overriding the short-term reward received from being busy, with the rewards that come from achieving something big and meaningful we can create a new, more helpful reward mechanism.

3. Do not use your inbox as a ToDo list. Delete, delegate or deal with them. To deal with emails and get them out your inbox, either respond immediately or diarise when you will respond. This way your inbox will be empty and temptations for short-lived and distracting dopamine highs are removed.

5.6 The fallacy of multi-tasking

One of the things we pride ourselves on, when we get promoted into management is our ability to multitask. Women also tease men about being less adept than they are, at juggling multiple priorities. I watched with amusement as a friend of mine was making a round of drinks for the guests, and every time he spoke, he stopped preparing the drinks, until his wife with frustration marched across and took over the duties, before we all died of thirst.

It turns out, our rational brains are just not capable of multitasking - they are what is termed a serial-processor. In other words, they physiologically can only do one conscious thing at a time. Unconsciously they are capable of amazing feats, all at the same time, but the intelligent, thinking tasks have to line up in single file for processing in our Pre-Frontal Cortex (PFC). When we think we are multi-tasking, we are in fact switching quickly between tasks. The more complex the task, the more information needs to be set up in our short-term memory, to quickly access for processing. As soon as we are distracted by a different task, a different set of neurons has to be fired up to load up that thought pattern. We often quite accurately describe what is happening with phrases like: "*now where was I?*" or "*I have lost my train of thought*", yet for some reason we still persevere in trying to do multiple complex tasks at once. Even the simplest activity like rubbing your stomach while patting your head, we find difficult.

Productivity in the modern workplace, where our jobs are to think, not to produce tangible things, has become woeful. We are often blissfully unaware of our inefficiencies as we tend to measure activity rather than results. Brain scans have shown that our IQ drops significantly with multi-tasking. A study by *Clifford Nass*, at Stanford University proved that even our switching ability gets worse, the more we do it. Unfortunately, as team leaders and managers we cannot just closet ourselves away, focusing on a series of single tasks until they are done. Despite the fact that it is the most effective way of completing the task, other people need access to our time, to complete their work. I have found the best way is to create some blocks of time in your day where you disappear into a meeting room or coffee shop and work on your top priorities in an uninterrupted and focused manner and at least ensure that for the most important things we do, we are doing it with our brains peaked to the maximum! The rest of the time, we have to bumble along with a damaged IQ, as we try to answer the phone while tapping away at the computer and pointing, using our nose, to a file on the shelf that someone has requested using sign language.

INSIGHT 6

COMMUNICATE MEANING WITH THE FACTS

Communicating is **a two-way process**. *We often tend to focus more on telling than listening, and this is usually at the heart of miscommunication. What we are communicating out has the contextual framework of a rich and complex set of beliefs and values, that defines its meaning to us. The meaning to the person receiving the feedback is usually interpreted through their framework of beliefs and values, and, therefore, the same set of facts and information shared, can be interpreted in two very different ways. The problem is that the movie clip which has the* **rich meaning of the story**, *is not attached to the communication event. As humans, we also build up our version of what the world means, and create a shortcut of what something means based on our internal rule-of-thumb - called a heuristic. Our patterns of generalising a situation to judge it without deep thought, form our biases, and while it can speed up decision-making to function more effectively in daily life, it can also wreak havoc with misunderstandings in communication, especially if it triggers some emotional reaction, linked to a past* *experience, that looks similar to this one, where we jump to the wrong conclusion.*

When communicating, focusing on your intended meaning - "what I'm trying to say..." - is less helpful than working to understand the context in which the other person has defined its meaning. What is important is not so much what is intended to be said, but what is heard! Deeper mutual understanding is achieved through sharing our respective stories, which have embedded in them the meaning to us, in addition to the factual information imparted.

Effective leadership requires mastery of **good listening**, *and learning to have* **effective conversations**, *even in, or maybe especially in, difficult circumstances.*

6.1 Pay attention to paying attention

Can you recall a teacher shouting, "*Pay attention!*"

Whether it was gazing out the window or staring at them with a blank look, our minds had wandered off, out of the classroom, even though our bodies were still physically present. Amazingly, we were sometimes able to protest that we were paying attention and proved it by repeating every word that was just said. The reality was, however, that we had only picked up the literal words and had no idea of the meaning of the discussion that had just taken place.

Through neuroscience we are now learning a lot more about how our brains work and what attention really means. Our brains can only really pay conscious attention to one thing at a time. For less complex tasks, we are able to create the illusion of multitasking by switching very fast between activities. For example, spoken sentences have lots of gaps, and our minds can process information in milliseconds. We are thus able to check our emails and write down a grocery list and still piece together the words that are spoken in a sentence.

Effective communication, however, requires us to interpret the words for meaning and this is an incredibly complex task, subject to all sorts of distortions.

In the workplace, our day usually consists of a mixture of routine and fairly menial work, balanced by activities that require deep, intellectual thinking. In the usual open plan offices, with our electronic always-on communications devices surrounding us, it is often literally impossible to pay attention to the task at hand. When we need to think deeply, or communicate effectively, we have no choice but to go somewhere where we cannot be interrupted and leave our smart phones behind.

There is something about human nature that, in order to feel motivated, we need to feel affirmed and understood. When we do not feel what we are saying is truly understood, we can become frustrated and discouraged.

Given how complex communicating is, and how open it is to biases, misunderstandings and deliberate distortions, is it any wonder that unless you are giving someone your absolute, undivided attention and fully engaged in understanding what they are saying, they will be crying out "*you are not listening to me*".

6.2 Why I am right and you are wrong

The government in Australia recently released its austerity budget and it seems a lot of people are very unhappy! Their popularity rating plummeted as all the various socio-economic groups counted the cost of throwing away the credit card. "*The age of entitlement is over*", declared the treasurer. "*Here, here*", said all those who believed that meant their hard-earned tax dollars would no longer go to lazy louts who refused to work. "*Boo, boo*", said all those who believed their government was abandoning the sick, the poor, and the unemployed. Political ideals often have opposite meaning depending on context. If you are employed in a well-paying job, and see half your income disappear in taxes to help the not-so-needy, you may have a different perspective to these announcements, than the twenty-something job seeker, after their umpteenth *sorry, no jobs here* letter.

In management, to improve communication we have to consider the context of the other person. Our beliefs are shaped by our life's experiences and we find it hard to understand how things may look or seem to someone else, through a different lens. Their life experiences may filter the information in a completely different way than the way we intended. It is helpful to walk in someone else's shoes before we judge them. But even then, consider if it is ever possible to really walk in someone else's shoes? Even if we do experience identical circumstances, the context in which we will frame that new circumstance, is shaped by a lifetime of unique experiences.

Having a starting position that we are right and the other person is wrong is often at the heart of all miscommunication. A different approach is to explain your context - how something looks to you, and then truly try to understand the other person's context - how it looks to them.

Communicating is a two-way process. It is explaining what something means to you, and then understanding what that same thing means to the other person.

6.3 Fancy a trip to the beach?

What comes to mind if I mention beautiful white beach sands? What if I enticed you with promises of the sunshine of the French coast and even included a trip to Paris? No doubt the majority of us would be excitedly imagining a fantastic holiday. This was not the case back on 6 June 1944. Reflecting on World War II, we are reminded of the terrible loss of life of thousands of Allied troops who stormed the beaches of Normandy, which arguably is the single most important event that turned the tide of the war. No doubt for the few hundred thousand people who experienced the terrible consequences of that heroic invasion the thoughts and memories of a sun soaked beach in Northern France, were anything but pretty.

There is often a debate about whether the red I see, is the same as the red you see. How would we ever know? When we communicate with other people, we try to impart what an event means to us, but how do we know what it looks like in their world? Keywords will trigger memories of the past or assumptions about the future that dictate how the other person will react to our message. I watched with interest this week when two managers reacted in opposite ways to the same idea in a brainstorming session. One saw a fantastic opportunity to improve staff engagement, the other saw an unnecessary expense that would indirectly have a negative impact on staff. There is no easy answer here. One way to be sure that what we are intending to communicate is understood in the right way by the other party is to ask them. Listen and observe carefully to learn more about the context of your message. Good communication is both an art and a skill and demands our full attention.

Just announcing the good news that we are all going to Paris via the beach will not always have the reaction you may expect!

6.4 Even great is not good enough

Jim Collins wrote an excellent book called *Good to Great*. In it, he talks about what makes companies truly great, rather than just good. A key theme of the book is the fact that, in order to be great, you have to do less good things, so you can focus on a few really great things. A colleague of mine, who in the 3 years of his tenure as CEO achieved over 25% growth in revenue per annum, was told by his bosses that "*it is just not good enough*". They expected more!

I recall the boom days in telecoms in the early 2000's. We look back with nostalgia on the growth of company share prices in the technology sector, and yet, at the time, I also recall the pressure to do better. Because the norm was almost exponential growth, even excellent growth was frowned upon as *not good enough*. One of the exciting things about business opportunity is there is no ultimate standard. This sense that *the sky's the limit* drives companies to achieve a lot more, with less, thus driving profits up higher and higher. Being a leader is tough, as you have to balance your leading role, with your follower role. The follower role is the one where you are responsible to your bosses for their expectations of you.

Often these expectations are unbounded!

The expectations are based purely on a *desire* to do better and many targets have no objective science behind them to prove that they are realistic or even possible. We are driven harder and harder to achieve goals that may not even be possible. This the reality of our society so there is no point in challenging it, and it is this constant striving to do better, whatever the odds, that drives progress, so it not a bad thing. Nobody ever achieved great things by setting conservative, and realistic goals.

The main point here, is that when you are in the team that is delivering these results, expect that whatever you do, it is not going to be seen as good enough – especially at the time. Years later, you may get credit for what was achieved, but at the time all you can expect on your score card is *can do better*. Set your own personal scorecard of success to value your worth as an imperfect, fallible human being who is doing their absolute best. Results, not trying hard, are rewarded, but your personal sense of satisfaction will be measured by what you have achieved, against your personal goals - with the cards you have been dealt – not necessarily by achieving the arbitrary external measures of success that have been provided for you.

6.5 The truth and nothing further from the truth

We have all seen those courtroom TV dramas where a witness has to swear to *Tell the truth, the whole truth and nothing but the truth*. Our society has grown tired of all the political spin to distort the truth and one has to be a little bit naïve to believe that the news is unbiased and telling you the whole truth. Imagine a society where the truth was the norm and in fact enforced as a public responsibility, in a similar way that speed is enforced on our roads. Recent advances in neuroscience are making that a possibility. Sam Harris in his book *The Moral Landscape* points out that "*deception is the principal enemy of human cooperation*".

We often think one thing and say another. In fact, part of us developing a mature personality requires us to do that. Regulating our responses, to something more socially acceptable than what may be rumbling around in our heads, is a learned skill. Sometimes, we also deliberately distort the truth to say things in a way to minimise the hurt that the blatant truth may cause. However, communication is compromised when we constantly distort what we say, to be different to what we mean. Honest, open communication is key to good communication.

We should avoid thinking there are only two options to a difficult conversation. Option one being to just say what needs to be said knowing we will ruin the relationship, or option two being to avoid saying what really needs to be said to protect the relationship. It is what Joseph Grenny, co-author of *Crucial Conversations*, calls a Fool's Choice. The book authors point out: *"Watch to see if you're telling yourself that you must choose between peace and honesty, between winning and losing, and so on. Break free of these Fool's Choices by searching for the* and.*"*

A few suggestions to achieve that include:

Start by establishing a **mutual higher-level goal**. This establishes context to the conversation, and avoids it spiralling downwards into negative conflict. When things get heated both parties can point back to the common goal *"We both want X, so let's figure out how to get there."* This also makes each party feel safe, as it is clear the overall outcome intended is in both parties' interest.

Stick to the facts and when things degenerate, get out of the content of the discussion and back to the context. Conversations go badly when each party brings their own biases and distortions about what something means to them. Challenging someone's belief system or judging his or her values seldom will result in a good outcome. The more you can stick to the facts of the specific situation and the joint outcome you want, and avoid judging generic behaviour that you may object to, the better the conversation will end.

Do not play games. Sometimes our behaviour in the conversation is more about proving we are right or even about punishing the other person for their views. We can also play emotional games based on the stories we tell ourselves about what is happening, where we may be victim, villain or rescuer. When we find ourselves playing games, we should remind ourselves of the desired outcome we want.

Good leadership requires us to get really good at having **good, open honest conversations** where we are able to speak the truth and say what we actually mean, and in the process, retain good relationships.

6.6 Winning hearts and minds

The concept of winning hearts and minds has wartime connotations of not getting the local population off side, when the soldiers are engaged in active battle. In management, it is far more important than we sometime realise, to ensure we win *both* hearts and minds in any decisions we make. It is helpful to almost imagine we have two decision-making control centres in our head. One says, what do I think about this? The other says how do I feel about it? Personality profiling suggests different people have stronger biases each way, but we all appeal to both.

In practice, it is easy to mix the two and it is not uncommon to see two people in a conflict because one is objecting based on emotional reasons while the other is justifying in rational terms. Let's say, the company has made a decision to temporarily transfer a key staff member to a project to help get it back on track. The manager is explaining what a great opportunity it is and stroking the ego of the candidate explaining the honour of being chosen for this role. If the candidate has a young family, emotionally they may be feeling this is bad news as they will work long hours and have to travel. Their head says this a great career opportunity, but their heart is upset about the impact on the family. A sensitive manager will first check what the candidate thinks and feels, before automatically assuming this good news will be received as such. People often ask me, in my coaching role, "*How do you know what Joe*

Soap really feels or thinks?" and the answer is a simple 3-letter word - just ASK.

Managers often do too much telling and too little asking.

Asking decreases our blind spots. If we ask questions that address both the mind and the heart our communication will improve....

6.7 Stop being so emotional!

In my younger days, as an engineer, I always prided myself in being analytical and logical. If someone said to me, *"you are so logical"*, I took it as a compliment. On the other hand, if someone said to me *"you are being emotional"*, I would take it as a harsh criticism that I needed to pull myself together and be more rational. More recently, I have been reading about neuroscience, and understanding that these two aspects are dominated by two different parts of the brain. Understanding personality styles, I also discovered that other people, in different fields, do not necessarily process information or make decisions the same way most engineers do. What is perfectly logical to them, is not necessarily logical to me. They may have a higher bias for emotional reasoning. It's about a balance and getting it right is a critical skill in leadership.

Passion seems to be a word that is more readily accepted as a positive trait than being emotional, yet what is passion other than an emotional emphasis on what you are doing? A leader without passion and a display of true emotions and feelings is hard to follow or be inspired by. I am talking about allowing ourselves the freedom to display some emotions and true feelings, and to be real – rather than being so politically correct and professional, that we appear aloof and cold. Doug Sundheim, author of *Taking Smart Risks: How Sharp Leaders Win When Stakes are High* says, "*Emotions are critical to everything a leader must do: build trust, strengthen relationships, set a vision, focus energy, get people moving, make tradeoffs, make tough decisions, and learn from failure. Without genuine emotion, these things always fall flat and stall. You need emotion on the front end to inform prioritisation. You need it on the back end to motivate and inspire."*

As human beings, we process information at both an emotional and logical level, and if we can learn to trust both sources, we will become better leaders. So, the next time someone says to me *"you are being emotional"*, I will take it as a complement!

Allowing your emotions to create some passion in what you are doing is a positive thing, but this is only true up to a point. When we overdo it our emotions get highjacked, and we behave seemingly irrationally. The first thing to come to terms with is that we are not nearly as rational as we (especially technical people) think we are. I am reading an interesting book by Daniel Kahneman, *Thinking fast and slow*, who explains that we can think of it as though we have two systems in our brain – a fast instinctive, emotionally driven one, and a slow, thinking rational one.

These two systems generally work in harmony, to help us function as rational, decision-making human beings, but sometimes they also clash. Why is it that sometimes we get worked up and feel like we are *losing it*? Our perfectly justified reactions in the heat of the moment, often seem a complete *over-reaction*, when we reflect on it, after we have calmed down. It seems that our fast thinking can sometimes overstimulate our emotional responses, and we feel, and indeed experience physiological changes in our bodies that replicate, a life-threatening scenario. Before we have time to rationally assess the true threat, our quick reacting emotional brain hijacks all the resources thus draining the fuel from our slow thinking brain, thereby leaving us unable to rationally assess the reality of the situation.

When we feel we are not thinking straight, in fact that is exactly what is happening. Our rational thinking has gone and so we behave in ways that may surprise or even embarrass us later on, once everything is back to normal and we are able to think with our rational part of the brain. At the time, no amount of appealing for ourselves or anyone else to calm down and be rational will help, as it's like calling for assistance from a vehicle that has run out of fuel. What helps is to break the cycle of emotional hijacking, by deliberately doing something else or removing ourselves from the situation and coming back to it, once our emotional balance is restored. Deliberately asking yourself to identify what is happening, without putting any meaning to it, can help to draw resources back to our thinking brain a little faster.

So, next time you see one of your team members acting a little crazy and overreacting to something, have a heart because they literally may be feeling like they are being attacked by a cave bear!

INSIGHT 7

SUCCESS IS IN THE EYE OF THE BEHOLDER

I know a guy who ever since childhood was very driven. Whether it was perfecting his serve in tennis, shaving millimetres off the clearance of the hurdles in athletics, or working on a difficult picking riff on the guitar, he was always the guy who was going to try harder, work longer hours and aim higher to be successful at whatever he did. Mediocrity was just not an option. He worked his way through university doing engineering and while the arts students were busy having parties and protesting at political rallies, he slaved away trying to get his head around partial differential equations in mathematics, software coding and optical physics. When he started his first job, this internal drive to be the best and be successful continued. Working his way up the ladder through various engineering management jobs he also published a technical textbook at the same time as having a very demanding full time job and a wife and three children at home. It was not unusual for him to get home, spend time with the family and then work from 9pm till 2am slaving away at his book to meet publisher deadlines.

His big management break came when he was headhunted to join a privately owned international company, headquartered in London who were on a mission to grow the business and sell it within 5 years. The company was highly successful and received awards for growth. Due to his hard work and determination to succeed, he was soon promoted to the top operational management role in the business and as COO worked closely with the equally driven CEO to achieve seemingly impossible things. Sixteen hour days became the norm and with the global demands on his time he ended up renting a flat right next to the office so he could maximise his time on the job, only travelling home on weekends. But this success was like a drug. He had more money and power than he'd ever had before. He was travelling around the world on business class flights and eating in top restaurants, all organised by his private secretary who basically ran his life for him, as he was so busy. With such a jet setting lifestyle, and the status of the being on the board of the company, he got regular reinforcement from those around him on how successful he was. In his world if there was a corporate ladder to climb, he was sitting on the top rung - He had made it.

One cold, rainy night at 10pm he locked up the office and walked on his own back to his London flat as the rain pelted down on his dreary black umbrella. He reached for his key to enter his empty lonely flat, and it suddenly hit him like a ton of bricks!

This is success?

He hadn't played squash, his favourite sport for months. His guitar had long sat on its stand untouched. Friends and family - something he had always prided himself on being a top priority - had in reality been pushed down the priority list, as he was always too busy. This job consumed his mind 24 hours a day, often waking up at 3am thinking about how he could improve things.

Standing there in the rain on that cold lonely night, he realised he was putting his life on hold to achieve success at work. In his mind, he was doing it for his family, for his future, but his heart knew otherwise. He had justified to himself and others that he was working like this, so he could retire early, so he could be financially independent and then really live his life.

Right there, right then, he made a decision. He would start living the life he wanted to live today! Not next week, not next year, not when he had achieved the next success marker. Now!

Despite having a 3-month contract, he resigned and negotiated an exit with a 48-hour handover. He set up his own business to create his dream job. He identified all the things that were a priority to him and started doing them. He started working on creating the dream life that he had imagined he would have when he retired. He learnt the lesson that success at work will only feel like success if it is not at the expense of success in all the other important areas of your life.

The guy I am talking about is ….ME!

I hope you have found this book, and the insights and personal lessons I have shared, useful. I trust you will apply whatever you found helpful in these seven leadership lessons of mine, to your personal situation and achieve success, as defined by you!

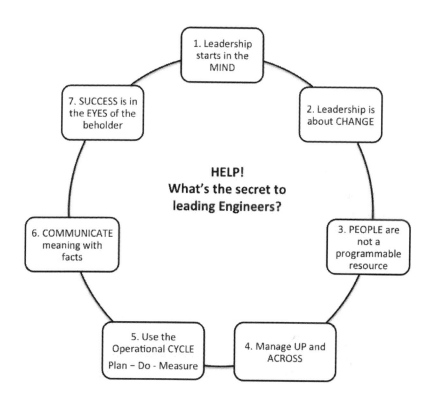

1. Leadership starts in the MIND

2. Leadership is about CHANGE

3. PEOPLE are not a programmable resource

4. Manage UP and ACROSS

5. Use the Operational CYCLE

Plan – Do - Measure

6. COMMUNICATE meaning with facts

7. SUCCESS is in the EYES of the beholder

HELP!
What's the secret to
leading Engineers?

REVIEW AND FEEDBACK

1. If you liked this book please spend two minutes writing a short review on amazon.
2. Write to me with any feedback. Email me at author@tmcglobal. com.au
3. You can also connect with me on my Facebook author page at https://www.facebook.com/Trevor.Manning.Author/
4. We learn by teaching, so if this has been helpful in any way, please share your new insights with friends and colleagues. Tell them about the book. Review the book, email and tweet about it and recommend others to follow my Facebook author page. Sitting on my hard drive or in the publisher's store this book has no value.

UPCOMING TITLES
BY TREVOR MANNING

Register for an advanced copy if you're interested in one of the upcoming titles by Trevor Manning:

Help! They made me the team leader
Help! I need to master critical conversations

To find out more search for Trevor Manning's author page on Facebook. Go to https://www.facebook.com/Trevor.Manning.Author/

Gourmet Ghosts 2

James T. Bartlett

City Ghost Guides

Gourmet Ghosts logo: U.S. Trademark No. 5,039,244

ISBN 978-0-9975829-0-1

Special Thanks To...

Nina Monet, Amy Inouye at Future Studio, and the History
& Genealogy Department at the L.A. Central Library.

Dedicated To...

My wife Wendall Thomas, who still loves and supports me.

Introduction

Welcome to *Gourmet Ghosts 2*, another look into the dark, deadly and weird history of Los Angeles. In these pages you'll find bars, restaurants and hotels where you can drink with the devil or learn about the strange side of the City of Angels – maybe even both at the same time!

Serial killers, suicides, snipers, scandals, scams, robberies, arsonists, murders and unexplained mysteries: they're all here, sometimes even in one location (see The Cecil on page 141; it's the Deadliest Hotel in L.A. and the focus of a bizarre death that went viral).

Just like I did for *Gourmet Ghosts – Los Angeles*, the first book in the series, I scoured the newspaper archives for true crimes known and unknown, spoke to employees and eye witnesses about what they had seen and heard, and again uncovered some very strange connections.

I unearthed new ghost stories as well, but because I found so many amazing stories and hidden treasures that I couldn't include (well, if I stuck to the idea that they had to be at a place you could go for a cocktail or a bite to eat), I decided to break the rules this time.

So, in some entries you might not find a bar or a restaurant, but you'll learn about a previously-unpublished death at the Hollywood Bowl, the place MLK's assassin plotted his deadly deed, the Rose Murderer – and others.

Really, how could I have kept them from you?

History, murder and mystery are a potent mix, so you can continue your investigations by getting a copy of *Gourmet Ghosts – Los Angeles*.

Inside that book you'll learn about "The Night Watchman" at the Last Bookstore, *La mujer sin cabeza* (the Headless Woman) at Musso & Frank Grill, "Millie" at the Paradise Cove in Malibu, and James Z. Oviatt, who is still haunting the building that killed him.

You can submit your own stories and read more at www.gourmetghosts.com and keep right up-to-date on Facebook, Twitter and Instagram too – just search for "Gourmet Ghosts."

Finally, the guide for how much you might expect to pay in these bars, restaurants and hotels is roughly as follows:

$ - Cheap, fun night
$$ - A few more bucks for the bang
$$$ - Standard L.A. prices
$$$$ - Serious cash

Apologies in advance if you go to one of the locations listed here and find that something's different. I did try to keep *Gourmet Ghosts 2* as current as possible, but sometimes things just disappear into the night...

Contents

Chapter 1
Hollywood & W. Hollywood

The Hollywood Sign

The Famous Suicide and the Unknown Accident

Perhaps the most famous icon in the world, the Hollywood sign was originally designed by forgotten sign-maker Thomas Fisk Goff (though a couple of other people claimed the honor too).

Born in London in 1890, Goff had settled in Los Angeles by the 1920s and was doing well as the owner of the Crescent Sign Company, so his commission from a real estate company looking to sell land under some hills was probably no big deal at the time.

Hollywoodland

Originally the hillside sign spelled out the word "Hollywoodland," the name of the development area, and Goff's design saw the 50 foot high, 400 foot long sign lined with 4000 flashing light bulbs to attract buyers.

It was only meant to last a year or so after it was unveiled in 1923, but by the time the bulbs went out and the promotion was over, "Hollywoodland" meant something much more glamorous.

But glamorous or not, the Hollywood sign has had a checkered history.

For a start, a drunken caretaker who lived on site once drove his car into the H in the early 1940s, and in 1949 the H fell down after a storm, the Hollywood Chamber of Commerce quickly offering $5,000 for a replacement so it didn't become known as 'ollywoodland.

They also agreed to the removal of the LAND letters, and though the sign has been destroyed in many blockbuster movies and alien invasions, by the late 1970s the rotting, much-vandalized sign faced destruction for real, despite having been declared Cultural Historical Monument #111 in 1973.

Luckily, it was saved with donations from an odd mix of celebrities including Alice Cooper, Gene Autry, Andy Williams and *Playboy*'s Hugh Hefner, all of whom paid around $27,700 per letter, and when Goff died in early 1984, he was doubtless still unable to believe what had happened to his sign.

Over the years the sign has been renovated – most recently with 275 gallons of paint to celebrate her 90th birthday – and even occasionally altered for charity events (or as a prank or protest), but today the priceless 350 foot landmark is closely monitored by the LAPD and Griffith park officials.

The Most Famous Suicide in Tinsel Town

While the Hollywood sign might seem to be the very symbol of fame and success, it was also the place where someone who had had seen their movie dreams crushed came to end their life.

SUICIDE LAID TO FILM JINX

Born in Wales in 1908, Millicent Lillian "Peg" Entwistle was just a young girl when her family – her father was also an actor – came to America.

She had some early success in Broadway theatre, and when she came to Los Angeles in 1932 for the play *Mad Hopes*, she got more good reviews.

She naturally then tried out for the big screen, but despite her blond hair, blue eyes and theatrical prowess, her luck ran out.

'Actress Takes Own Life in Hollywood Hills

Leaps From Towering Sign to Death Below

Around September 16, 1932, after leaving a suicide note with her shoes, purse and jacket, Entwistle climbed a workman's ladder to the top of the H and looked out over the city for the last time before leaping to her death.

An anonymous woman called in the discovery of the body, and left Peg's belongings on the steps of the Hollywood Police station. The body was later found at the bottom of a hundred foot ravine, and the cause of death was multiple fractures of the pelvis.

The *LA Times* published a picture of the smiling Entwistle and a melodramatic report on the "spectacular suicide," the story reading in part: "a house of cards that came tumbling down and revealed to her the futility of fleeting fame!"

The suicide note was published too:

"I am afraid, I am a coward. I am sorry for everything. If I had done this a long time ago, it would have saved a lot of pain. P.E."

Her ashes were sent to Ohio for burial next to her father, and her only movie appearance – a small part in *Thirteen Women* alongside Irene Dunne and Myrna Loy – hit theaters soon after her death, but it was not a success.

Ironically, her suicide at the age of just 24 did bring Peg posthumous fame.

She's been the subject of many books and even a 2014 opera called *Goodnight September*, and then of course there's the rumor that she lives on in spirit, still haunting the place where she took her final bow.

The smell of gardenias...

Apparently her ghost can be seen around the H of the sign, and even the smell of her perfume (gardenia) has been noticed here too.

Travel Channel show "Ghost Adventures" looked into this haunting, and in 2014 the Halloween edition of *Vanity Fair* quoted a jogger who, while running through another part of Griffith Park, began sneezing when she felt "the overpowering scent of gardenias."

More frighteningly, she then said that she saw a "woman with blond hair who seemed to be walking on air."

The Unknown Accident

But Peg wasn't the only person who died up here at the Hollywood sign.

A story that doesn't seem to have made the pages of any other books, it took place in March 1988 when Susan Diaz, 16, her brother Michael and several other people went climbing up under the Hollywood sign to take pictures.

Tragically, Susan and Michael both fell off a cliff and while Michael luckily wasn't injured, Susan had to be airlifted to a Burbank hospital by helicopter, where she later died of head injuries.

For many years the sign and its surroundings had been accessible, and people did climb the steep, rocky hills to get pictures, drink beer, make out, or simply go hiking, but that's just not the case today – and the death of Diaz is one of the reasons why.

So as inviting as it might be to get up close and personal with the huge letters, don't go up there – you might end up in hospital or a jail cell.

www.hollywoodsign.org

The Hollywood Bowl
2301 Highland Avenue
Los Angeles, CA 90068
Tel: 323 850 2000

"Death Before Ghosts"

Many tourists don't realize that you can actually get a great view of the Hollywood sign from many places in L.A., but perhaps one of the best vantage points is from inside the Hollywood Bowl, an outdoor venue that can seat around 17,500 people.

The amphitheater was first carved into the wilds of "Daisy Dell" in the Griffith Park hills back in 1922, with the iconic white arched shell coming in 1929.

Since then it has hosted opera, ballet, theatre, music, Monty Python and President Franklin D. Roosevelt (not at the same time), and essentially everyone save for Elvis Presley has taken the stage here at one time or another.

Elton John holds the current record for the most performances, but the record attendance was over 26,000 for a recital by French opera star Lily Pons in 1936.

Before the show starts – and one of the biggest attractions of visiting the Bowl – is that you can bring your own picnic and beverages, from soda to champagne, for al fresco dining in and around the 15 picnic areas, as well as in your seat.

There are of course restaurants including the fancy The Backyard and The Wine Bar, burger joint Kitchen 22, Marketplaces, Street Food, and stores where you can buy cookies, sandwiches, popcorn, cheeses, beer, wine, coffee, snacks and of course souvenirs.

However, aside from the bats that fly overhead when the sun goes down, there aren't many ghostly stories associated with the Bowl (though there have been alien invaders; a skunk in the seats, a family of raccoons on the arches, and even a fox who came on stage during a show!)

But one night it was the location for a suicide that seems to have been lost to history, one that, perhaps if more people knew about it, might be said to rival poor Peg's in terms of dramatic style.

Just take a quick glance at photographs of the dead body; it made me gasp out loud when they appeared on the microfiche at the Central Library.

DECORATOR COMMITS SUICIDE
ON HOLLYWOOD BOWL STAGE

On March 26, 1938, the *LA Times* reported on the last moments of a 45 year old interior decorator:

"Under the curving concrete shell whence the music of the immortals ascends each season to the star-studded skies, Emanuel E. Linhart went, not for the accolade of the multitude, but for a tryst with death."

Found sprawled out on the stage by a janitor, Linhart had a pistol with one bullet missing lying next to his body. He had shot himself in the head, and while the *LA Examiner* had an amazing picture, the *Los Angeles Evening Herald-Express* headline read:

Hearst Communications, Inc

The motive behind his suicide was unclear, though it emerged he had won $3,500 on the Irish sweepstakes a few years before.

Perhaps he had gambled or lived beyond his means, and had hoped for another moment of good luck.... but that luck never came.

$$$ & $$$$ Various; hours vary

www.hollywoodbowl.com

Frolic Room
6245 Hollywood Boulevard
Hollywood, CA 90028
Tel: 323 462 5890

Strange Guests

Though it's a small dive bar, the Frolic Room has perhaps one of the most recognizable neon signs outside – it seems to feature in all articles and tour guides about Hollywood (and movies like *L.A. Confidential*).

It has a long history too, officially coming into being in 1934, though for years before that it had been the secret unofficial bar (the speakeasy) of the Pantages Theater next door.

The Pantages was built in 1930, during Prohibition, so naturally there were no signs – or even a front door to the bar – but people "in the know" would come up a side walkway (which is now where the women's bathroom is) and go in to the storage room.

In that storage room, which is right at the end of the bar, you can still see the now bricked-up outline of a door that led directly to the theatre stage.

The Pantages Theater was built as a vaudeville and movie venue, and the bar was always part of that. They're still the landlord of the bar today, though the Frolic Room itself is separately owned.

As for the inspiration for the Frolic Room's name, it is said that one "Freddy Frolic" was the genial host for actors, guests and others at this illegal joint.

In 1949 Howard Hughes bought the Pantages and set up his offices on the second floor, and from then until 1959 it was the venue for the Academy Awards – and surely plenty of star-studded parties.

Later in the 1970s and 1980s, it suffered as the surrounding area of Hollywood fell prey to pimps, hookers, addicts and the homeless, though patrons still stayed loyal, and today it's close to being a hip place as well as a dive.

Inside, the bar is dark, the jukebox loud, and the welcome friendly. Once I'd ordered a beer, bartender Gita Bull was happy to talk about her time here – some 20 plus years, she says.

She came to Hollywood with her parents when they emigrated from Romania, and she fondly recalled the days of clubbing on the Sunset Strip, when "you could just talk to celebrities; they came out and partied just like us."

She also remembered talking to one of the bartenders who worked here back in 1947. He told her that in those days they used to fix sandwiches in the back and didn't have a jukebox – just a record player. Frank Sinatra used to come in from recording at Capitol Records up the road with fresh-off-the-press vinyl records and play them.

In recent years, Gita said that Keifer Sutherland, who used to live in an apartment opposite, was a regular, though he hadn't been in much recently.

"I think he got divorced or moved," she said, adding that she got mail addressed to him c/o The Frolic Room.

Black Dahlia sitting at the bar...

She added that Charles Bukowski used to drink here (as he did around most of Hollywood) and that the Frolic Room was the last place Elizabeth Short – better known as "The Black Dahlia" – was seen alive.

Apparently she came here after being dropped off at the Biltmore Hotel downtown (the last place she was officially listed as being seen), had her last drink, and then met a man she left with.

Gita thinks the horrific (and still unsolved) murder was a date gone wrong, and that Short was accidentally killed and the man cut up her body and dumped it on waste ground.

She added that the "48 Hours" television show had come out from New York to do a story on it, and that there's supposed to be a tunnel from The Frolic to a long-gone bar across the street.

This is a common story at many bars – especially those that served liquor under the table – and while some tunnels have been found, many, including one from the Frolic Room, have not been located.

Handprints & Someone Trying To Escape?

Nevertheless, she did have a number of strange stories about ghosts and unexplained events, admitting that she always "felt uneasy" when she was here at night.

She recalled her friend who had been a bartender here in the late 1940s saying that once he had been wiping down the bar when a full handprint emerged where he'd just been cleaning; another time footprints emerged on the cement floor, clearly visible among the peanut shells.

She also mentioned something that had happened to her and to a co-worker – but years apart. Neither had mentioned it to the other until a mutual friend who heard both stories made the connection.

"Years ago" Gita was here alone setting up the bar for the day when a man walked in and asked to use the restroom:

"Then, for around 30 or 40 seconds, the women's restroom door started shaking – as if someone was trying to get out."

Thinking the man had gone into the wrong restroom and "was crazy," Gita didn't do anything – until the hapless man, white-faced and looking terrified, shot out of the men's restroom (not the women's), and ran out of the bar.

It rang similar to the story of her co-worker, who was there one Thursday night, closing up, when he went upstairs to the liquor room where the bottles are kept in a locked area.

The lock on the liquor room began shaking violently, "and he was so scared he put down the bottles he was carrying and ran out," she says.

There's a mural opposite the bar towards the back – a wall reproduction based on the works of cartoonist Al Hirschfeld – and she recalled that a few years ago they had a young artist in restoring it.

This artist would work 6am to midday in order to work in quiet, but on the first night she heard loud banging and thumping upstairs (perhaps Howard Hughes wanting some peace and quiet?).

She was "red faced and crying, really upset, and wanted to leave," so, in order to calm her fears ("and because I wanted her to finish the work," Gita laughs), "I told her it was the sound of a compressor."

In the fictional world the Frolic Room is the favorite hangout of Kane Pryce, hero of supernatural thriller novels by FJ Lennon, though Lennon himself has written about his own haunting experience at the Frolic Room on his blog.

The Man in the Mirror

In 1999 he was at the bar and not drunk ("yet") when he went to the jukebox. On coming back to his seat he "glanced into the mirror that runs the length of the bar. It wasn't my reflection looking back. The fellow staring at me was in his fifties; a chubby-faced, jowly guy with a thick bushy mustache and bald dome with a ring of hair."

Gita didn't mention any strange faces in the mirror, though she does feel that the Frolic Room is "definitely haunted to a certain degree," and pointed out something above the bar near the entrance to the bathrooms.

It was a photograph of former regular whose seat was in the far left corner by the wall, and Gita said that he had said "'After I die, I'm going to come back here,' though there's no sign of him yet!"

One story she didn't mention – perhaps understandably – was the murder of the Frolic Room's much-loved doorman in 2010, who was found in the doorway with blunt force trauma to the head, perhaps inflicted by a patron whom he had been in a confrontation with earlier that night.

It shocked the local community and was quite a sensation, yet no one has faced charges for the crime

There's no Happy Hour and no food here, but if you're a fan of Hollywood History, a trip to the Frolic Room really shouldn't be missed.

$ / Daily 11am-2pm

Hollywood Historic Hotel
5162 Melrose Avenue
Hollywood, CA 90038
Tel: 323 378 6312

Murder-Suicide & Parking Lot Tragedy

Opened in 1927 as the Hollywood Melrose Hotel, it was an early design by 28 year old Art Deco and Moderne architect S. Charles Lee, who became better known for designing motion picture theaters.

He completed several hundred across California and Mexico in his career, and was behind the Los Angeles Theatre, the Bruin Theater and the Max Factor Building (now the Hollywood Museum), to name just a few.

Stretching an entire block and unmissable in striking red brick, today the Historic Hollywood Hotel is a budget hotel – albeit one that offers a view of the Hollywood sign from many of its rooms.

Over the years it underwent several name changes, styling itself the Melrose Arms and the Monte Cristo Island Apartments before it became the Hollywood Historic Hotel.

It was for sale back in 2008 for just under $15m, but the owner opted instead to restore the building, sanding the entire façade to bring back the red brick, refurbishing throughout and tweaking the 62 room's original bathtubs, sinks and mirrors just a little to take it back to its 1920's heyday.

Handily, that owner of the hotel, Edmon Simonian, was also the owner of one of the businesses on street level, a furniture and stone gallery.

He had arrived in America in the late 1970s with his wife and young daughter, and soon set up business in the building.

Quickly finding his skills in designing, carving and manufacturing wood furniture to be in demand, he was able to buy the whole building within 20 years.

In April 2010 the new-look hotel was reopened as the Hollywood Historic Hotel, a name that might have paid tribute to the fact that in 1992 it was added to the National Register of Historic Places.

There are gold-painted gargoyles and shields on the bright white outside porticos, royal red dominates, and red and gold combines on the boxy, glitzy front doors. The lobby is the same – perhaps a little gaudy for some, but it definitely has charm.

Back in the day it was patronized by tourists, dignitaries and celebrities alike – it's just a block from Paramount and Raleigh Studios – but like the movie business, this hotel has had its ups and downs too.

For example, the *LA Times* of December 16, 1933 reported a murder-suicide here.

Distraught at failed attempts to reconcile with his divorced wife Maryon, Hollywood-based police officer Harold H. Richardson, 34, entered her apartment here, shooting her while she slept and then turning the gun on himself.

OFFICER KILLS WIFE AND SELF

Lifeless Bodies of Couple Found in Apartment

What appeared to be a suicide note from Richardson offered few clues, save for a note about where he had left his car and the line:

"Mother: Forgive me. My life is not worth anything, so take care of Maryon and me."

The *LA Examiner* said that relatives "tentatively planned a double funeral," and ironically (or perhaps deliberately) this sad story was positioned right under a big picture of movie icons Douglas Fairbanks and Mary Pickford, who had recently announced their divorce.

Barely a year later in September 1934, the newspapers were devoting pages and pages to the arrest of Bruno Hauptmann, the kidnapper/murderer of Charles Lindbergh, Jr, the 20 month old son of aviator Charles, yet the *LA Times* still reported the news that one of the apartments here had been raided by police; three people were arrested and a "small quantity of narcotics" and an "opium smoking outfit" seized.

One of the arrested, Garrett "Dolly" Joseph, 34, was charged on suspicion of robbery and violation of the State Poison Act, and bragged to detectives that he was a member of the "Purple Gang."

They were a violent outfit that was suspected of making a deceptive phone call that led to the infamous St. Valentine's Day Massacre of seven rival gang members by Al Capone's men in Chicago in 1929.

Years later, with the papers full of the chaos, Nazi suicides and horrors of the concentration camps as WWII was coming to an end, a small report in the *LA Times* in April 1945 reported that Flossie Fay Dell Daniel, 27, took an overdose of sleeping tablets in her apartment here.

Sleeping Tablets Held Death Cause

She left a rather cryptic note saying "she was tired" and "sought forgiveness for her act," and presumably the person to whom the note was addressed – "Mom" – would know what those last words meant.

It was nearly 30 years before this address hit the headlines again, and this time it was in relation to a deadly double shooting. Out on patrol, LAPD officers heard gunshots around 2.30am on March 21, 1974 and found Robert Cox, 44, lying critically injured in the parking lot by his apartment here.

One Man Found Slain; 2nd Wounded

Just yards away was the body of another man –
already dead, shot in the head – but Cox said he didn't
know who he was.

Police were working on the assumption both men
were victims of an unidentified robber, as Cox had handed
over his wallet before being shot in the back, while the
dead man had had his pockets turned out.

The hotel doesn't seem to be one that attracts
celebrities (it's a distance away from the main areas of
Hollywood), and further speaking to manager Betty, who
has worked here for 17 years, she said she didn't have any
strange stories to tell – at least about the hotel:

*"I lived in places with strange happenings and strange
things, but not here."*

That said, some guest reports on the Yelp review
site mention an odd experience or two.

In March 2016 reviewer "Katherine Niswonger"
wrote about their alarm clock radio buzzing with strange
static and a window seemingly closing on its own in the
night (though both may well have logical explanations).

A reviewer from October 2013, "Jason B," was
more direct:

*"First off I wanted to say that there is no doubt in my mind
that this hotel is HAUNTED!!!!! Beware and do not book at
this hotel!!!"*

At around 4am on the second night of his stay, they
were woken by a "loud, scary and frightening scream from
a woman" that seemed to come from the floor above theirs
– they were staying in room 2013.

He continues that he heard what sounded like a
woman being beaten and saying "Something like 'Just stop
it already, just stop!'"

Looking out of the window he saw nothing, but he called down to the front desk – and within minutes the noise had stopped. Nonetheless, Jason B was shaken:

"I can't help but to believe that it was ghosts doing all that. Something like a murder must have occurred in that hotel in the past! Please do NOT STAY!!!"

A murder did happen here – the murder-suicide by Harold H. Richardson – but it seems he committed his act in near silence.

Perhaps then what Jason B had heard was simply a nasty argument between the couple in that room, though if you really want to see dead bodies, the hotel is just a couple of blocks south of perhaps the most famous cemetery in Los Angeles: Hollywood Forever.

Founded in 1899 at originally 100 acres in size (though it quickly sold around 40 of them to nearby Paramount), it is one of the oldest in the city.

Its graves, crypts, memorials, cenotaphs and niches – both the extraordinarily grand and charmingly simple – are the resting places for cartoon voice genius Mel Blanc, director Cecil B. DeMille, Douglas Fairbanks, Beatle George Harrison, director John Huston, Dee Dee and Johnny Ramone, Bugsy Siegel, Rudolph Valentino, Fay Wray and countless others.

It's a beautiful spot, and in the summer there are regular music and outdoor movie screenings here. They encourage visitors too – there's an interactive site map, tours and more – and it's well worth a visit!

As for eating at the hotel, the Nue Studio Café (part café, part salon and part boutique) closed recently, though I was assured that mid-2016 will see the opening of an American-style restaurant here – so watch this space…

www.hollywoodhistorichotel.com

Hollywood Plaza Hotel
The Chocolate Bar Pastry Cafe
1637 Vine Street
Hollywood, CA 90028
Tel: 323 962 3898

Alaska's Most Lurid Murder Case
& "The Hillside Strangler"

In its golden days, the Hollywood Plaza welcomed almost every single movie, television, music and radio star. Ernest Hemingway stayed here on his only visit to Hollywood in 1937 for example, and while the modern equivalent might be the Chateau Marmont further west, today you'd hardly know this grizzled building had such an illustrious past.

For many years it has looked dilapidated and forgotten, with small cafes and restaurants coming and going too: even now there's still a sign for the long-gone "Stars on Vine" restaurant.

Hopefully the new Chocolate Bar will bring some people back to this location, even if you can't stay here like so many other famous people did.

Located just a few yards from Hollywood and Vine, the cross street at the center of Tinsel Town in the early days, this 10 story hotel opened in October 1925 (15 days ahead of schedule), and was the brainchild of Jacob Stern.

In many ways Stern had helped start the movie business here when he rented half a barn at Selma and Vine to a young upstart named Cecil B. DeMille in 1913.

Hollywood Heritage Museum

Within a decade that "barn" was the headquarters of Famous Players-Lasky Studios (it's now the excellent Hollywood Heritage Museum), and when people began really flocking to Hollywood, Stern began developing the Hollywood/Vine area.

Architects Walker & Eisen designed the Plaza in a vaguely Italian/Spanish style, and inside there was luxury everywhere: chandeliers, red and gold silk drapes, marble floors and thick carpets.

The 200 rooms had their own bath and dressing room decorated in a variety of colors, and as was the fashion at the time there was a smoking room, a Ladies' Reception Room on the mezzanine, and other handy places like a lobby barbershop, beauty parlor and a cigar counter.

The hotel wore its ambition on its sleeve too, soon starting up a monthly Salon that featured lecturers, artists, musicians and dancers, and the lobby was given over to revolving art exhibitions.

AMUNDSEN TO LECTURE ON EXPLOITS AT POLE \

Most excitingly, the hotel got the nickname "The Adventurers Club" partly because the Aero Club had their offices here (and they even planned a mast on the roof for airships to dock with).

Over the years visitors included aviator/mogul Howard Hughes, explorer Roald Amundsen, baseball legend Babe Ruth (who broke the net on the hotel's golf practice range), and boxer "Slapsie" Maxie Rosenbloom (who was a long-term resident, staying until the hotel closed in 1973).

Back in January 1928, journalist Bob Barber of the *New York Times* gave one of these talks, and recounted his experiences on the EC LaRue expedition down the Colorado River.

During that adventure he had a found a skeleton sitting in a chair in a cabin, an unfinished game of makeshift whittled chess pieces in front of his bony corpse.

DEATH MATES CHESS PLAYER

Barber thought that the opponent hadn't enjoyed the contest – he'd probably shot the poor man still sitting there – and said that documents he found showed that the game had taken place in 1894.

It was the actors who got the biggest headlines at the Plaza though: Bette Davis stayed here when she first arrived in L.A., and Ronald Reagan made several movies while he lived here. George Burns had a suite here for some 20 years too, and he and Gracie Allen used it as an office between appearances on radio, television and stage.

It was at the Plaza where Burns met then-unknown Marilyn Monroe, who had been described as "the most beautiful girl you've ever seen" by her agent. It was the only time, Burns said, an agent had been telling the truth.

Doris Day stayed here during her break-up with husband George Weidler, and other notable guests included Tommy Dorsey and his band, which included a young man called Frank Sinatra. Sinatra stayed here again in 1942, when he was recording his first album.

A restaurant is always vital for hotels, and the first one here was Klemtner's Blue Plate Café, the first in a long series of eateries. It was replaced by the Pig 'N Whistle Café in 1928 (and there's still a "Pig" on Hollywood Boulevard next to the Egyptian Theatre; you can read about it in *Gourmet Ghosts – Los Angeles*).

Then, in 1931 the secluded palm grove at the back of the hotel became the Russian Eagle Garden, a secluded and romantic place that even appealed to the famously reclusive Greta Garbo, whose regular table was just to the right of the entrance. Charlie Chaplin, Oliver Hardy, Gloria Swanson, Ernst Lubitsch and Fay Wray dined there too.

Rags-to-Riches

In 1934 an amazing story hit the headlines when the *LA Times* reported that former bellhop Ray Cremona had come back and taken the Royal Suite here.

Four months previously he'd found out he was the heir to $250,000 and five hotels in Europe, so had naturally quit his job and gone on a tour to see them.

"We missed the States," he told the *Times*, and was planning to sell all the foreign hotels. The *Times* noted that the low value of the dollar and political unrest in those countries – plus the fact that American cigarettes cost 55 cents there – also played a role in the decision. He had a gift for his former employer too: coins from all of the countries that he had visited.

In 1936 the hotel changed hands for $2m and new owner Thomas Hull spent $100,000 remodeling "The Pig" into the Cinnabar, a swanky Art Deco nightclub that attracted guests like Ida Lupino, Errol Flynn, Jack Benny, Jean Harlow and Tom Mix – but not for long.

Like many other nightclubs in Hollywood over the years, it didn't last – and in September 1937 the It Café opened its doors.

Owned by Clara Bow, a sexy redhead and one of the biggest stars of silent movies – and the woman who was first given the nickname "The It Girl" – it was the kind idea of her husband, actor Rex Bell, who hoped a return to the spotlight might help her get over a recent miscarriage.

From day one "It" was thick with celebrities – but of the proprietress herself, there was often no sign.

Like many celebrities-turned-restaurateurs she had promised to be there in front and back of house, but barely weeks after the star-studded opening night she found out she was pregnant – and she didn't want to take any chances this time, so stayed home.

It was all over within a year, and then a couple of years after that came the first recorded death at the hotel.

Autopsy Ordered in Visitor's Death

The date was February 4, 1940 and the *LA Times* reported that 27 year old salesman Edward Sherman had been found dead in his room.

He had been ill and was attended to by a physician in the night, but the cause of death was unknown.

By 1944 the eaterie space had been refurbished into a casual dining room called Les Comiques that, despite the name, was aimed more at tourists than the elite – a sign of how Hollywood was again changing.

"Everything new but the name"

The Hollywood Plaza changed hands in 1951, and a big piece in the *LA Times* in May the next year reported on the five month remodel. The new owner, Lee Hotels, spent $400,000 unfortunately erasing most traces of the original elegance and making it "modern," the restaurant now called The Westerner Lounge Grill and coming complete with a horseshoe bar, murals and a band. There was a coffee shop and a store in the lobby too.

A couple of years after that a real scandal hit the Hollywood Plaza, the details so gossip-friendly – a blonde, a suicide, a scandalous affair, a rich older husband, a secret abortion, and of course murder – that all the Los Angeles newspapers covered it extensively, and it even hit the headlines across the USA.

DEATH OF BEAUTY

The date was March 10, 1954 and it was reported in the *Los Angeles Herald-Express* that 31 year old blond socialite Diane Wells had taken an overdose of 30 sleeping pills in her room here, barely a day after she had checked in as "Doris May."

Before this she had been staying at the Drake Hotel (now the Scientology Building – see its own entry later in this chapter), but then she had walked just a little further along Hollywood Boulevard and turned down Vine: it was going to be the end of a sad story for someone that the *LA Times* had previously described as "a woman in a million."

She was jointly accused of murdering her rich (and older) husband Cecil while he slept in their marital bed in Fairbanks, Alaska, late the previous year.

The real shocker (at least at the time) was that her co-conspirator was her lover, a "Negro jazz drummer" named Johnny Warren.

Warren, 33, had told police of many "trysts" with the blonde Wells after they had met at a dance, when she looked at him in a way that "led me to believe she might appreciate attention." He added that she said (he) "was the man for me" when he yawned during a strip tease act.

Wells maintained that on the night of the murder there had been a home invasion during which she had been badly beaten about the head, but authorities clearly thought she and Warren had cooked up a plan together.

Both the accused were released on bond and Wells got permission to come to L.A., where she and her son initially stayed with her friend Joan Mansfield. As the trial date got closer though, Mansfield and another friend both noticed she was getting more and more depressed.

After she checked into the Drake Hotel they warned the manager to "keep an eye on her," but it seemed Wells decided to go where no one would look for her.

Room 711

The only note found in room 711 at the Plaza was on a scrap torn out of a telephone directory. It had a rather crudely-drawn heart and arrow on it and read:

"My Valentine, I love you."

February 14 was the day she had checked into the Drake Hotel, and perhaps that romantic day had made her write that message – we'll never know for certain.

Then, the *Herald-Express* – who Wells gave her last interview to – reported that the autopsy revealed she had been pregnant, and had had a miscarriage or an "illegal operation" soon before she committed suicide.

Wells and Warren strongly denied the murder plot (and Wells the affair too), but she told the *Herald-Express*:

"I'm afraid the District Attorney isn't going to let go. It's such a big case, he's afraid to drop it. But my friends there are trying to see what they can do."

It seemed Warren was going to face the jury alone, but rumors from Alaska that there wasn't enough evidence (and later talk of a "third suspect") meant that he in fact never stood trial – though the charges weren't dismissed until after 1959, when Alaska became a US state.

It was several years before the Hollywood Plaza made the newspapers again – this time in March 1958 when Thomas A. Reilly, a 21 year old airline clerk visiting from New York, had a heart attack and drowned while swimming in the pool. He and his work colleague had checked in only the day before on a "vacation jaunt."

By the mid 1960s the Plaza's hotel days were over, and it was converted into senior housing, the swimming pool filled in for safety.

Nevertheless, Robert Stern, grandson of original owner Jacob, insisted the palm trees at the back of the building stayed – and they're still there today.

What stories they could tell of the people that sat underneath them below the Hollywood skies....

A number of small cafés and restaurants hoping for some of that old magic tried their luck here over the following years – unusually unsuccessfully – and then in the 1980s there was a another deadly twist here.

Buono Tied to Another Slaying Victim

Surprise Witness Says She Thinks She Saw Him Talk to Woman

In March 1982, former hostess Paula Heller testified that she saw Lissa Kastin, a ballet student and waitress here at what was then called Healthfare International, talking to two men at the back of the restaurant: Angelo Buono Jr. and Kenneth A. Bianchi.

The names Buono and his adoptive cousin Bianchi might seem unfamiliar, but you will probably recognize them by their joint nickname – the Hillside Strangler.

Between them they kidnapped, tortured, raped and killed abducted 10 girls and women in late 1977 and early 1978, leaving many of the bodies in the city's hills.

Victim #3 of the Hillside Strangler

That night was the last time the unfortunate Lissa was seen alive, and her nude body was found on November 6, 1977 near the Chevy Chase Country Club. She had been strangled with a ligature.

The only person to escape the killers was Catharine Lorre, who they gave a ride to sometime in 1977.

When they found out she was the daughter of actor Peter Lorre, famous for his role as a child murderer in Fritz Lang's acclaimed movie *M* (1931), they let her go.

Perhaps mercifully, she didn't realize the danger she had been in until after their arrest.

Bianchi and Buono were both sentenced to life in prison, Buono dying of a heart attack in September 2002.

Finally – or so it seems – the last time the Hollywood Plaza saw a dramatic moment was in October 1984, when the restaurant here (then called Koko's) was hit by a second fire in two weeks.

No one was injured, though 12 elderly building residents were treated for smoke inhalation, and police found the blaze suspicious: the smaller fire the week before had been deliberately caused by an incendiary device.

On a recent visit I noted the Hollywood Plaza sign outside was a neon one before I entered the small lobby, which had gorgeous, ornate old-style elevators and an all-floor mail chute (though I wasn't allowed to take any pictures).

I did however speak to several members of staff: Helen who seemed to be a manager, a maintenance guy in a blue uniform, and guy wearing eyeglasses.

They said they didn't know any strange stories, though Helen did say that she'd heard Elvis Presley had once stayed here (which is quite possible).

I was about to leave when the guy wearing the eyeglasses said something short but cryptic:

"I'll tell you one thing. That's all. No one likes to go on the roof. You'll have to research that. But no one likes to go up there."

Sadly I couldn't find anything in the archives about anything that happened on the roof (the swimming pool where Thomas Reilly died wasn't located there), so for now what he was referring to remains a mystery.

Outside again I spoke to the friendly Security Guard, who mentioned that the elevators here:

"Open and close all the time. Day and night, they're always opening and closing."

As you might guess, the Chocolate Bar – in its first location outside New York – is heaven for fans of pastries, cookies, and almost anything bad for you.

So, as someone with rather a sweet tooth, I can recommend almost everything on the menu – as long as it has chocolate! It's open for breakfast until late, so is perfect for munchies at any time.

$ / Daily 6am-midnight
www.chocolatebarpastrycafe.com

Church of Scientology Building
6724 Hollywood Boulevard
Los Angeles, CA 90028

Now Scientology, formerly Christie/Drake

To its believers, Scientology is a religion of science and psychotherapy-based practices centered on ideas expressed in the 1950 book *Dianetics* by science fiction writer L. Ron Hubbard.

In the eyes of many others though, Scientology is a wealthy, litigious, controversial, cult-like operation that's shrouded in secrecy, albeit with many famous (and often outspoken) members including movie stars Tom Cruise and John Travolta.

This book isn't the place for a major debate about Scientology, but it's true to say that Scientology "audits" members, utilizes an E-Meter to measure people's electrical resistance, and tells the story of *Xenu*, a ruler who, many millions of years ago, brought billions of *thetan* people to Earth in spacecraft.

Doubtless there's more to it than that, and a simple Google search will let you learn as much as you wish.

Either way it's important to many, though while the Church says there are millions of members worldwide, the real number is probably in the many thousands or so.

In 1955 Hubbard wrote about Celebrity Centres – Scientology churches that are open to the public but aimed at artistic, political and sports individuals who have a media platform and a chance to affect change and talk about the aims of Scientology.

As you might imagine, the castle-like first of these buildings was opened in Hollywood in 1969, but in fact it seems that the Church of Scientology is one of the area's largest owners of real estate.

Their mammoth blue compound is hard to miss on Sunset Boulevard, but they also have a large theater that promotes Hubbard's other works (dozens of adventure, fantasy, western and mystery stories, many of them adapted and performed as "old style" radio shows), and some other businesses too, as well as the expected offices, classrooms and chapels.

As you can tell from the tower design and the outdoor fire escapes, one of their buildings was a small hotel once known as the Hollywood Inn, but today it's an information center with a vertical blue sign on both sides and is staffed by smart, smiling young people.

It certainly seems to be welcoming if you're interested in finding out more about their beliefs, but what they might not know however is the long history of the building – and the people who have died inside these walls.

Commissioned by Haldane H. Christie, an auto parts manufacturer who sold out to Henry Ford and moved to L.A., the Christie Hotel was part of his many real estate holdings in Hollywood.

It was lauded as the first luxury hotel in the area when it opened in 1922, and standing at eight storeys and 100 rooms, the Georgian Revival building had annexed the nearby Glidden Hotel as part of the development, which was designed by Arthur R. Kelly.

It had stores on the street level as well as a busy café called The Greenwich Village (the first of several names for café's here during that period, including the wonderful Anteo's Café Diable).

Christie however sold the hotel in 1925, and it was again sold in 1931 to hotelier R.J. Matheson, who planned extensive improvements.

Christie himself died in March 1941, and a few years later in 1944 it was sold for $1m to Robert Schreiber.

Christie Hotel, Hollywood, to Change Hands

It was reported by the *LA Times* that Schreiber was already "scratching his head trying to think of a name," and he eventually decided on the Drake Hotel.

New Sparkler Comes To Coast

Located at the center of booming movie business, the hotel had immediately been a celebrity draw. Soon after it opened, the *LA Times* noted how motion-picture contest winner Miss Allene Ray was staying here as she was looking to "enter pictures."

Noted for her ability to horse-ride and her "wealth of golden hair," she appeared in dozens of action movies in the 1920s.

Sadly, barely two years after it had opened its front doors, the movie business also bought the first tragic event to the Christie. On May 22, 1924 director Lew Mason turned on the gas in his room, leaving a note that read:

"It's too much, too fast."

Suicide Pact?

On hearing the news, chorus girl Cecil Werner, 22, who said she "went with" the director, swallowed a bottle of chloroform in her apartment a few blocks away.

Her suicide notes to family and friends mentioned financial worries, and read:

"It all seems so futile to me…. not worth the reward."

Police said that when Mason was found – barely still breathing – he had a picture of a girl in his hand, and that it looked like Werner.

Less than two years later, Werner's apartment building was razed to make way for something that still is one of the most famous locations in Hollywood: Grauman's Chinese Theatre.

ERIN COUNT IS HELD ON OLD CHARGE

Another sad romantic story at the Christie happened just a week later on May 31, when the *LA Times* reported that Randall D. Taaffe, a well-dressed con man calling himself "The Irish Count" had been arrested here.

It turns out his tales of military service and a large Irish estate had been fake, and that he'd also left a broken-hearted girl in Paris.

Former Oilman Ends Life in Eight-Story Plunge at Hotel

In February 1941 there was another suicide here, the *LA Times* reporting that Walter Caward, 49, a former oil broker, had "ended his life in a spectacular fashion" by jumping from the window of his eighth floor room just minutes after checking in.

Detectives noted that Caward's wife had died suddenly a few months before, and that he had suffered a nervous breakdown after a recent serious operation.

Hotel Elevator Operator Killed

There was a more horrific death in early September 1943 when Albert Bellerose, 28, an elevator operator who had only worked at the Christie for three days, was killed.

His head and neck were "crushed" when he was somehow dragged into the narrow space between the lift and the shaft.

Witnesses said they heard a scream, and saw his legs extending from the top of the elevator door. The fire department had to be called to "extricate his body."

The 8th Floor Curse?

After being renamed the Drake Hotel in early 1945, it was only three years before they too faced suicide.

JOBLESS GIRL, 19, PLUNGES EIGHT FLOORS TO DEATH

Theater cashier Dolores Elaine Mollette was only 19 when she jumped to her death from a window in May 1948. Her mother told police Dolores was suffering from a heart ailment, and had told her she was going out to look for a job.

A few years later on Valentine's Day 1954, a blonde woman signed herself in as "Barbara Walker" – and staff had no way of knowing that she was at the center of a lurid murder case in Alaska.

The full details can be found in the entry for the Hollywood Plaza Hotel, as that was where Diane Wells (AKA Barbara Walker) did actually commit suicide, though she stayed here until the day before, and left several suicide notes behind.

Diane & The Drake

The Wells case was a real humdinger: a murder, a scandalous affair and a secret abortion, and it made the papers all across America, especially when, in March, Wells checked out of the Drake and walked a couple of blocks to the Hollywood Plaza Hotel, where she took a fatal dose of sleeping pills that night.

The notes she left at the Drake included one that said her actions were to spare her 5 year old son Marquam (known as Mark) the "terrible publicity" of the upcoming trial, in which she was accused of murdering her rich car dealer husband Cecil at their home in Fairbanks, Alaska, the previous year.

She was accused alongside her lover, "Negro jazz drummer" Johnny Warren, the aspect of the story which – in those days – was more of a sensation.

Both denied the murder, and Wells insisted her husband had been killed in the robbery in which she had also been injured – but the authorities weren't convinced.

They were both released on bond, and Wells got permission to come to L.A. to get treatment for her injuries (and to "get away for a while," she told the *Los Angeles Herald-Express*).

She initially stayed with friend Joan Mansfield and even enrolled Mark in school, but was apparently more and more despondent before she checked into the Drake Hotel.

The return date to Alaska – and the trial – loomed large though, and the *LA Times* reported that despite the efforts of Mansfield and her other friend William Colombany, who had taken a number of sleeping tablets out of her purse, tragedy seemed to be on the horizon.

Another suicide note she left behind at the Drake was addressed to the Tate family in Seattle – executors of Cecil's will – and asked them to: "Please raise Mark as your son. He has never been baptized. It is my wish for you to have him."

However, this note also seemed to confess to the murder (kind of):

"For one thing – I am guilty, too, for ever seeing Warren, if Warren is guilty. One thing is sure, Cecil is dead and I must be the cause of it, one way or another."

Less than two years later in September 1956 the Drake was sold for $450,000, the owners incorrectly listed in the *LA Times* as "noted motion picture producers" the Christie Brothers, who had run Nestor, the very first movie studio in Hollywood.

Al Christie made the movies while brother Charles kept things running in the office, and later their Christie Film Company made comedies for Universal and others.

Sadly they lost it all in the Stock Market Crash and the following Depression, and were gone by 1933.

Ghost Owners

That said, the Christies are kind of "ghost owners" of the hotel that coincidentally used to bear their last name. There's a plaque noting them in connection to what is now Hollywood Historic Site No. 38, but as the *LA Times* reported in 2011, since 2009 the great-grandson of the correct Christie, Haldane, has been trying to remedy that error – without luck, so far.

Either way, it was back in 1974 when the Church of Scientology paid well over a million dollars for what was then the Hollywood Inn, and archive references to this address after this are few (though they do show there was a performance space here, at least in the mid 1980s, when it was home to the Pacific Renaissance Theater).

The Scientology welcome center was once empty for a while too, but it was renovated extensively from around 2012 – but as for a restaurants or a bar, it's possible you might well be offered a cup of coffee if you visit.

www.scientology-losangeles.org

Sunset Tower Hotel
8358 Sunset Boulevard
West Hollywood, CA 90069
Tel: 323 654 7100

The Little Girl & The Man In The Chair

Brought to life by architect Leland A. Bryant and opened in 1931 at a cost of $750,000, this classic Streamline Moderne form of Art Deco on the Sunset Strip has been a magnet for celebrities ever since it opened.

Today, the lobby and the bar and restaurant are located in what used to be gangster Bugsy Siegel's 1930s apartment, and it has also appeared in a number of hit movies including 2003's *The Italian Job*, *Get Shorty*, and *Strange Days*.

Its first literary mention was in Raymond Chandler's 1940 novel *Farewell, My Lovely* (1940), and it then also appeared on screen for real in the movie version (called *Murder, My Sweet*) a few years later.

Also, in 1947 Truman Capote wrote in a letter that he was staying here, and that it's "where every scandal that ever happened happened."

No doubt he had also heard the rumor that the Sunset Tower was known for having the "best-kept call girls in Hollywood."

At 15 storeys in height – and boasting one of the highest penthouses in town – the Sunset Tower was scandalized by Siegel in 1944, the *LA Times* reporting that the "Hollywood sportsman" had been charged with placing bets via long distance calls from his "assistant film director" pal Allen Smiley's apartment.

Justice Convinced 'Bookie' Operating at Sunset Tower

Also in the room was actor George Raft, though it was only Siegel and Smiley who were charged with a "bookie" crime (and while the fine of $250 might not have troubled Bugsy's wallet, being formally asked to leave the Sunset probably hurt him more).

In 1955 the *LA Times* trumpeted a million dollar makeover for the Sunset, and in 1968 there was an upgrade too – including the introduction of a "pay-as-you-need" maid service – but despite being placed on the National Register of Historic Places in 1980 the Tower had begun to fall into disrepair, and 1982 it was partly converted into condominiums.

In 1985 it was saved from possible demolition on a promise from Peter de Savary, who pledged $25m to restore it back to its halcyon days – earning an award from the Los Angeles Conservancy in 1988 for his efforts.

Some years later de Savary sold the hotel and it was renamed the Argyle, then in 2004 it was purchased by Jeff Klein.

He bought back the old name and went for a look of modern luxury: outdoor heated pool, a spa and fitness center, and the Tower Bar & Restaurant and a smaller Terrace Café.

The Sunset Tower has suffered from a case of misidentification – a slip of the tongue you could call it – over the years too.

In August 1944 it was incorrectly reported as the venue for the "Battle of the Balcony," a punch-up between bandleader Tommy Dorsey and Siegel's right hand man Smiley, who brawled with actor Jon Hall after Hall seemed to be getting too friendly with Dorsey's wife Patricia.

The fight actually happened at the Sunset Plaza, further down the street, where Smiley had ended up after being banished from the Sunset Tower alongside Siegel a few months before.

Location aside, they were all charged with felonious assault and brought to trial, but the only winners were the scandal-hungry media, as the charges were later dropped.

A few years later, Smiley was at Siegel's side again when Siegel was shot and killed while reading the *Los Angeles Times* at a house in Beverly Hills – his murder was never solved.

Other scandals here included one about John Wayne, who was said to have bought a cow up to his penthouse during a late-night party (though it's highly unlikely he managed to get the beast in the elevator), and a very strange tale of a disappearing actress.

Hunt for Blonde Singer Centers on Taxi Driver

Husband Seeks Clew to Route Chilean Took Apparently During Period of Depression

Maria Gatica was a striking Chilean singer who hailed a cab to take her home to the Sunset Tower where she packed a hatbox of nightwear and then asked him to drive her somewhere unknown.

Police began an immediate search for the driver, reported the *LA Times* of April 12, 1948, and a possible "clew" (as they spelled it then) was that she had recently been to the doctor complaining of headaches – and had expressed a desire to go to Mexico City.

Though she was booked at the swish Macombo Club she had missed several recent shows, and was said to be depressed about her lack of success – and the fact her pregnancy may delay that further – though her husband Gene Fell admitted "she had done this before," and felt she was still in the area.

A couple of days later the mystery was solved, when it was revealed that Gatica was now working, quite happily, as a housekeeper.

The 26 year old said she took the job to learn how to run a home, learn to cook and get used to family life. Her employer's apparently knew all about it, and had only insisted she let her husband know where she was.

That was one of the odder tales connected to the Sunset Tower, though there were certainly some far more deadly moments here over the years.

Business Owner Reported Suicide

On Christmas Eve 1944 the *LA Times* reported that George G. Steere had climbed into the bathtub and shot himself in the head while his wife was out shopping.

Blonde Slashes Wrists, Attempts Suicide Leap

Despondency Over Failure to Reach Stardom Overnight Blamed by Girl

Then, on November 23, 1953 the *LA Times* reported that a "beautiful buxom blonde from Boston" named Renea Roussau had made a hysterical and screaming attempt at suicide earlier that morning by slashing both her wrists and, when police and a doctor arrived, making a desperate dash for her seventh floor apartment window.

The 19 year old was said to be impatient for fame (even though she'd only enrolled in drama school the week before), but the manager of the building shrugged and offered another explanation:

"Girl gets stood up. Happens all the time."

After being administered with a sedative, the doctor promised "She'll be all right in a few days."

Barely seven months later, Sheriff's deputies were again called to the hotel when Mary Binner took an apparent – unsuccessful – overdose of seconal tablets.

She was a guest of Texan James McKinley Bryant, who told police he was in the kitchen preparing steak when he found a note from Binner addressed to him and another woman that was asking for "forgiveness" – and then realized she had locked herself in the bathroom.

As for ghostly stories from inside the Sunset, the reputation they have for discretion prevented one person from being willing to be credited as anything more than "anonymous," though he did talk of several strange things known amongst the employees.

The Little Girl On The 12th Floor

The most striking were "lots of stories" about "a little girl" running around on the 12th floor. "Guests have reported seeing her too," he said, adding that a former housekeeper had a specific room on the 12th floor that she wouldn't go into:

"One time she had gone back into the corridor to get materials from her cart and, on returning to the room, saw that all the dresser drawers had been pulled out."

The Penthouse...

He also mentioned how another guest wanted to check out in the middle of the night after saying that "the paintings were looking at her," and then he spoke about the penthouse floor:

"There are two penthouse suites, and a chair in the hallway outside the door of both of them. One day an engineer was working in one of the suites, and when he came out he saw an elderly man sitting in the chair opposite, reading a newspaper or book. They nodded to each other and the engineer went to the elevator nearby. Turning back again as the doors opened, he saw that the man had vanished – but he wasn't a guest, as neither room was booked, and the corridor was a dead end."

As you might imagine, dinner or drinks in the Tower Bar is a very fancy affair – you are in a legendary gangster's apartment after all! Designed by internationally renowned decorator Paul Fortune, this 80 seater is a calm, walnut-paneled room lined with black and white photos from the golden years of Hollywood.

There's a fireplace too, live piano some nights, and special seating that's ideal for a discreet (or illicit) night out; you might want to reserve it in advance!

The food mixes northern Italy with a French bistro and wraps it in California stylings, but the real star of the night is arguably the view – you can take in the whole city from the terrace, which is also, of course, poolside.

The 2010 comedy *Dinner For Schmucks* shot a few scenes here, though perhaps its most famous appearance was in 1992's *The Player*, when studio executive Griffin Mill (Tim Robbins) met a mysterious screenwriter by that very same pool.

It's very old school Hollywood here (and there's a good chance you might see a famous face), but a mere mortal like me can only recommend the Tower Smash cocktail, which I picked because of the great name initially, but with tequila, basil, lemon and ginger, it also had the kick I was hoping for.

Alternatively, the Afternoon Bites won't break the bank – pay homage by trying the Tower Bar sliders or the Terrace club sandwich.

SSSS / Sun-Thu 6.30am-11pm, Fri & Sat until 11.30pm
www.sunsettowerhotel.com

Crossroads of the World
6671 Sunset Boulevard
Los Angeles, CA 90028

The Murder of the "Wolf of Spring Street"

When it was built in 1936 it was touted as the first outdoor shopping mall in America, and had an international theme – hence the name.

That theme was literally built in, as you can tell from the Streamline Moderne ocean liner main building, which looks like it has just docked alongside a number of foreign-styled bungalows.

The seven bungalows represented Spanish, Italian, French, Moorish and European architecture (as well as colonial New England and early California for American visitors), and they were planned as café's and unique stores on the street level, with offices above (one of which was once leased by Alfred Hitchcock).

There are other maritime elements here: portholes, a catwalk, a statue of a large pelican, a "lighthouse" at the back – and of course the huge Art Deco tower, which soars 30 foot above Sunset Boulevard and has a spinning white and blue globe with a bright red neon sign.

A landmark in Hollywood from day one, it was designed by Robert V. Derrah at a cost of $250,000, and his love of the sea is evident in another of his L.A. buildings, the Coca-Cola Building in South Central, a bottling plant that he built before the Crossroads and also looks like an ocean liner sailing the streets.

The mastermind behind the Crossroads was Ella Crawford, who clearly had a love of – and connections with – the world of movies and the theatrical.

On opening day, October 29, 1936, the *LA Times* reported there were foreign musicians, native dancers and folk singers, while stars including Cesar Romero and Boris Karloff greeted guests at their native bungalows.

The opening night was as glittering as a movie premiere, though it's hard to believe that the guests didn't know this building was born out of violence – and that Crawford's determination to build the Crossroads was because her husband had been murdered here.

Clark Left While Spencer Dying, Witness Swears

That was the *LA Examiner*'s headline several years before in August 1931, when Angelenos followed the story of a double murder at this address.

Former deputy D.A. David H. Clark had been accused of killing Ella's husband, Charles H. Crawford, a gangster and politician who was known as "The Wolf of Spring Street," and another man named Herbert Spencer, at Crawford's real estate office here.

Autoist and Former Jurywoman Identify Suspected Slayer; Story of Kidnaping Told

A witness said he had seen Clark leaving soon after hearing several gun shots – and it emerged Clark had bought a .38 Colt revolver the day before (and they were the same caliber of bullets found in the victims).

But Clark claimed the two men had pulled a gun on him, telling him to back off against the underworld, and wanting him to help them frame the Police Chief.

It sounded like the perfect noir, and it certainly had all the ingredients: the handsome D.A., the crooked guys, a gun, dead bodies and a question: murder or self-defense?

Clark was tried twice – a mistrial and then acquitted – but just months after the Crossroads had been opened by widow Ella Crawford he went missing and was found in France, apparently "insane."

He didn't escape criminal punishment forever though; he was later was convicted of a murder at a party, and died soon after starting his sentence in Chino Prison in 1954.

Crossroads of the World was a memorial of a sort for Spencer, and it seemed like a glamorous, winning concept. You could buy cigars, or handkerchiefs, or Asian art, or French dresses, and then get a haircut in the latest style. Celebrities and the public loved it – for a while – but it soon became more offices than stores.

It did get Historic-Cultural Monument status in 1974, but by then it was dilapidated and due to be demolished for – of course – a skyscraper, but developer Morton La Kretz bought and restored it, adding fountains and some other touches to the old style.

It was a music business favorite in the 1970s and onwards too: Jackson Browne, Bonnie Raitt and Crosby, Stills & Nash recorded and rehearsed here, as well Fleetwood Mac, Gladys Knight, Patti LaBelle, BB King, and America, who put the Crossroads Tower (surrounded by palm trees) on the back cover of their album *America's Greatest Hits* (1975).

Over the years it also featured in movies and TV shows like *Indecent Proposal*, *L.A .Confidential*, "Dragnet" and "Remington Steele," and in plenty of commercials and pop videos.

Also, if you're ever in Florida at Disney World, you'll see a reproduction of the tower and globe inside the entrance to Disney's Hollywood Studios.

Today it's home to music companies, production companies, writers and more movie-related businesses, though there's no restaurant or bar here to hang out at.

Even so, during the day it's usually easy to wander the "streets" of this unique and rather weird piece of L.A. history and remember the deadly way it all began…

www.crossroadshollywood.com

Updates –
Hollywood & W. Hollywood

The Cat & Fiddle closed towards the end of 2014, and has yet to reopen elsewhere, so where is the ghost of "The Smoking Man" – former owner Kim Gardner – going to be when that happens? His favorite spot for a cigarette (by the main gates) is still there though, so perhaps he'll have new owners and guests to watch over in the future.

Chateau Marmont – for readers wanting specific facts (or looking for the right room to stay in), it was bungalow #3 where John Belushi died aged just 33 after overdosing on a cocaine and heroin "speedball" on March 5, 1982.

The Magic Castle, as the name suggests, is a mecca for magicians. A private club that's part museum, part theatre and part library, it's also home to several bars – and at least two ghosts.

One is former bartender Tate Loren, who is regularly seen by guests in the Hat & Hare Bar, and there's also magician Chris Michaels, who died in 1986 while waiting in a chair to go on stage. Today Chris is fondly blamed for all technical problems.

Another late magician called Billy McComb is apparently still here too – you can sometimes smell his pipe in one of the theatres – so after dinner, try the drink they invented in his honor, "Billy's Nutty Irishman," which is coffee with Baileys and Frangelico.

There's a fun Harry Houdini séance room here too (though it's more Disney than anything netherworld), but it is true to say that this room was also the place where the mansion's original owner, banker and real estate magnate Rollin B. Lane, took his dying breath – in those days it was his bedroom.

Joe Berg, Master of Illusion, Dies

Finally, recent research uncovered an *LA Times* report from February 1984 about Joe Berg, a legendary trick inventor and owner of a magic store on Hollywood Boulevard, who had a heart attack while walking up to the Magic Castle (it is up a very steep hill!), and died a few days later. He was described as "a master of illusion, mentor of magicians and architect of trickery."

There have also been reports of a little girl in a white dress here, but that might be inspired by "Invisible Irma," who will play the piano just for you and graciously allowed herself to be photographed for souvenir postcards.

Sadly, February 2016 bought unexpected news about the real lady of the Magic Castle, Irene Larsen, who died aged 79. The very first member on the books, she helped set up the Magic Castle alongside brother Milt and her husband Bill, and as well as being Bill's stage assistant for years, she was a lifelong advocate of the magical arts. If there's any place in Hollywood where she might come back, this will be it…

Right next to – or rather, right above – the Magic Castle is **Yamashiro**, a huge, gorgeous Japanese mountain palace that recently celebrated its 100th birthday.

Inspired by a palace located in the Yamashiro Mountains near Kyoto, Japan, it was opened in 1914 by the Bernheimer brothers as a home – and virtual showcase – for their amazing oriental antiquity collections.

Inside the 10-room teak and cedar mansion the rafters were lacquered in gold and tipped with bronze dragons, and inside there's a sacred inner court garden.

Rooms were draped with luxurious silks and ancient tapestries, the garden landscaping was rumored to have cost $2 - 4m (a huge sum of money even then), and the hillside terraces were decorated with 30,000 varieties of trees and shrubs, waterfalls and hundreds of goldfish.

Miniature bronze houseboats floated along a maze of tiny canals, and though some of those features have passed into history (or storage), the famous 600-year-old pagoda is still here.

Operated for many years as a restaurant, Yamashiro is also home to many ghost stories – and the place where many security guards only worked one night before quitting in fright at what they'd seen and heard.

You can read all about it in *Gourmet Ghosts – Los Angeles*, though a recent sale and claims of exorbitant new monthly rent costs saw Yamashiro close – and then unexpectedly reopen barely a week later.

We visited just before the closing day, and as we were handed the menu we were told that it was much shorter than usual – a bad sign we thought, though perhaps it wasn't after all.

Either way, if you want a chance to sit at Table 9 in the Sunset Room, see Norman the ghost bartender or maybe hear the vanishing woman in the gardens, you should go soon – before anything else changes.

One thing is true though: previous owner Thomas Glover Sr's ashes were laid to rest in the north east corner under a tree in the inner court garden – so his spirit will always be here.

Back down on Hollywood Boulevard, a further search of the archives added more names to the list of people who have died at the **Roosevelt Hotel**.

On September 3, 1932, the *LA Times* reported Fred N. Baylies died of a heart attack in his room here, and on December 14, 1949 the same cause ended the life of 51 year old Major John Gaston, a millionaire financier and former Marine.

> **Hollywood detectives were informed the body was found slumped on the floor between twin beds, when a maid entered the room during mid-morning. Doctors said he had been dead about 12 hours.**

Perhaps the most famous long-term resident at the Roosevelt is the spirit of actor Montgomery Clift, who stayed here while filming the movie *From Here to Eternity* in 1953. He's still heard playing the bugle (his character was the army company bugler) and pacing up and down the corridor practicing his lines.

Also, one time a female guest stayed here and complained about the coffee pot, television and lights in her room switching on and off.

When it happened again in her new room, she checked out despite it being in the early hours of the morning. It turned out she had an Ouija board, and was trying to contact Clift.

Barely a block away from the Roosevelt is the **TCL Chinese Theatre**. A landmark in the movie world, it has hosted glittering movie premieres for decades and decades, and is the place with the handprints in concrete (the Dolby Theatre, where the Oscars take place every year, is just a stone's throw away too).

There was no evidence of any murders or suicides at the Theatre – or so it seemed…

In researching this book I found out that someone did die at 6925 Hollywood Boulevard, albeit a couple of years before the Theatre opened its doors.

There are more details under the entry for the Scientology Building, but on May 22, 1924, chorus girl Cecil Warner took a fatal dose of chloroform on learning of the suicide of her apparent lover, director Lew Mason.

Also, *Gourmet Ghosts – Los Angeles* reported on the murder death of actor Victor Kilian in March 1979, who had (unwisely) invited a man he met in a bar near the Chinese Theatre back to his apartment for drinks.

His battered body was found the next day, and it seemed that robbery was a probable motive – until, the very next day, it was revealed that another elderly actor named Charles Waggenheim had also been beaten to death in his home in the Hollywood Hills that same week.

Though there was talk of a serial killer, police arrested Stephanie Boon, a young nurse who looked after Waggenheim's invalid wife Lillian, two months later.

Despite Lillian being unable to say anything about what she may or may have not seen, Nurse Boon was sentenced to jail in January 1980.

Nurse Sentenced to 8-Year Term in Slaying of Actor

The *LA Times* noted that police theorized she had attacked Waggenheim with a table leg when he confronted her about stealing checks from him.

However, despite a $2,500 reward being put up by his friends, Kilian's killer was never caught – and it's said his ghost has wandered around the Boulevard by the Chinese Theater ever since.

Barely a few blocks from the Chinese Theatre is **Miceli's**, L.A.'s oldest Italian restaurant, which was opened in 1949 by Carmen Miceli, his wife and brothers. Sadly, in late November 2015 Carmen passed away aged 92.

Staff have long said that the spirit of waitress Antoinette "Toni" Heines, celebrated in stained glass in her old section, is still here, so why wouldn't Carmen want to check in every now and then too?

Chapter 2
Mid-City & Beverly Hills

El Carmen
8138 West 3rd Street
Los Angeles, CA 90048
Tel: 323 852 1552

Rock Stars & Ghosts

Originally appearing in one of the "Couldn't Get A Table" sections of *Gourmet Ghosts – Los Angeles*, El Carmen (at the time) didn't seem to have enough evidence to back up claims that it was haunted, nor any stories in the city's archives.

That changed after publication when several more stories – and people from the restaurant's past and present – shared their experiences, so now El Carmen has made it into *Gourmet Ghosts 2*.

Apologies then to those who have already read the story behind this popular 3rd Street joint, but there's definitely new information here, and so it's worth checking out again (and a great excuse for a margarita!)

El Carmen originally opened at 3rd Street and La Brea on September 15, 1929 in a location that was then almost at the edge of town, even out of reach of the city's famous trolley cars.

There's a plaque on the door that says it opened in 1927, though apparently that was a kind of marketing play at the time to make it seem as old as rival restaurants like El Cholo and El Coyote (the latter of which is featured in *Gourmet Ghosts – Los Angeles*).

Either way it was a big gamble for the owner Encarnación Gomez, who had ended up opening the doors on her own *taqueria* after a tragic and unexpected turn of events in her life.

Barely two years previously she had been preparing to return to Mexico and take her place as First Lady alongside her husband General Arnulfo Gomez, but then the man that people called *El Hombre Sin Vicios* ("The Man Without Vices") was captured and executed in Mexico City, leaving her isolated and almost penniless.

Determined not to be beaten she pawned her jewelry, gathered together some family recipes and did something that – at the time – was unthinkable for a widow: she went into business.

The Depression hit almost instantly, but her friendly welcome and great food soon saw directors Cecil B. DeMille and D.W. Griffith regularly sitting at the counter, and they helped keep the doors open during that time.

By 1947 artist Diego Riviera, singer Mario Lanza, choreographer Busby Berkeley and actors Vincent Price and John Wayne could all be seen here, and they followed when she moved to the current location back in the 1950s.

Moving into the 1960s and 1970s, and El Carmen became a favorite of some huge rock stars of the era. A woman who worked here then as a water girl recently came back for the first time in decades as part of her work for a tequila company, and she had some tales to tell.

After mentioning that both the bull's heads (which are over the front and kitchen doors) were in fact original fixtures, she then told several amazing rock anecdotes.

Jimi's Enchiladas & Fleetwood Mac Form

Firstly she recalled how an under-the-weather Jimi Hendrix – possibly during his time in Los Angeles in February/March 1965 – called in from his hotel bed to order some enchiladas.

Also, she said how Mick Jagger of the Rolling Stones gave an interview saying that he hated L.A. except for El Carmen, where a "crazy Mexican lady walks round with a spoon behind her ear, tasting everyone's food."

That was probably "Mama" Encarnación, who manned the till for 40 years, or perhaps her sister Hortencia, who was a chef here too.

In December 1974, El Carmen really was the location for a moment in rock history. Mick Fleetwood and John and Christine McVie were looking to add a new member to their band, guitarist Lindsey Buckingham, though he had insisted his singer girlfriend Stevie Nicks became part of the line-up too.

Fleetwood later described it as a night where there "was something magic in the air, and we all felt it. We also got drunk on the margaritas!" and by the time dessert had arrived, the most famous incarnation of Fleetwood Mac had more or less been born: just six months later they released their classic album *Fleetwood Mac*, which sold well over 5m copies.

Back in El Carmen's past times, Encarnación's granddaughter Montserrat Fontes recalled shooting a .22 gun into the then-deserted land out back, while grandson Paulino was the manager for several decades before he sold the restaurant in late 1997.

Following the sale half the space was then sold to Doughboys next door, and El Carmen became a small, snug bar with a *lucha libre* (Mexican wrestling) theme, complete with Mexican movie posters, masks and even an occasional visit from "wrestler" Tito La Brea himself!

It's a welcoming, colorful and intimate joint, and since there aren't many tables, booking ahead is always a good idea if you don't get there early.

This is even said to be the place where the "combo" plate was invented (a cheap mix-and-match meal where you make your own taco).

As for me, I highly recommend the *flautas* and guacamole; the latter is perhaps the best in town, in my own humble opinion – and that's no mean feat!

However, most people come in to pick from the hundreds of tequilas on offer, and many too for the *Hora De Fiesta* (Happy Hour).

It runs from 5-7pm every weekday and often sees the small bar packed with people getting salsa, chips and something with a kick from the knowledgeable bartenders.

    Gourmet Ghosts – Los Angeles originally relayed a story from bartender/supervisor Paige Gentry, then a new employee, who had had a very unusual experience:

"Last Sunday I was in the bar by myself, listening to the jukebox and getting ready for opening. Suddenly that very jukebox switched off. This is something that never happens – it runs off a separate amp and power source that's never turned off – yet when I went in back to check it again, it was turned off."

    But it was another story she told me that I later managed to connect with the bar's past:

"We have a jar of candy in the office, but my bag and hoodie were on the opposite side of the room. When I picked my bag and hoodie up later to leave, there were Reese's Pieces inside."

These may have just been an anonymous gift, but on further investigation I was told not only about staff members seeing strange shadows, boxes falling from shelves and shiver-inducing drafts by the back door, but that years ago there used to be a bowl of candy by the till.

Paulino, a member of the Magic Castle, told me in a later email that while he felt his grandmother's spirit would have "moved on," if there was any "malevolent ghost" it would perhaps be Hortencia or aunt Martha Gomez, step-daughter of Encarnación.

"She was a force to be reckoned with," he said about Martha, adding that whenever he was about to leave the restaurant she would walk to the till, grab the candy jar and offer him candy. "On a few times, she simply dumped a handful of candy on top of my check," he added.

Also, Craig Owens – the photographer, writer and researcher behind Bizarre Los Angeles – contacted me recalling the candy too, and remembering that on one of his many visits here "the day the cook had a stroke on the sidewalk outside the front of the restaurant. He didn't die, but he was pretty damaged and had to be taken away by ambulance."

Going there every week to visit and eat, he doesn't remember anyone ever talking about ghosts or whether the place was haunted, but he admitted that the candy story was a great coincidence – even though:

"(Martha) could be a personality that would turn off a jukebox. But then again, that family was raised on opera. We exchanged phone numbers when the restaurant was sold and we did speak a few times, but then we drifted apart."

He said that Martha, then 80, was "very upset" when the restaurant was sold.

She passed away in 2003, but perhaps it's possible that she – and maybe even Hortencia and Encarnación – are still keeping an eye on things.

Maybe they'll choose you as one of their favorite customers and leave you a sweet treat or two…

$$$ / Mon-Sat 5pm-2am, Sun from 7pm
www.elcarmenla.com

Beverly Hilton Hotel
Trader Vic's
9876 Wilshire Boulevard
Beverly Hills, CA 90210
Tel: 310 887 6055

The Howard Hughes Mystery

An institution in Beverly Hills – it's home to the glittering
Golden Globes award ceremony and where politicians and
Presidents stay when they're in town – this hotel had
perhaps the worst year imaginable in 2012, when music star
Whitney Houston, 48, drowned in her room's bathtub.

Whitney and Room 434

The resulting press hurricane – the city was already
full of media to cover that night's Grammy Awards – gave
the hotel such negative publicity, even though it was utterly
blameless in what happened that February night (the corner
ruled Houston's death accidental, with heart disease and
cocaine use listed as contributing factors).

Rumors swirled around Houston's death at the time,
but perhaps more tragic (and even weirder), was the fact
that her daughter Bobbi Kristina, 22, died in very similar
circumstances.

She was found face down in the bathtub at her Georgia home in January 2015, and died several months later after never really regaining consciousness.

Perhaps inevitably, fans of Whitney Houston now think she haunts the hotel, and though the room number was quickly changed, unsuspecting guests might be staying there without knowing it.

Then, just a few months after Houston's death, the Hilton was the stage for another bloody tragedy.

Murder-Suicide

An elderly couple who had been living at the hotel since December the previous year – and were apparently struggling with financial problems – were found in their room dead from gunshot wounds to the head.

Oddly, it was the night before yet another ceremony – the 39th Annual Daytime Emmy Awards – was scheduled to be held in the ballroom, though the police didn't look for a criminal motive, as there was a suicide note.

Had they died somewhere other than this recently-infamous hotel, it's unlikely their sad story would have got more than a passing mention in the newspapers.

Back in 1977, there was another famous death here – actor Peter Finch, 60, passed away soon after suffering a heart attack in the lobby.

Just weeks later he became the first person to receive a posthumous Oscar as Best Actor for his role in *Network* (his famous line being "I'm mad as hell, and I'm not going to take this anymore!"), the award being collected by his widow Eletha.

Nola Hahn, Onetime Pal of Gamblers, Ends Life

There was another suicide at the Beverly Hilton back in 1957. Nola Hahn, 60, owner of the Clover Club on Sunset Boulevard and "crony of big-time gamblers" according to the *LA Times*, checked into a room and took a fatal dose of barbiturates, the chambermaid finding his body sprawled across the bed the next morning.

Hahn's wife had died a year previously, but his suicide note offered no clues, reading simply:

"Nobody to blame."

Perhaps the strangest story associated with the Beverly Hilton is that of the 1974 murder of Alfred Wayne Netter, who died due to the deadly plans of his business associates John H. Meier, Gordon Hazelwood and William McCory.

Murder Indictment of Ex-Hughes Aide Told

Secret Charges Reportedly Involve Slaying of Business Associate at Hotel

Hard to find out anything about in the archives, it's tempting to wonder whether it was kept under wraps at the time because the accused Meier was a former scientific advisor and confidante to billionaire recluse Howard Hughes.

Either way, the trio was finally charged in a secret indictment in 1981, a month after Meier had been released on parole from his 30 month sentence for obstructing justice.

It was a punishment handed out after he used forged documents in a 1972 civil trial in which he had been accused of "bilking Hughes" (said the *LA Times*) out of over $8m.

Like many other murders, Netter's killing was motivated by greed. There was a life insurance policy taken out on the group's idea of using a VCR-type machine in theatres, and the deadly scheme seemed to come to its conclusion over dinner.

Savage Knife Attack

Netter ordered food for two from room service, and though the second guest wasn't positively identified, it was McCory who was accused of stabbing Netter fifteen times in a "savage knife attack."

While an arrest warrant was issued for McCory, the *LA Times* reported that Hazelwood had been offered immunity in return for his cooperation; he had inferred that he had "certain documents in his possession," apparently.

McCory was never found however, and in 1986 Meier took a plea-bargain in which he admitted to harboring a suspect (whether it was McCory or Hazelwood no one knows) and was sentenced to two years, then freed because of time served. All other charges were dropped.

Not surprisingly the hotel isn't keen to recall its darker past, let alone talk of ghosts or things out of the ordinary (up until its 2007 "renovation" their noted tiki bar Trader Vic's was a favorite for illicit liaisons too), and their PR company said they had "nothing to contribute."

However, a report in *Angeleno* magazine in 2013 quoted psychic medium Thomas John saying that the hotel does feature some of the strange electrical anomalies and missing objects that are common to buildings of this kind that have heavy foot traffic.

Psychic Revelations

John also mentioned two apparitions that have been seen by many employees over the years in the eighth floor ballroom.

The male apparition is said to be a former electrician, and the woman is rumored to be a former guest, while "Jeopardy" and "Wheel of Fortune" creator (and former owner) Merv Griffin is supposedly here too.

However, despite the hotel certainly being a place of suicide and murder, there are no clear connections between those stories and the archives.

A Waldorf Astoria hotel is being constructed on the site right next to the Beverly Hilton, and is due to open in 2017. That means more glamour for Beverly Hills, but it will still be many more years before the 1954 time capsule sealed under the Hilton lobby will be dug up.

Time Capsule Placed in Beverly Hilton Hotel

Designed by architect Welton Becket as an "ultra smart" hotel of 582 rooms, the Beverly Hilton had an unusual gimmick to help speed up construction; it built all those rooms (right down to the furniture and decoration) somewhere else, and they could simply be craned into place like Lego bricks.

Walt Disney was said to be a fan of this idea, and commissioned Becket to do the same for his futuristic Contemporary Hotel in Walt Disney World in Florida.

We already know what's in the capsule; a prayer written by Conrad Hilton, menus, a phone directory, a local newspaper, a world almanac and one more item, which is the only thing we can be certain will still be recognizable to everyone when the capsule is opened: a Beverly Hills Police Department parking ticket!

If you visit, regardless of what food you order, you really must have a Mai Tai (rum, Curaçao, lime juice an syrup) in the Polynesian-themed Trader Vic's, a lounge that serves island appetizers and over 75 exotic cocktails.

Trader Vic was in fact Victor Jules Bergeron, Jr., the genius behind the kitschy chain that, while tiki may go in and out of fashion, is still a favorite for many.

The Trader Vic's here isn't as over-the-top (in terms of décor) as, say, the Tonga Hut and others, but it has been a watering hole for celebrities for decades.

There's a short daily happy hour 4-6pm, but I tend to make for Tuesday (Korean taco day), and Wednesday, which is the night for dim-sum (they're available for longer, between 5-8pm).

$$$$ / Sun-Thu 11am-midnight, Fri & Sat until 1am
www.beverlyhilton.com

May Co. Building (AMPAS Museum)
Ray's & Stark Bar/LACMA
5905 Wilshire Boulevard
Los Angeles, CA 90036
Tel: 323 857 6180

The Ghost of the Murdered Wife

Due to open at the end of 2017 as the museum of the Academy of Motion Picture Arts and Sciences (the organization behind the Oscars), this was originally the first branch department store of the California-based May Company, and the new museum will retain its distinctive golden tiled cylinder.

Opened in 1939 at a cost of $2m, this helped it quickly became a landmark on Wilshire as the May Co. opened stores all over the State, with the company only going further afield in the late 1980s and then merging with JW Robinson's in 1993 to form Robinson's-May.

Designed by Albert C. Martin, Sr, also the architect of the downtown Million Dollar Theater and co-designer of L.A's City Hall, it is one of the city's most notable Streamline Moderne buildings, and is a Historic-Cultural Monument.

In the 1980s there was talk of trying to link it up with the proposed mall development at the nearby Farmers Market, but that never came to pass – and soon after the merger with Robinson's it was sold to the Los Angeles County Museum of Art, which was located next door, and served as LACMA West exhibition and events space until it was announced that AMPAS were moving in.

Arguably the May Co's most famous store – it has featured in the background of many movies and television shows – it was however already LACMA West when it had a birds-eye view over one of the most famous murders in Los Angeles history.

R.I.P. Biggie Smalls

On March 7, 1997, rapper Notorious B.I.G was shot four times when the SUV he was travelling in was stopped at a red light on the junction at the corner of Wilshire and Fairfax and someone pulled alongside and opened fire. The murder was famously never solved, and has been the focus of a number of conspiracy theories ever since – just take a look online!

There have been some unusual – and even deadly – events actually inside the May Co. building though. The June 27, 1988 edition of the *LA Times* told the story of an amazing find that had been unearthed when work was being done on the men's restroom.

Pocket-Sized Crime Story Told in Shaft

At the bottom of a ventilation shaft workers found 125 wallets and purses – the ill-gotten gains of thieves who had presumably used it as a dumping ground after taking out any money they had found inside.

Police said that while some wallets still had ID inside, only a handful could be connected to theft reports, and that those reports came from the last few years – and not all inside the store, either.

Horrified patrons witness murder-suicide at May Co.

Almost exactly a year later, there was a real spasm of violence within the refined department store – and *LA Times* readers were shocked to learn that the victim and suspect were an elderly couple.

Evelyn Wasserman, 79, was about to play cards with her friends in the large, pink, fifth floor dining room of the store when suddenly her estranged husband, 87 year old Jack, approached her, shot her in the neck and chest, and then turned the gun on himself – and all without ever saying a word.

"They all started screaming, these old ladies," said Ruthie Brodey, one of the large groups of people the store happily allowed in to play cards while sipping coffee.

The couple had separated recently and Evelyn had told friends she was afraid of Jack's temper after he had become isolated and accused her of "stealing his money."

A sensation across Los Angeles, it inevitably lead to stories that the building was now haunted by this tragic couple, forever united unhappily in death.

Interestingly, I did find evidence to back up this story from one of the building's employees, someone I shall only identify as "C".

In both 2012 and 2014 I exchanged emails with C, and initially he or she very much implied that the staff knew all about a ghost in the building, even naming the ghost as that of a woman "killed by her husband in the top floor restaurant here. We talk about her often," C said.

Clearly there's a link here between the story and the spirit world, but C also mentioned that people have also reported seeing or feeling different things in the building.

However, once the building was leased to AMPAS, C became increasingly reluctant to go into further details, even saying that a promised tour of the building now wasn't possible anymore.

Make of that what you will – it very much seemed to me that staff did think there was something unusual or ghostly here (certainly at one time) – but since the AMPAS museum isn't open for some time, there are some other ghostly stories associated with LACMA itself to be getting on with...

The old Ahmanson Building (which towers above Ray's and Stark Bar) is said to have a haunted third floor.

Staff apparently don't like going up there when the museum is closed or late at night because a ghostly woman in a white dress has been seen in the corridors.

The Woman in White on the 3rd Floor

Women in white, black or even red dresses are a rather common apparition (there are several examples in *Gourmet Ghosts – Los Angeles*), and it's possible the story of the unfortunate Evelyn has spirited itself from one building to the next.

It may also have had an influence on the story that staff in the Leo S. Bing Theater (go on a Tuesday afternoon when they show classic movies for $4!), have said they've seen an elderly woman who sits in the back corner of the auditorium, but who vanishes when you go near her.

If nothing else, this part of the Miracle Mile definitely has the potential to explode into a deadly fireball, thanks to the methane gas that's trapped underground and regularly bubbles up into the famous La Brea Tar Pits – and also leaches up through the sidewalks around the museum.

Finally, if you ever happen to be in the park at night, keep an ear out for the screams of "La Brea Woman."

The only human remains ever found in the tar pits and estimated to be over 10,000 years old, she was aged around 25-30 when she died.

Though it seems she was definitely interred there, her death wasn't suspicious: it didn't seem to have been an accident, and she wasn't the victim of a murder either.

You don't have to go into LACMA to see the iconic "Urban Light" sculpture outside, or to have a drink or a meal at Ray's & Stark Bar. The Ray's part is a small indoor space with tables and chairs whereas the Stark Bar, right alongside, is a cool outdoor space with funky red chairs, curved sofa chairs and a 1970s vibe.

Believe it or not, the longest water menu in America is available here – choices from Italy, Canada, Denmark, New Zealand, Norway, Fiji, Spain, France, Germany, the UK and the USA – and all of them described in depth.

I was more impressed by their selection of gins, and the many California wines, spirits and cocktail available from seems like a deceptively small bar. There's a Happy Hour here (Mon-Fri 3-6pm) and I recommend Ray's Swizzle cocktail (bourbon, ginger syrup, mint, lime) and their wood-fired margarita pizza.

$$$ / Mon, Tue & Thu 11.30am-8pm, Fri until 10pm, Sat & Sun 10am-8pm, Closed Wednesday
www.lacma.org
www.patinagroup.com/rays-and-stark-bar
www.oscars.org/museum/about/building

Tom Bergin's Tavern
840 South Fairfax Avenue
Los Angeles, CA 90036
Tel: 323 936 7151

Tom's Still Everywhere!

Tom Bergin's would definitely have been in *Gourmet Ghosts – Los Angeles*, except that at the time it was closed, then reopened briefly and then closed once again, so instead it was featured in the "Extra! Extra!" section of the website www.gourmetghosts.com

It was rather an uncertain period in the story of one of the oldest continually-operating bars in Los Angeles, and some people wondered if it was even going to make its 80th anniversary.

Happily though, a Tom's regular called Derek Schreck and his business partner Jordan Delp finally ponied up and bought the place in 2013.

They opened the doors again early the next year, and so the anniversary was indeed celebrated in February 2016, with many of the punters already looking forward to the legendary St. Patrick's Day event here the following month (come early, and be prepared for plenty of madness!).

Despite Irish pubs seeming to be everywhere in the world, there's actually not that many in Los Angeles. San Francisco has plenty of course, as does San Diego, though Tom Bergin's, which looks like a quaint old cottage, has nevertheless managed to carve out a niche as one of the most famous Irish pubs in the country.

Inspired by his uncle who had a tavern with the same name in Boston, lawyer Tom Bergin first opened the doors of Tom Bergin's Old Horse Shoe Tavern and Thoroughbred Club on February 12, 1936 at the original location, which was a few blocks away from here.

Tom's Tipple

Barely a year after opening, Schreck explained, Bergin ordered a custom label single malt scotch (you can still see some of the labels around the bar), though he didn't have a regular drink himself: "Tom drank a lot of everything – he was Irish!"

Over the years the Thoroughbred Club and Horse Shoe were dropped from the name, though the horseshoe-shaped bar is still present and correct. In fact, it was considered such an important part of the bar that during the move to its current spot in 1949, some of the regulars carried it to make sure it made the move safely.

Decades later, Tom Bergin's allegedly made a vital contribution to television when it inspired writers Les and Glen Charles, who felt that this bar was a place "where everyone knows your name."

Of course, they came up with the idea for "Cheers," the sitcom which ran from 1982 to 1993 on NBC and still regularly plays around the world.

In early series of the show there was a character called "Coach" (played by Nicholas Colasanto until his death in 1985), and he was based on Tom Bergin's head bartender Chris Doyle, who still occasionally works here, despite being semi-retired.

A feature you'll immediately notice is that the walls and ceiling are liberally plastered with green shamrocks, all of which have names on them.

Getting your own hand-painted shamrock in Tom Bergin's is a huge honor in this town, and the tradition began in 1950, with honorees including Cary Grant, Ronald Reagan and Keifer Sutherland, though John Wayne and Bing Crobsy also popped in here too.

Tales of spirits and banshees are everywhere in Ireland, and online at least there are a couple of stories about paranormal sightings here, though during research for *Gourmet Ghosts – Los Angeles* I spoke to then-owner T.K. Vodrey, and the only strange visitor he knew for certain was of the living, breathing, equine variety.

It was on St. Patrick's Day 1978 when a horse was brought in here to promote a Walter Matthau movie called *Casey's Shadow*, an inspirational tale about a no-hoper nag who becomes a champion. Speaking to the *LA Times* in 1987, Chris Doyle recalled that day:

"We poured a couple of bottles of Guinness into a bucket, and the damned horse loved it… we had to drag him away from the bar!"

There's a big sign outside that says "House of Irish Coffee," and, like many other places, Tom Bergin's claims to be the first place in America that served the warming drink of whisky, coffee, cream and sugar.

Whether that's true or not, you have to try one – or of course a pint of Guinness, which is properly poured and thoroughly respected here (which isn't always the case).

The menu is above what you'd expect from a pub (well, this is L.A.), and alongside sandwiches, burgers, fish dishes and Shepherd's Pie there's also a kale-based salad, whisky-injected smoked and shaved beef (a "Naughty Cow"), crispy brussels sprouts and more.

I usually go in for a pint of Guinness, but I can recommend the hearty meatballs (lamb sausage, fig, tomato and horseradish/mustard aioli) and if I was ever there for brunch, I'd have to try the salmon Scotch egg with panko and curry mayo.

When I spoke to Schreck in late 2015, he admitted that as a former history graduate he was a fan of historic properties like Tom Bergin's, so just couldn't resist the chance to buy it when he had the opportunity. More than that, he says that he "did a lot of the renovation myself."

Died Happily At The Bar

He also revealed what seemed to be a little-known story about a former patron who died here in the early 1980s. She was an elderly lady – a regular – and passed away quietly while sitting in her usual seat at the bar.

"She was often there until after close," says Schreck, "so nobody thought too much of the fact she was still there."

There was a plaque affixed to her seat in tribute, but it became too damaged and worn to be read, so during the renovation Schreck moved it, and it's currently in a file in his office.

Confirming other reports that Tom Bergin still haunts the bar he created, Schreck spoke at length about his own experiences:

"Soon after I had had bought the bar and was working there alone, I felt the essence of smoke, right where Tom used to sit at the bar."

That smell of smoke (and of course the pub is non-smoking) has also been smelled by others, emanating from Tom's favorite booth in the corner.

The most common sighting of Tom's ghost happens in the dining room at the back, where many members of the cleaning crew – and bartenders – have seen a man in a three-piece suit sitting by the fireplace:

"We like to think that it's Tom still keeping an eye on the place, though over the years I've had four night time cleaning crews quit because of what they have seen. Some bartenders have quit too, some of them saying that they even heard Tom's ghost whisper their name."

Neon Spirit…

Perhaps the most likely place to see Tom's spirit is in that noticeable neon sign. "We spent $60,000 restoring it" says Schreck, explaining that the "Tom Bergin" lights up green while the rest of it is white:

"The sign's all on one electrical circuit – you turn it on, you turn it off – but we've noticed that, especially when the bar is quiet, the "Tom" blinks off and on, and we just cannot work out how it happens!"

Clearly, Tom wants you to come in for a pint.

$$$ / Mon-Thu 5pm-2am, Fri & Sat 11am-2am, and Sun 11am-11pm, but be aware: the kitchen always closes earlier…
www.tombergins.com

E. Clem Wilson Building
Olio - The Crêpe Kitchen
5223 Wilshire Boulevard
Los Angeles, CA 90036
Tel: 323 933 3403

Ghosts and Ghost Signs

Perhaps one of the most recognizable buildings in L.A., the E. Clem Wilson is at the corner of La Brea and Wilshire (the spot for a Metro subway station on the Purple Line, due to be completed in 2023 – you'll doubtless see the construction work).

Designed by Meyer & Holler (the team behind the Chinese and Egyptian Theatres in Hollywood), it opened in July 1930. It's very much in the Streamline Moderne style of Art Deco, and perhaps could be described as looking like a kind of castle, with several fortress levels leading to the summit.

That summit also originally had a tall mast for airships to dock with, and the building was funded by Elihu Clement Wilson, an Ohio native who came to Los Angeles as a child, and made a fortune in oil tool manufacturing.

He died in 1950, just months before film crews used the exterior of the building to stand in for *The Daily Planet* offices in the television series "Adventures of Superman."

With the building in such a prominent position and standing 190 foot tall, it was an ideal place for advertising – so in the 1970s a rather unattractive box structure was added atop it.

That meant the Mutual of Omaha insurance logo could be seen by drivers along Wilshire, and then later people from miles around were with urged with bright, electronic signs to try Asahi beer and, most recently, anything made by Samsung.

In early 2015 the Samsung letters were removed, and it became what is known as a "ghost sign."

Found in many cities across the world, they're simply the remnants of usually huge painted signs that once stretched up and along the side of large buildings, rising above street level and hopefully catching the eye of pedestrians below.

Today we're far more used to digital billboards, but you can still go to downtown L.A. and seek out lots of these forgotten (and usually hidden) gems from another era.

Many are carefully crafted around windows and roof tops, often using arrows to make the point that almost everything you ever wanted (was once) available at the store below.

The "ghost" part of the name is because they have become badly faded, flaked away or even been partly hidden by later construction, but look up (or take a trip down well-lit alleys) and you might find a relic of the past.

Modern apartments have started to re-introduce this trend of large wall signs, though it's fair to say the ghost sign on this building (what locals would might even call the Samsung, Asahi or even Omaha Building, depending on their age) is rather unique, and certainly the most visible in the area.

When the E. Clem Wilson building first opened one of the ground floor tenants was the Owl Drug Company, though today (doubtless due to the Metro construction), it seems to be in transition.

There's a small shop called Olio (delicious sweet and savory crepes, salads and paninis with a Mediterranean influence), a computer repair store, a barbershop, a rug and ornament store, two currently-empty units and the former restaurant Luna Park.

Ghost Restaurant

Known for its PBR in a paper bag and its cheese fondue – both real favorites of mine – Luna Park closed suddenly in late 2015 (so suddenly there were eviction and Sheriff's notices on the door).

Like the Spanish Kitchen on Beverly Boulevard that you can read about in *Gourmet Ghosts – Los Angeles* (which, coincidentally, is also again empty), Luna Park also became a "Ghost Restaurant."

For weeks after the closure the lights remained on inside – the televisions above the bar too – and it was even a while before the neon sign outside was turned off.

But the lights remained on for many more months, like they were ready to open for business in just a moment – and sure enough, in June 2016 a notification of a new restaurant went up in the window.

On visiting the Wilson building – faded marble walls and a postal chute running down from the top floor to the battered, golden mail box in the lobby – I made my way to the basement parking garage, where the electricity outlets and transformers were located.

Electric Shock
Beheads Worker

It was down in this basement in May 1945 that a Bureau of Power & Light engineer named Orin LaRue was working on one of the transformers when it accidentally exploded and he was electrocuted by 4800 volts, the shock setting him alight and – horrifically – ripping his head clean off his body.

Today the electricity transformers are behind a solid door, and while the valet had no strange stories himself, he did tell me that the cleaner Martina, who has worked there for seven years, has mentioned some odd things happening:

"She's usually here at night, when there is no one around, and she's said that she had often heard the sound of a baby crying."

Double Suicide

There may well have been the sound of tears here in the past, because in September 1936 rug importer John Keshishyan slashed his left wrist while he was in his office here – and he'd also taken a huge dose of sleeping tablets the night before.

RUG IMPORTER CRITICALLY ILL AFTER SUICIDE ATTEMPT

He was rushed to hospital and listed as in a critical condition, while his suicide note merely listed his home address details.

It was a place perhaps of domestic unhappiness for him since June 1932, when his wife Claire "took poison" and killed herself there, apparently despondent over the "loss of the family fortune."

Mrs. John S. Keshishyan Takes Poison

Husband Finds Her Dead in Palatial Home

Keshishyan reportedly found her "lips blue and her body cold," and called Dr. Thomas A. Hogan, who police then found pouring the contents of a bottle into the drain because "he feared the bereaved husband might obtain it."

Sadly it seems that Dr. Hogan's fears came true, and though there is a rug store – Baker Rugs – in one of the street level units here (though it too is about to close), on investigation it didn't seem that there was a connection.

$$ / Daily 9am-5pm
http://crepepluskitchen.com

Café Jack
508 South Western Avenue
Los Angeles, CA 90020
Tel: 213 365 8882

Tarot Cards Ahoy!

Themed restaurants are common everywhere, but not many have tarot card reading on the menu.

Set back off the street, there's no mistaking Café Jack when you see it: it looks like a mini-version of the doomed ocean liner that's somehow come to rest in this part of Koreatown.

As you might have guessed from the name plate on the ship's bow – and the choice of maritime stylings (to say nothing of pictures and posters from the blockbuster movie) – this restaurant was inspired by *Titanic*, and the character of Jack Dawson (played by Leonardo DiCaprio).

I visited here for the *LA Weekly* and mentioned in my article that, with all the maze-like additions of tables snaking around the ship and the crazy, collage-style décor and fittings, it seemed like survivors from a shipwreck had built their own little settlement here using whatever they could find.

Owner/captain Jack Shin bought this empty lot on 5th Street and spent what he admitted was close to around $500,000, then, with just one "helper," built his unique homage to the 1997 weepie.

They used real boating material for the liner itself, and then painted and nailed for a year, adding finds from antique stores and flea markets alongside all the nautical touches before opening the doors in 2007.

Ramshackle is how I'd describe Café Jack today; on a more recent visit it seemed a little worse for wear, but the locals still hold it in their hearts (you might see a business meeting here, or students working at one of the tables), but then there's a hidden attraction too.

Inside it seems that there are seemingly endless decked corridors, and you'll find a little bit of everything: private "cabin" rooms, snugs, patios, large communal tables, a piano, shiny lights, and even window murals with tiny balconies complete with potted plants and bird feeders.

There are also lots and lots of hearts: stuffed hearts, heart lights, heart pillows and heart objets d'art because Shin really is a *Titanic* movie nut.

He's watched it hundreds of times and in the interview he called Café Jack "my home, my dream, where every day can be happy. I live here!"

Due to the locale the menu is largely Korean food, though you can stick a pin in the menu and hit something tasty adorned with the prefix "Jack." There's plenty of sushi, pasta, chicken wings, curries, and other choices too, while many – especially teen visitors – come here for the teas, shaved ice, coffee, juices and boba smoothies.

It's a popular place to hang out and talk – just press the bell on the wall for service – and of course you can sing your heart out (karaoke's available here as well).

As for the spirits, they're not alcoholic (there's no beer or wine here), but instead they come from Shin's otherworldly abilities. You might even see a small placard – in Korean – that shows his skills: he gives tarot card readings every night from around 7pm.

Apparently he's extremely famous for his accuracy, and in fact the café relies more on the income from his practice than the food and drinks it sells – which nonetheless still seems a little pricey.

It has been 10 years since Café Jack opened and nearly 20 since the movie, so while tourists tend to be a rare sight these days, something is still bringing people here – and it seems to be that universal desire to learn about your luck, love, fate and future.

If you want a reading, book well in advance – and I hope the wind blows fair for a good luck of the draw!

$$$ / Mon-Thu & Sun 12pm-1m, Fri & Sat until 2am
www.cafejackla.com

Chapter 3
Downtown

Ace Hotel
929 South Broadway
Los Angeles, CA 90015
Tel: 231 623 3233

Ghostly Women and Human Legs...

Since they opened in 2014, the Ace Hotel has very much been the hip and happening place to be – and stay – in downtown Los Angeles. At least part of that is because they're inside the ornate United Artists Building, home to the gorgeous United Artists Theater, something that's quickly become a major events venue in this town.

Built in 1927 for the maverick movie studio (United Artists was set up by actors Charlie Chaplin, Douglas Fairbanks, Mary Pickford and director D.W. Griffith to give them much more artistic control), the building was designed by C. Howard Crane of Walker & Eisen.

The building's style is Spanish Gothic – a favorite of Pickford – and was inspired by the Segovia Cathedral in Spain (do make sure you look up at the many evocative statues and small, comedic figures dotted along the building – like that bespectacled guy!).

Since Broadway was then the centre of the city's glittering movie palaces, they wanted the first and flagship United Artists Theater to be here too – and if you ever get the chance to go inside, make sure you do: it's exactly what you'd imagine a golden picture house to be like.

For a short time this was the tallest building in town, though it hasn't always been exactly what Charlie and his friends envisioned.

In later years it changed owners and was known as the Texaco Building, and later in 1989 the evangelist preacher Gene Scott leased the theater for Sunday services.

On the building at the back is the distinctive red "Jesus Saves" neon sign, which originally came from the Church of the Open Door (which itself used to be behind Checkers Hotel), and which Scott bought with him when he moved onto Broadway.

Scott later purchased the United Artists Building outright, holding services there until his death in 2005 – and apparently amassing an enormous collection of bibles.

His widow Melissa carried on services for TV, radio and online audiences, but in 2011 it was sold to the developers who wanted to create the boutique Ace Hotel (182 rooms, a pool, a restaurant and bars) and make the theater a concert and events venue.

From day one the Ace Hotel has seen celebrities come and go, but there was a different structure here from at least 1891 (when Mrs. F.C. Woodbury apparently invited her friends round for a "pleasant evening" playing whist), and the darker history of this address goes back to the late 19th century too.

The Ghastly Discovery Made in the Rear of a House on South Broadway Yesterday Morning.

As reported in the March 3, 1895 edition of the *LA Times*, housekeeper Mrs. Moore had come across something "mysterious" that morning.

The headline read "A Mysterious Leg" and told how she had noticed a "peculiar odor" coming from the back yard and was preparing a bonfire to burn some trash when she found a bundle wrapped tightly in paper – the 1893 Christmas edition of the *Ladies' Home Journal*, no less – and, on cutting the string, found inside the decomposed remains of a human leg.

Coroner Campbell concluded that it was the leg of a woman and seemed to have been an amputation or "dissection from a dead one" (no one was able to tell which), but he did say that it was "too valuable to be thrown about in such a way" by a medical student.

CASE OF CARELESS DISPOSAL OF HUMAN REMAINS.

Murder was considered, but it seemed that unless there were "further discoveries" in connection with the limb, "the thing" would probably be buried.

The long article then concluded with the revelation (something that surely should have been mentioned earlier), that *another* human foot had been found buried here a few months previously!

A couple of years later in March 1897, a long article – really what we today would call an "advertorial" – told the tale of "A Chinese Romance' between the rich, eligible Fan Li and her poor but handsome gardener, Ah Sing.

Their Romeo and Juliet-style courtship saw Ah Sing afflicted by sunstroke and cured by melon broth made by Dr. Tom Foo Yuen, who lived at 929 South Broadway and treated all kinds of disease "with extraordinary success."

REMOVAL.

Dr. T. Foo Yuen, the Imperial Chinese physician of No. 17 Barnard Park and late of No. 903 South Olive street, has moved to No. 929 South Broadway, where he would be pleased to meet his old friends and patients.

This short announcement in August the previous year had welcomed "old friends and patients" to his new surgery here, so maybe they hadn't been coming to see the "Imperial Chinese" physician as much as he wanted.

Murder On The 13th Floor

Moving forward to the years of WWII when this was the Texaco Building, it was barely a week after it had been declared an air-raid shelter when death came in the front door – and then there was an attempted murder-suicide in an office on (appropriately) the 13th floor.

Furious that he was about to be fired (seemingly because his nosy nature had caused a number of employees to quit), 52 year old Lawrence P. McClellan "went berserk" and shot at his boss James T. Wood, Jr, before turning the gun on himself.

Man Kills Self as Superior Shot

Wood wasn't seriously injured – though he did lose a number of teeth – and puzzled fellow employees said there wasn't any previous bad blood between the pair, who had worked together for many years.

It didn't change anything though: McClellan had shot himself behind the ear with his .25, and was dead when the ambulance arrived.

On a recent visit there I talked to Amelia Posada, the florist/designer at the Birch and Bone store that's in the outside theatre lobby, and she revealed a number of ghost stories about the building:

"I always feel the absolute presence of something when I'm in the theatre. It's overwhelming."

There's a Ladies and a Men's Lounge in the theatre too, and Amelia said that the air always feels "thick and heavy" in the Ladies Lounge, and that an employee named Conrad, when he's in the Men's Lounge, always find that his shoelaces are undone.

Crying Child & Woman in White

She also mentioned a hotel guest from Japan who reported hearing a child laughing and crying in their room's bathroom, and how they were "freaked out" by the sounds.

Additionally, she said that a woman in a white dress had been seen, and that maintenance staff and maids regularly say certain floors and rooms feel haunted: one person who was waxing the floor in the Segovia Hall, an event space on the second floor, had a very unsettling experience:

"He heard the clicking of high heels, and then he turned round and saw a women standing nearby. He went to talk to her – and she simply vanished."

If you only have time for a cocktail at the Ace, you have to go to Upstairs, their rooftop bar. Lined with low couches and sofas – the crowd often end up sitting by the pool – it offers not only amazing views and a regular DJ, but a chance to see and be seen and enjoy nibbles like charred plums, hummus, quinoa, and apricots.

Downstairs is the all-day, French-style, black-and-white tiled L.A. Chapter brasserie just off the hotel lobby. Here you can get pancakes, California fave avocado toast, burgers, oysters, burgers and a kale and seaweed salad.

$$$$ / L.A. Chapter 7am-3.30pm and 5.30-11pm, Upstairs Bar 11am-2am
www.acehotel.com/losangeles

Barclay Hotel
103 West 4th Street
Los Angeles, CA 90013
Tel: 213 626 5231

Slashing Serial Killers & The Deadly Elevator

The oldest continually-operating hotel in Los Angeles, the Barclay Hotel was called the Van Nuys when it opened in January 1897, and it was the height of luxury at the time.

There was a telephone and electricity in every room, lush furniture, elaborate carpets, sixty private bathrooms (en suite) and ten public ones.

"Of special interest to the ladies" said the *LA Times* was a "neat device" for the heating of curling irons, and in the grill-room and bar guests were going to be entertained by Romandy's Orchestra during meal times. Even the basement had a billiard room and barbers.

The proprietor was Milo F. Potter, and the hotel was named after owner Isaac Newton Van Nuys, one of L.A's wealthiest businessmen (though not the founder of the city of Van Nuys).

If you look carefully at the stained glass windows in the lobby, among the banquets and dancers you'll see some seahorses holding up a crest with the initials "V. N." and there's still a reminder of the past on the wall outside.

Designed by architectural firm Morgan and Walls, this six-story Beaux Arts-style building with Romanesque stylings cost nearly $300,000, and the lobby is still home to many original pieces including the plasterwork, columns and door arches.

TERRIBLE ACCIDENT AT THE NEW VAN NUYS HOTEL.

Sadly, tragedy came to the hotel barely six weeks after it had opened.

MANGLED BEFORE HE FELL.

In a horrendous accident, waiter Charles G. Gamble was killed in a way that many people might have terrible nightmares about.

As reported on March 4, 1897, he and the elevator boy, Robert White, were going down to the first floor and "joking" together when White turned the lever the wrong way, and it began going up again.

Having "lost their presence of mind," White jumped out of the still-moving elevator at the third floor and Gamble, apparently frightened, tried to follow him out – but too late. Caught in the doorway, the rising elevator then pinned his legs:

"They snapped like pipestems…"

The *LA Times* went on to graphically describe how Gamble's body was dragged up by the foot until "that was smashed" and he fell head-first to his death, his skull fractured in multiple places and his left eye actually torn from the socket.

Amazingly Gamble was still alive, but "after nearly an hour of intense suffering," he died in hospital.

BELL BOY KILLED.

Tragically (and creepily) a second hotel named the Van Nuys Broadway and also owned by Potter (it was located on nearby 4th and Broadway) was the scene of yet another stomach-churning elevator accident a couple of days into the new century.

"His internal organs were crushed…"

Bell boy Earl Newton, aged just 16, was on top of the elevator cage when he accidentally pulled on the power rope, causing the elevator to rise and trap him between the shaft and the ceiling on that floor.

His internal organs were instantly crushed, and the blood rushing to his head turned his face purple.

It was however a good day for the Van Nuys on Main in 1901, when President William McKinley stayed here (just a few months before his assassination), but then, unbelievably, there was a second elevator death at the Van Nuys in September when Joe Kato, a Japanese assistant janitor, couldn't overcome his curiosity about the open elevator shaft, and peeked into the darkness.

CURIOSITY KILLED HIM.

Predictably – and horribly – he was hit on the head by the 4800 lb counter weight that went down as the elevator went up, and was killed instantly.

Almost exactly a year later there was more bad news behind-the-scenes here when a petty argument about a dirty chef's smock resulted in a fight between baker Hugh Roberts, his brother Evan, the hotel's butcher, and assistant steward Lloyd Alcott, who picked up a sharp bread knife when Evan came at him with his fists.

Bloody Fracas at Van Nuys Hotel.

When Evan returned to with his brother, Alcott ran out of the kitchen and was chased through the hotel and then onto the street, slashing wildly as he ran.

Sometime in the fracas he had in fact stabbed both his pursuers – Evan fatally, as he died soon after from a deep wound in his side.

Alcott turned himself in and faced a murder charge, but was set free before trial when it was determined he had acted in self-defense.

Only a couple of months passed before the Van Nuys was in the news again: H. Lee Borden, 71, the eldest son of the late Gail Borden, the inventor of condensed milk, had died of angina pectoris (heart disease) in his room.

It was said Lee "could shoot as long and as straight as most of the young men."

YOUTH TAKES CYANIDE.

In June 1909, the Van Nuys Hotel recorded its first suicide, that of Arthur Sugg, a traveling salesman aged just 17. He had been ill for a number of weeks and, apparently unable to take it anymore, bought potassium cyanide and took the deadly cocktail in his room.

Barely two months later, Ada Otis, who had moved to Los Angeles for a fresh start following divorce from her drinking, gambling husband, made the same choice.

She had taken a room at the Van Nuys and thrown herself into social events, but despite seeming happy it wasn't enough, and she took poison in her room and died four days later in hospital.

Her wealthy merchant father sent a private detective from Chicago to investigate, and her friends didn't get to read her suicide note until a few days later:

"I feel that the whole game of life is not worth the candle that it takes."

Two years after that another death – this time from natural causes including heart disease – saw the authorities called to the hotel once again.

Led a Secluded Life in Los Angeles Hotel.

Major W. Arthur Phipps was a land and mining millionaire who had lived in luxury at the Van Nuys for over five years – and was seen as one of the city's most notable eccentrics.

Apparently convinced the Mafia-like extortion "Black Hand" gang was after him he rarely left the hotel, and when he did he was surrounded by what we'd know today as an entourage, "valets and attachés" who ensured that "the coast was clear," reported the *LA Times*.

His poor wife Emma was seen even less, but hopefully finally had some freedom now he was dead.

SECRET AGENT OR DEAD MAN?

Then, July 1915 saw some very unusual excitement at the hotel when it was reported that Ludwig Steiner had been missing for two months, having left all his possessions – including jewelry – in his room here.

Ludwig Steiner.

Steiner had asked for a job soon after he checked in, and, impressed by his skills in several foreign languages, was hired by Potter as a clerk.

Steiner said he was from Austria, had travelled widely, and had been arrested as a spy in Japan, though some felt he showed "signs of melancholia," and noted he had few friends.

The *LA Times* and other newspaper archives gave no further clue about what happened to one of the Van Nuys's most notable residents, though an internet search did pull up the 2015 obituary of Ambassador Ludwig Steiner, a noted Austrian post war diplomat and politician.

So did Ludwig leave Los Angeles for his beloved homeland? Sadly not: that Ludwig was born in 1921.

The Van Nuys was quiet for a number of years until January 1924, when there was an incident here that, like the tragic elevator accidents and the "Butcher Murder," again involved a member of staff.

WIFE IS BLAMED IN·SUICIDE NOTE

Man Seen Seeking Revenge by Ending Life

As the *LA Times* explained, mining engineer William Edward Collier, 39, had swallowed cyanide in front of porter George Alger, who was helping him pack before checking out. Determined to get revenge on his wife Ida, who had recently served him divorce papers, Collier left a long, bitter letter for her, excerpts of which included:

"I leave you with your conscience…. You murdered my soul. Now I kill my body. Murderess! Betrayer of souls! So as you go through life think of the soul roasting in hell because of you…"

A few months later in July, George Purdy Bullard, the first Attorney General for Arizona, died here of heart disease at the age of 55.

He was visiting Los Angeles on vacation with his wife, but had fallen ill the week before. She accompanied his body back to their home in Phoenix.

In March 1929 the hotel was sold to Consolidated Hotels, Inc – one of the companies belonging to Ben Weingart, who had bought the Stillwell Hotel a few years before – and it meant the closure of the hotel dining room (one of the city's most famous, according to the *LA Times*) and plans for a drug store on street level.

Old Van Nuys Hotel Will Be Renovated and Reopened by New Company

Whether those plans were a success or not, in July 1935 the hotel changed hands again.

New owners the Barclay Hotel Company of course renamed it, and were to spend $25,000 on modernization and refurbishing by architects Morgan, Walls and Clements; the plans included a cocktail lounge in the lobby.

WOMAN DYING AS RESULT OF SLUGGING IN HOTEL

In early 1937 there was another criminal event here. Smudged fingerprints found on a window casing were the only "clew" for police looking into the case of Elizabeth Ries, 71, who was found in her fourth floor room with a fractured skull.

It seemed the assailant had climbed in via the fire escape, and that this was a violent robbery – Ries seemed to have been struck with a brick, and her purse was missing.

She was found semi-conscious sitting in a chair by a maid, but hopes were not high for her recovery according to investigator Det. Giese:

"Even if she recovers she may never be able to tell just how and when she was assaulted."

Amnesia Case Clew Found

Police returned to the hotel in October that year, only this time it was to for an "Amnesia Case," according to the *LA Times*.

A young woman had been found sitting on a bench at a gas station, and staff at the Barclay Hotel recognized her – she had recently disappeared from her room, leaving behind her belongings and a note addressed to the manager:

> "For weeks I've been looking for a job and haven't found one. Now I'm at the end of my resources. No money, no job. I haven't eaten in three days. I haven't any money to pay for this room.
>
> "Isn't it funny? I've a college degree and it means less than nothing. Life's like that.
>
> "Marvelous w o r l d, isn't it? Thanks for your kindness.

It was signed "Doris Fowler," and while it seemed the recently found girl, aged 22 or so and speaking with a Southern accent, was her, she claimed she did not know who she was, or where she came from.

She could type and quote a poem by Tennyson, but "then she sank into a sea of forgetfulness...."

Visitor Falls to Her Death

There was another unhappy occurrence here in February 1944, when Marjorie Smith, 20, fell from the third floor window.

She and her two friends had come from Colorado and were looking to get jobs in one of the many wartime plants in California, but Smith had apparently been sleeping on a bed near the window when she turned over – and rolled out to her death.

Later that year, the Barclay Hotel suffered its most infamous horror.

'Ripper' Says Lust to Kill Made Him Hack Pair to Death

The *LA Times* of November 17, 1944 noted that Otto Stephen Wilson, 31, had readily confessed to the brutal mutilation murders of two women, adding after he signed the papers that:

"I have always been emotionally unstable and with my sexual complex I went completely insane and could not possibly control myself."

Still a notable stain on L.A. crime history, it saw the press going to town with reams of coverage and headlines including "Steve the Slasher" and:

ROMEO SLASHER

Wilson explained that he met his first victim, Virgie Griffin, 26, in a Main Street bar and offered her money to come back with him to his room at the Barclay where:

"(He) became enraged and, after killing her, started to dismember her body but could not finish the job."

His actions – carried out with a razor and knife – were sadomasochistic and akin to Jack The Ripper; long slashes along the body, removing entrails, and cutting off an arm and other body parts. He spent that entire night:

"... carving the body and drinking whisky.... A kind of craze had gotten hold of me."

After putting her remains in a closet, the next day he went to see a Boris Karloff movie – chilling called *The Walking Dead* – picked up Lillian Johnson, 48, strangled and then cut her to pieces in another hotel called The Joyce (now a parking lot) before going to a bar to drink wine.

Wilson had been arrested in that bar while police were investigating the killing of Johnson, his cut hands and possession of a book of matches from the Barclay Hotel making him an obvious suspect.

He had a long criminal record including convictions for assault and burglary, and though he denied involvement in several other recent murders, the devastated husband of Griffin didn't care:

"Just let me with him for about two minutes – I'll save the State a lot of expense!"

With both murders discovered, a suspect arrested and a confession gained within less than a day, it seemed an open-and-shut case.

The story ran and ran of course, with Wilson's defense employing three alienists (the term used then for a psychiatrist) to support Wilson's claim that he was not guilty by reason of insanity.

However, witness Eva Dunn, a maid at the Barclay Hotel, said that Wilson had told her not to come in and clean his room because his wife was "tired," and had tipped her a dollar for not doing so.

That "wife" was Virgie Griffin, and it emerged that Wilson had warned off staff at the other murder site in a similar way.

He was executed in the gas chamber at San Quentin in September 1946.

Woman Killed in Barclay Hotel Fire Identified

Thankfully the hotel was out of the news for many years after this horror (though room 332 was the location for a fictional killing (an ice pick in the neck!) in Raymond Chandler's 1949 novel *Little Sister*), but then in March 1972 there was a deadly fire here.

It killed three people, injured a handful more, and initially it seemed to be the work of convicted arsonist Harvey Lynn Beagle, 30, who confessed to setting the blaze as firemen were still putting it out!

DA Won't Prosecute Man Who Said He Started Hotel Blaze

His claims were quickly dismissed when two witnesses came forward to say they had been drinking with him when the fire started – and when it was determined that the fire had started in room 625, where first victim Geraldine Fox, 50, was found.

It seemed a discarded cigarette was to blame, as her husband Arthur told investigators that he had woken to find the bed on fire on his wife's side, and had then tried (unsuccessfully) to drag her to safety, suffering burns to his face and hands in the process.

Just over two years later there was another fire at the Barclay. It also started on the sixth floor, and 160 people fled to the street, with one man briefly treated for smoke inhalation.

They had been alerted by the new fire alarm system and protected by fire-resistant doors installed as result of new laws after the (now long-gone) Ponet Square Hotel fire of 1970, which saw 19 people killed.

Sadly, the four year period allowed for landlords to make these changes didn't help the 25 people killed in a blaze at apartments on West 6th Street in 1973 (the building was razed soon after), but they certainly saved many more Angelenos afterwards – including at the Barclay that night.

By now the hotel had fallen a long way from its heady days as the Van Nuys, and in the 1970s it seemed to be a magnet for flame.

There was a double fire (in rooms 301 and 405) in November 1979, the third floor resident hospitalized for second-degree burns, and then again in March 1981, when there was no-injury fire in a room on the fifth floor.

Hatchet Attacker Indicted in L.A. Slasher Murders

Those fires were a footnote though to another dark moment in the history of the Barclay Hotel, when it was connected with Vaughn Orrin Greenwood, a 32 year old man who was known as the "Skid Row Slasher" for a number of brutal slayings.

Between December 1, 1974 and January 31, 1975, Greenwood was charged with killing nine men, many of whom were derelicts and transients.

He was also charged with two more murders going back to 1964, though on his arrest he was already in Fulsom Prison serving 32 years to life for a knife and hatchet attack on two men – and for burglarizing actor Burt Reynold's home in Hollywood.

Greenwood's killings included three at or near the Los Angeles Central Library and several more at downtown hotels – including here at the Barclay, where drifter Samuel Suarez, 49, was slain in his fifth floor room.

Greenwood's attacks were brutal; many stabbings, throats cut deeply, and bodies arranged in poses, their shoes removed and salt scattered around – there was even evidence he drank some of his victim's blood.

Almost exactly a decade after Greenwood's reign of terror, the Barclay was the location of another death – only this time it was what some might see as karma: Marvin Walker had apparently been trying to take a stolen TV set out of a fifth floor room window when he lost his balance and fell to the sidewalk below.

In more modern times there was a shooting here in September 1997 – one man was killed and another was critically wounded – but *Gourmet Ghosts 2* doesn't report fully on events after 1985 or so out of respect for the people and the families involved.

The hotel was put up for sale in May 2016, though that was too late for local favorite Bar 107, which lived an eclectic life (way back it was the rowdy 400 Hundred Saloon, while as Bar 107 you never know quite knew what you'd see on the walls: swords, animal heads, wrestling souvenirs, beer ephemera and other crazy stuff).

It closed in mid 2015 after much protest, but you can still see the doorway, which is shaped like a human-size keyhole and has been painted black.

Bar 107 was also supposed to be the home to a ghost or two – at least according to the excellent Ghost Hunters of Los Angeles (GHOULA) website, which noted that the back room was a haunted spot.

Apparently phantom hands grabbed, pushed and pulled punters there – especially in the DJ booth and areas above the ground floor.

Maybe that was just happy drinkers dancing one night, or perhaps it's poor Charles Gamble, flailing around as he falls to his death?

There's nowhere to eat or drink at the Barclay or in its street level units at the moment, though a look through one of the half-covered-up windows shows there was a diner or restaurant here once, though today it's only rented out for filming.

Television shows "The Closer" and "Castle" have been here, and another empty space here was made up to look like a bakery for "CSI: New York" (the building has a look that's very reminiscent of the Big Apple).

Also, the lobby was made into the Café 24 Heures for *As Good as It Gets* (it was where Jack Nicholson's "Melvin" dined every day and where Carol (Helen Hunt) worked), into a hip coffee shop for *(500) Day of Summer*, and was even an exotic gambling saloon in *Inception*.

Even at a rumored price of $40m, it seems the Barclay might become a high-end boutique hotel, though the new owners would have to abide by the rules related to it being Historic-Cultural Monument #288, and re-house the several dozen SRO (single resident/low income) people living here before it can rent out the 165 rooms.

Big-money changes like this are a sign of the times in many downtown hotels, so when you pass by, take a look up at the Barclay – on one wall is a ghost sign that still announces: "ROOMS $1.00 AND UP."

No matter what the future holds for the Barclay, the somewhat-forgotten grande dame of downtown that's been seen in *Rocky III*, *Armageddon*, *Mr. & Mrs. Smith* and also *Catch Me If You Can* (as well as being the lair of two violent serial killers), has certainly earned its moment of infamy in these pages.

Brockman Building
Bottega Louie
700 South Grand Avenue
Los Angeles, CA 90017
Tel: 213 802 1470

Acid Threats & The Human Fly

Standing 12 storeys high at the junction of 7th and Grand, the Brockman Building was named after its funder John Brockman, a German immigrant, soldier and successful miner who owned local property and wanted to make the area a focus for retail and offices.

Designed in the Classical and Romanesque Revival style by George D. Barnett, it was one of the first buildings to reach the city's 150 foot height limit when it was raised in 1912.

Today the Brockman Building is home to luxury apartments, but for years it was home to many companies – especially doctor's surgeries – and in early September 1919 it was the scene of a dramatic struggle seen by crowds of bus commuters below.

LEAPS FAR TO SUDDEN DEATH.

Dr. B.F. Church, 55, had been visiting his own doctor on the 10th floor of the building when there was suddenly a deadly fight for life between Church and the nurse, J.B. Scheneweg, who had risked his life in trying to save Church when he had suddenly raced to the open window and tried to jump out.

Scheneweg grabbed Church and had been holding onto his legs as he momentarily dangled 100 foot above the startled crowd below, "but released his hold after he had been dragged half way out of the window."

Church smashed though the glass awning over the main entrance before being "dashed to death on the sidewalk" said the *LA Times*, which reported that Church had "every bone in his body broken" and that "mental troubles" were believed to have been behind the suicide, adding that Church had been a resident of the Kimball Sanatorium for eight months.

SURGEON STEALS HANDSOME WIFE?

Weird Story of ".Abduction" of Pretty Mrs. Peppers.

Fake Kidnapping?

Not even a year later, there was another dramatic event when police issued a warrant for the arrest of Charles H. Peppers, a surgeon with offices here, in the alleged kidnapping of his own wife Amelia.

The *LA Times* of August 11, 1920 reported on Peppers and two other men who "sprang from an alley" and knocked over mother-in-law Mrs. M. T. Holmberg before bundling Amelia into a waiting car.

Amelia's screams had attracted the attention of a policeman when they stopped at a gas station in Ventura, and he rescued her and then escorted her to a hotel.

Described by the hotel owners as "a perfect little lady, very pretty," Amelia, 24, thought that Peppers was planning to place her in a sanatorium (an act that would nullify her divorce proceedings against him), and was in a "semi-hysterical" condition.

A few weeks later, the headline "Police After Cave Man Now" revealed that Peppers, who had been charged with battery but released, had not appeared at his court date – but then neither had anyone else. Apparently Amelia had meant to drop the charges, but the paperwork was absent and so Peppers was now a wanted man.

POLICE AFTER CAVE MAN NOW.

At the arraignment, Peppers said that the "whole trouble" was "too much mother-in-law," and that he was innocent of any "cave-man stuff."

Their story ended without further trouble it seems, as all charges were dropped, and the divorce papers were signed: Peppers was said to be "broken up" about it all.

A few months after the funeral of John Brockman himself, who had died aged 84, there was another threat made against someone in the Brockman Building.

In May 1925, the *LA Times* reported that Mrs. T.C. Conley, who worked at the office of Dr. Ralph Hagan, had been the subject of threatening phone calls from an anonymous woman.

WOMAN TELLS
ACID THREATS

Feminine Voice Warns Her in Phone Call

Advises Her to Leave Post or Lose Eyesight

Initially Dr. Hagan had taken a call saying he should fire Conley, and then a similar call was placed to the manager of Conley's apartment building. Now it had been Conley herself who had been told:

"(I'll) get you some place and put your eyes out with acid."

Conley told police she felt it was "some paranoiac suffering from a fancied grievance," though she admitted she was afraid to go home.

Was it a love rival? A jealous wife? A nasty prank? Sadly the archives don't offer any answers to what must have been a chilling experience.

That said, the building you see before you today almost fell to the wrecking ball nearly 30 years ago.

The upper floors had been vacant for many years after long-time ground tenant Brooks Brothers, a clothing store, had moved to a new location in 1989 (though their logo still remains in marble in the apartment's lobby).

That "B" may have been good luck though, as today the building is better known as the home of Bottega Louie, a 255 seater white and gold marble restaurant and patisserie that has high ceilings, loud conversations and great food.

It's been busy since it opened in the former Brooks' space in 2009, and recommended dishes include their eggs Benedict – my favorite – while there's pretty much been universal approval for their pizza.

Harold and the Human Fly

There don't seem to be any ghost stories associated with the Brockman, though there's certainly a strange one – and it's related to silent movie legend Harold Lloyd and his most famous stunt, when he hangs from the hands of a clock high above Broadway – you know the one.

That stunt was filmed at a number of places in downtown (as well as in a studio), though the roof that Harold's character finally manages to heave himself up to safety – and to his girl, Mildred – is the Brockman.

It's been reported that Lloyd was inspired to create that sequence for his 1923 silent romantic comedy *Safety Last!* after seeing "human fly" Bill Strother climb the exterior of the Brockman as a stunt.

Lloyd was famous for his stunts, and in this movie his character, who has lied to his girlfriend about being the manager of the fictional De Vore Department Store, ends up suggesting a climbing stunt to attract new customers (with his pal "Limpy" Bill (Strother) doing all the hard work of course), though thanks to a meddlesome truncheon-wielding cop, that's not how it works out…

Strother stunt-doubled for Lloyd in some of the shots, and though it was his only on-screen role, he helped create one of the most famous – and thrilling – scenes in movie history (2m views and counting on YouTube).

Strother was a North Carolina native who began building-climbing from around 1910, when skyscrapers started being built across America.

Often climbing for charitable causes he summited buildings all over the country, including the 57-story Woolworth Tower in New York, though perhaps inevitably he was injured in a fall in 1930, and later ran a boarding house for military personnel in Virginia.

HUMAN FLY PERFORMS

Scales Lane Mortgage Building; Is Cut in Effort

As for his ascent of the Brockman, I was unable to find solid evidence of that in the newspaper archives.

He did climb the Biltmore Hotel – even standing on his head on window sills and balconies as he did so – in late 1923, but it was probably his effort in June that year that Lloyd saw (or heard about), and that took place at the Lake Mortgage Building at 8th and Spring Street, leaving Strother with "cut and bleeding" hands.

Strangely, Lloyd was missing two fingers on his right hand as a result of an accident on a movie set some years before (he wore gloves to hide it), which makes their genius precision – and physical slapstick – above and beyond much of the CGI-fakery we see today.

Check out Lloyd/Strother's work on YouTube, and even if you just pop inside Bottega Louie, have a look at their chocolates, cakes and colorful macarons – it's hard not to leave without a box of something delightful under your arm!

$$$ / Mon-Thu 8am-11pm, Fri 8am-midnight, Sat 9am-midnight, Sun 9am-11pm, weekend brunch 9am-3pm, Patisserie Mon-Thu 6.30am-11pm, Fri until midnight, Sat 8am-midnight, Sun 8am-11pm
www.bottegalouie.com

The Cecil Hotel (now Stay on Main)
640 South Main Street
Los Angeles, CA 90014
Tel: 213 213 7829

The Deadliest Hotel in L.A.

Astonishingly, the archives reveal that The Cecil has been home to baby murderers, arsonists, snipers and not one but two serial killers. It was also the last address for over a dozen people who committed suicide.

However, that suicidal statistic isn't actually very unusual.

In researching the darker history of L.A., it has been common to find that hotels are often the place where people go to end their lives.

Not only can you register anonymously (at least to an extent), they're rather impersonal places where you can put a sign on your door ensuring you won't be disturbed.

And, of course, all hotel rooms are tidied and cleaned up by someone you don't know.

Though it was bought and rebranded as Stay on Main in 2011, several of the old signs are still in place, and so this will probably always be known as The Cecil, the most infamous hotel in Los Angeles.

Yes, despite the glamorous looks and silver screen appearances of other hotels like the Biltmore and the Bonaventure, The Cecil is known world-wide – but for all the wrong reasons.

Out of respect for the families involved *Gourmet Ghosts* books try not to mention recent tragedies, but the 2013 deaths of Elisa Lam and Richard Ramirez made it impossible not to mention them in relation to the history of this hotel.

Lam, a 21 year old Canadian student visiting the city, was found naked and dead in one of the hotel's rooftop water tanks in February 2013, and her mysterious and tragic story soon went viral thanks to security camera footage of the last time she was seen alive.

A Chronology of the Night Stalker's Spree

In June that same year, serial killer Richard Ramirez – known as "The Night Stalker" – died in prison, where he had been on Death Row for a catalog of brutal crimes including the murder of at least 13 women, sexual assaults, burglaries and attempted murders during a 16 month period in 1984 and 1985.

His appalling crimes and brutality can be easily researched elsewhere, which was one of the reasons The Cecil didn't make *Gourmet Ghosts – Los Angeles*.

It had no restaurant or bar either then (just an odd, half-equipped bar that I was told was now a "guest lounge" and the dusty Main Street Café that was "closed"), though today there is a small place called Natural Selection on one side where you can get coffee, wraps, sandwiches, burgers, rice bowls and snacks at breakfast/lunch time.

Newspaper reports do mention that Ramirez lived at the Cecil – apparently on the 14th floor, where he was fond of smoking marijuana and playing loud music – during at least some of the time he terrorized Los Angeles, and it's said he even threw his bloody clothes away in the hotel's dumpsters.

A horrible coincidence like that would be bad enough for any hotel – and certainly put it on the crime and tourist trail – but The Cecil seems to be such a home for violence that it really is possible to wonder whether this building is cursed, or that there are negative forces inside.

It didn't start that way though. Finished in late 1924 by the Weymouth Cromwell Co, this 14 story concrete hotel was one of the largest in the west at 700 rooms, and was one of many aimed at business travelers visiting the fast-growing Los Angeles.

Even today, Art Deco chandeliers loom overhead and the marble floors, stained glass ceilings and faux Roman statues in the lobby reflect the style of its original design – one that attracted many the moment they opened their doors.

In 1941 the *LA Times* reported on one of their notable early guests, 65 year old Jacob Horner, who had been recalling his golden days as one of General George Custer's cavalryman in the bloody campaign against the Sioux in 1876.

Mentioning how a shortage of horses had meant he and many others couldn't ride into battle with Custer at Little Big Horn – the battle that saw Custer and his men defeated and killed – Horner called modern warfare "machine murder" and said:

"It's murderous slaughter!"

Later that same year The Cecil was leased to the Alberts Hotel Corp, who had other hotels in L.A., Texas, San Diego and Arizona, for 15 years at a cost of $600,000.

The *LA Times* noted that they planned a $50,000 improvement program, but by the time that lease came to an end The Cecil was suffering the same problems as many of its hotel rivals.

Development and population growth outside of downtown had hit all the large hotels there, and The Cecil had a dip in popularity – one that it perhaps never recovered fully from.

By the 1950s it was better known as a lower-end residence, though refurbishment decades later in 2007 – and the renaming in 2011 – tried to position it as a budget hotel for young tourists looking for a cheap, central location: tourists like Lam, as it turned out.

With many thousands of guests per year, hotels are inevitably going to be the scene of accidents, natural deaths, suicides, crime and even pure bad luck.

Few of them ever have anything to do with the hotel or its staff, but even from the early days there seemed to be drama at The Cecil, even when their guests were elsewhere.

Asserted Hotel Prowler Cought in Hunt for Police Murderer

Barely 18 months after opening, on June 10, 1926 it was reported that elderly former mining operator William F. McKay had died in his room here, and in February 1927 there was more drama when John Croneu, a resident who was suspected of killing a policeman but was in fact a burglar, was arrested in his room.

There was bad luck for a Cecil resident later that same year when passenger Edmund Bennett Jr. was "crushed" in a small plane accident in Alhambra: the pilot survived.

Then, in April 1929 Dorothy Robinson, 33, was taken to hospital suffering from poisoning after she had been "in a dazed condition for three days."

Apparently her husband had died a month before, and she had suffered a collapse, the drug (presumably barbiturates), prescribed for her nerves.

Police didn't record the case as attempted suicide though; perhaps it was an accidental overdose.

Asserted Seller Captured in Decoy's Hotel Room

In August 1931 a resident named George Ford, 40, was arrested at another hotel after attempting to selling 10 pounds of opium, a score worth $10,000 and said by the *LA Times* to be "one of the most important captures made here in many months."

PAIR FACE EACH OTHER AT JAIL

Jackson Tells Paul Elgin "I Never Saw You Before"

A few months later in December 1931, Herbert Jackson was arrested – and made to face – the man he had impersonated for nearly three years, Paul Elgin, whose name he had used to scam around $150,000 worth of bonds.

Elgin had lived at The Cecil for over two years, and when Jackson gave police the same address, it was the clue that linked fake with real.

More bad luck saw 30 year old hotel resident Virgil Tallman killed when he was hit by a car in Glendale in early 1935, though it seems a quarrel led to the death of Nick Damiano at the barrel of gun held by Harold Daniels.

They confronted each other in the bar where Daniels worked, and after Daniels drew a .38 and shot Damiano there was a scuffle and he was injured too – but survived.

The pair were apparently friends from back in Minnesota said the *LA Times*, who also mentioned that Daniels came to the bar with his wife Shirley.

Search for Man Ends in Finding Body at Hotel

As for the first suicide at The Cecil, it shows how often people check into a hotel to end their life.

The *LA Times* of November 19, 1931 reported that the search for W.K. Norton, 46, who had been missing from his home in Manhattan Beach for nearly a week – was over. He had checked in as "James Willys of Chicago" and, once in his room, had taken a number of poison capsules.

Less than a year later, another suicide was listed among several in the *LA Times*. Benjamin Dodich, 25, had shot himself in the head in his room, and his body had been found by maid Carrie Brown the next morning – though there was no suicide note.

In late July 1934, former Army Medical Corps sergeant Louis D. Borden, 53, slashed his throat with a razor in his room here; he left a note behind mentioning his ill health.

Strangely, right above a newspaper article about his suicide was a story and the smiling picture of a person who had used the last name "Borden" as a disguise.

Ethel Harriman Russell had christened herself Ethel Borden on signing a contract with Metro-Goldwyn-Mayer as a "scenario writer."

Why this was worthy of an *LA Times* piece was unclear; it seemed to be because she was the daughter of a prominent former Democratic National Committeewoman – heaven forbid that she was getting involved in the sordid world of movie-making!

Victim Crushed in Nine-Story Drop at Downtown Hotel

Less than three years later in March 1937, it was reported that Grace E. Magro, 25, had jumped from a ninth floor window here, hitting telephone poles as she fell.

Police were unsure if it was suicide or an accident, and bizarrely it seemed that *USS Virginia* sailor M.W. Madison, who was sleeping in the same room as her, had no explanation either. The telephone wires were "entangled about her body," and she died later in hospital.

SHIP FIREMAN IN SUICIDE LEAP

In January the next year, Roy Thompson, a 35 year old marine fireman, took "a suicide leap" from the top floor. He had been registered here for several weeks, and his body was found on the skylight of a building next door.

Sailor Ends Life by Taking Poison

Another sailor, Erwin C. Neblett, 39, of the *USS Wright*, took poison in his room here in May 1939, and in January the following year teacher Dorothy Sceiger, 45, employed the same method – and was said to be "near death."

Mother Held After Baby Found Thrown to Death

It wasn't until September 1944 that The Cecil hit the headlines again, and this time it was a disturbing case of baby murder; Dorothy Jean Purcell, 19, was accused of throwing her newborn son out the window.

> His only christening was an entry on the coroner's records—"John Doe No. 31."

The small body was found on the roof of an adjacent building, and after hearing testimony a juror called "almost beyond belief," it was determined she be charged with homicide.

"I don't know why I did it, but I thought he was dead."

Apparently unaware she was pregnant, Purcell didn't want to wake her sleeping partner, shoe salesman Ben Levine, 38, when she woke with stomach pains, so she went to the nearby restroom and delivered the baby herself.

Believing the child to be dead, she threw it out of the nearby window.

Young Mother Freed in Baby Death Plunge

This tragic and horrifying story came to an end in January the following year, when Purcell was found not guilty by reason of insanity.

Three "alienists" (the term at the time for a psychiatrist) reported that she was "mentally confused" at the time – though sane at present – and she was ordered to report to hospital for a thorough examination.

In November 1947 death again came to The Cecil when Robert Smith, 35, of Long Beach fell from his seventh floor window – "fell" often being the term used to infer suicide – but there was a more oddly amusing story on December 5, 1952, when it seemed that The Cecil had been the headquarters for the "Grandma Bandit."

Oh, Grandma!

Wanted for three bank holdups was an elderly lady who had eluded police for months, and whom they thought might be Cecil resident Alfred H. Hughes, a pickpocket who tried to rob the nearby North American Airlines office, albeit not in disguise.

Police thought they were on the right track when they found a woman's black hat, scarf and dress in his room, and despite Miss Helen Owen, 40, saying she was a friend of Hughes and that the clothes were hers, police were still keen for Hughes to take part in a line-up – in full costume!

Robber Suspect, 60, Not Grandma, Police Decide

He refused, and soon evidence proved he wasn't the little old lady whose exploits had hit the headlines across the country. Nevertheless, Capt. Harry Didion, head of the robbery squad, booked Howard and Owen on suspicion of robbery anyway.

It seems that this mysterious "bandit" was in fact Ethel Martin Arata of Monrovia, California.

The 52 year old divorcee was arrested on Christmas Eve 1952, and the far-flung *Long Island Star-Journal* reported that one of her robbery notes had read:

"I am desperate, I need money."

Claims She's 'Heiress'

Grandma Bandit Admits 2 Jobs

Arata apparently said "I am not grandma," when she was arrested, but then claimed to be heiress to a $20m Philadelphia inheritance, though she had not got the money because of "legal tangles."

Such unusual notoriety might have bought a rare smile at The Cecil, yet it was barely two years before another person died here.

Woman Killed in Seven-Floor Hotel Plunge

On October 23, 1954 it was reported Helen Gurnee of San Diego had "plunged to her death" from the window of her room. Checking in as "Margaret Brown of Denver" the week before, her body had landed on the hotel marquee, and needed to be reached by ladder.

A man named Melvin Hinkley, 26, was taken to General Hospital soon after – he was apparently hysterical after witnessing Gurnee's death.

Unusually, the newspaper report mentioned the room Gurnee was staying in – number 704 – a detail that's usually kept back in order to prevent curious visitors from asking to stay there (and unknowing future guests from maybe getting a ghostly surprise!).

Woman's Death Leap Kills Man on Street

In 1962 there were two suicides and a bizarre accident here. In February Julia Frances Moore, 50, jumped from her eight floor window – she had recently arrived from St. Louis and had nearly $1,800 in a bank account – and then in October there was a double tragedy when Pauline Otton, 27, "leaped or fell" from her ninth floor room and landed on George Gianinni, 65, killing him too.

More barely-believable Cecil bad luck, it saw police initially thinking they had taken part in a suicide pact, but then it emerged that Gianinni had his hands in his pockets and his shoes on; the impact would apparently have wrenched them off his feet.

Convicted Arsonist Held in Hotel Fire Fatal to 3

Earlier that year in March, the *LA Times* reported that convicted arsonist Harvey Lynn Beagle II, 30, a resident at The Cecil, had been arrested and charged with a fatal fire at the nearby Barclay Hotel.

The fire had killed three people and injured at least seven more, but, inconceivably, Beagle had approached firefighters *as they were tackling the deadly blaze* and complained that a newspaper report had undervalued the cost of a previous fire he had set – and served time for.

Understandably skeptical, the police arrested him anyway despite the fact they were looking into the possibility this $65,000 blaze was accidentally started by a guest smoking in bed. This proved to be the case: Geraldine Fox, 50, who lived on the sixth floor, was its first victim.

Bird Lover Slain, but Friends Remember

A couple of years later in June 1964, the first adult murder took place at The Cecil. Well-known for feeding the birds in Pershing Square, Goldie Osgood – or "Pigeon Goldie" – was a popular resident at the hotel.

Hotel Prowler Kills 2nd Woman

She had been raped, stabbed and strangled, and police – and the *LA Examiner* – were potentially linking it with the similar killing of Veva Brown, 50, at the nearby Rosslyn Hotel the year before.

They quickly made an arrest in relation to Osgood's murder though; Jacques B. Ehlinger, 29, had been seen walking through the Pershing Square wearing blood-stained clothing, had admitted knowing Osgood, and that he was near the hotel at the time of the killing.

The *LA Times* reported that local retired nurse Jean Rosenstein, a friend of Goldie, had been given donations to buy some flowers, which she laid in Pershing Square and noted:

"We just wanted her to know we remembered."

The Cecil was quiet for some time afterwards, except for Christmas Day 1970, when the *LA Times* reported that security guard Robert Alan Thomas, 28, had been arrested outside on suspicion of firing shots at the California Highway Patrol – though without causing injury.

Ex - Mental Patient Seized in Rooftop Sniping Spree

But in the early hours of December 1976 there was a major incident here when Jeffrey Thomas Paley was arrested on the roof after firing random shots at the sidewalk.

A former mental patient, Paley said "I never intended to shoot anyone," but wanted to show how easy it was to buy a weapon "and shoot a lot of people."

No one was injured by the dozen shots or so from the .22 semi-automatic rifle – though one man in a Bank of America office had a narrow escape – and it later emerged Paley had called the *LA Times* to tell them of his plan.

Police then zeroed in on the Cecil and he quickly surrendered, though he was revealed to have several hundred rounds of ammunition.

Man Held in Huntington Beach Slaying

It wasn't until 1988 that The Cecil was again in the papers when Robert Sullivan, 28, was arrested in his room here and charged with the stabbing death of his girlfriend at their home in Huntington Beach.

But then three years later, another serial killer checked in at the front desk.

Serial Killer No. 2

It's more than likely Johann "Jack" Unterweger knew that Richard Ramirez had stayed here during his reign of terror, and perhaps he wanted to bask in that deadly shadow – an extreme example of why hotels rarely give out many details when something bad happens.

Unterweger was originally from Austria, and had murdered prostitutes there and in Czechoslovakia and Germany, his first murder taking place in 1974 and spanning perhaps a dozen victims overall.

Once again there's plenty of information online about Unterweger, so we'll just focus on his time in L.A.

Amazingly, Unterweger came to the city as a reporter hired to write about crime and attitudes to prostitution in Europe and America.

Though jailed before for murder in Austria, he had written books, plays, poems and an autobiography while in prison, and had become a cause célèbre among his country's intellectuals – though authorities still made sure he served the minimum 15 years of his life sentence.

His much-lauded and believed rehabilitation was a fatal sham though, and he continued killing after his release before being sent to L.A. in 1991, when he joined police ride-alongs in red light areas as part of his "research."

Trail of Killings

Three prostitutes were beaten, assaulted and strangled by Unterweger while he was in L.A., though in 1992 he was finally sentenced to life without possibility of parole in his homeland.

He committed suicide while in prison in 1994, and though not as well-known as many other notable serial killers, he has been the subject of books and an opera called *Seduction and Despair*, which debuted in 2008 with John Malkovich in the lead role.

More recently, it was rumored that actor Michael Fassbender – known for *Prometheus, X-Men: First Class,* and many other movies – may be playing Unterweger in an adaptation of the 2007 non-fiction crime novel *Entering Hades: The Double Life of a Serial Killer* by John Leake.

After those horrors there were years of calm in the Cecil, but then came the sensation of Lam's death.

Elisa

The strange and gruesome circumstances – Lam's decomposed body was discovered following complaints the tap water "tasted funny" and had been in the water for close to three weeks – were bizarre enough, but then it seemed there was more to the story.

Lam, who had a history of bipolar illness but was found to have no alcohol or drugs in her body, was listed as an accidental drowning, but when the CCTV footage came to light it only raised more questions, including worries about a possible murderer on the loose.

Easily found online, it's several minutes of a seemingly confused or afraid Lam – not wearing her eyeglasses – entering one of Cecil's elevators just minutes into the New Year.

It's uncomfortable and confusing to watch, and when you know it's the last sighting of a girl who was later found dead, you can only imagine the worst.

Viewed many millions of times on YouTube and elsewhere, it is the subject of many conspiracy theories – all of which you can read online.

Some of them note how similar it is to the plot of the movie *Dark Water* (2005), or how weird it was that a local initiative against an outbreak of tuberculosis utilized a test called LAM-ELISA.

It went on and on, Lam almost being forgotten as a young woman who had died in tragic circumstances and instead becoming a digital oddity.

There was the inevitable movie version – or doubtless something "inspired by" it – announced by Sony Pictures, and creators Brad Falchuk and Ryan Murphy of "American Horror Story: Hotel" candidly admitted that they were influenced by downtown hotels with a sinister reputation – like The Cecil.

Their fictional "Hotel Cortez" was haunted, and was home to the "Ten Commandments Killer," though Richard Ramirez (played by Anthony Ruivivar) checks in and begins killing at one stage, and episode four saw a number of actors playing other real serial killers arriving there too.

It seems like Stay on Main will never really be able to distance itself from its past, and that death will always be part of the woodwork.

As recently as June 2015 there was yet another suspected suicide here, when it was reported a 28 year old man's body had been found outside the hotel.

A man identifying himself as the assistant manager said the dead man wasn't a guest and could have been an intruder, but either way it was just another name added to the long list of people who died at the Cecil Hotel.

Unless you're staying here, even going inside to look at the lobby can be difficult. On my most recent visit I was immediately approached by a suited security guard with an earpiece.

He aggressively questioned me several times about what I was doing, what I was writing, whether I was checking in, and then telling me I couldn't take pictures – or even go further – into the lobby.

"I'm a Believer" by The Monkees was playing on the sound system, and it seems The Cecil has a problem with people even coming in just to look at the most notorious (and haunted?) hotel in town.

But maybe things are looking up for the future; it was announced in mid-2016 that a $100m renovation of the 301 residential units will transform them into what are called "micro-units," and should also include a gym and a rooftop pool. Work begins mid-2017 and will take a couple of years.

$$ / Mon-Fri 10am-6pm, Sat to 2.30pm, closed Sunday
www.stayonmain.com
www.eatatnaturalselection.com

Double Tree (formerly the New Otani/Kyoto Grand)
120 South Los Angeles Street
Los Angeles, CA 90012
Tel: 213 629 1200

"The Japanese O.J. Simpson"

A favorite with Japanese tourists since it opened at a cost of
$30m in August 1977 – when it was called the New Otani –
this hotel is located in the Little Tokyo area of downtown
Los Angeles, and was doubtless named after the famous
hotel in Japan.

    A hidden treasure in downtown, it's perhaps best
known for its stunning half-acre rooftop Kyoto Gardens,
which were inspired by the Japanese Garden created by 16th
century samurai lord Kiyomasa Kato.
    Located on the Garden Level (naturally), they're
worth a visit by themselves, just to step out of the hustle
and bustle and go into a little oasis of greenery, cascading
waterfalls and tranquil ponds. If you're a resident at the
hotel, they're also the perfect spot for some sunbathing.

The hotel has been a social hub and a meeting point for politicians, dignitaries, business people and celebrities since the early days – and the fact it's barely two miles from the Los Angeles Convention Center doubtless helps fill the 400-plus rooms too.

The Japanese theme continues in the Rendezvous Lounge in the front of the hotel, which is for residents (and the public) from early afternoon onwards.

It seems that they cater to plenty of lawyers and attorneys here, as you can have Justice Wings, a Barrister Burger and a Good and Evil Angel Cake if you're feeling victorious (or maybe drowning your sorrows), though I recommend their Racer IPA braised barbeque pork ribs.

Also, if you follow a few corridors towards the back of the hotel there's an adjacent Starbucks and a gastro pub that shows a lot of sports, opens early for residents to have breakfast (it's owned by the hotel), but is also open to the public as well.

Called Justice, it's rather a nice secret little spot, especially if you catch some cheaper bites and drinks during their weekday 3-6pm Social Hour 3-6pm (why not have a Big Ass Pretzel with Pub Cheese?).

They offer almost exactly the same menu as the Rendezvous Lounge, with a cocktail menu that's even more amusing; raise a glass with a "Drug Mule," "Thyme and Punishment," "Subpoena" and others, though I suggest a "Beet The System" (slow hand white whiskey, St. Germain, apple bitters, lemon and fresh beets).

In its short history the hotel has changed hands a couple of times, firstly in 2007 when it became the Kyoto Grand Hotel, though bankruptcy meant it was sold again in 2011, opening after renovations in 2012 as one of the hotels in the Double Tree by Hilton chain.

Becoming branded hasn't reduced its popularity though. Electronic dance music producer and DJ Skrillex worked on a song while he stayed here in 2011, even recording the vocals (by Sirah) in his room.

The song was called "Kyoto," and the lyrics even included "Chillin' in the Kyoto Grand with my man Skrill." The track appeared on his *Bangarang* EP, which won two Grammys in 2013.

Only open barely 40 years, there are no reported sightings of ghosts at the Double Tree – at least not yet – though there have been some deadly times here.

In fact, you could argue that that the first bloody moment happened here way back in 1896.

BLED TO DEATH.

At that time this address was the location of the Matthews Implement Company, and according to the *LA Times* of August 6, it was the site of a gruesome accident.

A gray horse broke free and galloped down South Los Angeles Street, colliding with a wagon outside the store and impaling itself on the wagon's pole. A crowd assembled and tried to help the dying horse, but a stream of blood "as thick as a man's wrist" couldn't be staunched, and the animal bled out on the street.

Moving ahead many decades to barely two years after the New Otani had opened its doors, and there was a suicide here in April 1979.

Leaper Victim Identified

Charles Cassell, 34, of Hollywood climbed onto the roof and, though police fired a Taser to try and stun him, he nevertheless jumped to his death just out of reach of two officers. Apparently he had been "despondent over marital problems."

Nearly two years after that, the biggest scandal to hit the New Otani came to light.

Ultimately dubbed the "Japanese O.J. Simpson" case, it led to two dead bodies and a story that was a sensation in Japan and became a diplomatic hot potato too, amidst fears that Japanese tourists might see L.A. as a dangerous place to visit.

Miura Named as Sole Suspect in 2 Slayings

In a Tokyo court, importer Kazuyoshi Miura and waitress/model Michiko Yazawa were both indicted in the attempted murder of Kazumi Miura, Kazuyoshi's wife, which had happened at the New Otani in August 1981.

Japanese Police Arrest Mate of Woman Attacked in Hotel, Then Shot on Street

According to the *LA Times* of October 4, 1985, Yazawa, 25, had confessed to using what she called a "hammer-like instrument" on Mrs. Miura, who survived the attack only to be gunned down on a Los Angeles street three months later, dying many months after being flown back to Japan in a coma.

Miura was also accused by L.A. District Attorney Ira Reiner of the murder of a former lover, Chizuko Shiraishi, 34, whose body was found in Los Angeles in May 1979, but not identified until March 1984.

Miura was by then back in Japan – a country notoriously difficult to extradite criminals from – and, in the midst of a media circus, had denied all the charges.

LAPD and Tokyo detectives were collaborating, but there seemed to be differing views on exactly what had happened.

Some felt that Miura, heavily in debt, was keen on the large life insurance policy his wife had (and he did take $21,000 from the bank account of Shiraishi – a debt she owed him, he said), while others felt that Miura was innocent, and that there were countless witnesses to Yazawa's confession.

Another alleged lover of Miura's, Yazawa's confession however said that he paid for her to fly to L.A. and that she sneaked into Mrs. Miura's room at the New Otani posing as a dressmaker, and, when her back was turned, hit her on the head with a weapon.

Mrs. Muira had bravely seen off her would-be-assassin (that time, anyway), and her husband, who told hospital staff she had fallen in the bathroom, denied he had persuaded Yazawa to try and kill her. No "hammer-like" weapon was ever found either.

As for Mrs. Miura's actual murder some time later, Miura explained that was the result of a street robbery by two men who shot first (he had himself been injured during the crime), but some authorities felt that it was another fatal set-up he had arranged.

Miura – who quickly married again and seemed to enjoy his notoriety – didn't avoid prison though.

In 1987 he was sentenced to six years for that attempted murder – a rare Japanese conviction for a crime committed abroad – while Yazawa received 2½ years.

Then, in 1994 he was convicted of his wife's murder and sentenced to life imprisonment – though this was overturned on appeal in 1998.

He had nearly 10 years of freedom – during which he stayed a media celebrity of sorts – until 2008, when he was arrested by authorities in Saipan.

Part of the Northern Mariana Islands (a US
territory), he had unwisely announced on his blog that he
was going there for on a business trip.

Suicide – and still unsolved

There's no statute of limitations on murder in
California, and so again Miura found himself in a court
fighting extradition.

It was an unsuccessful battle, and he found himself
in an L.A. jail cell on October 10, 2008 – and committed
suicide that same night, hanging himself with his t-shirt.

The *LA Times* of October 21 reported that his
defense attorney had questioned the coroner's finding of
suicide, but either way the story was over – though the
murder of Chizuko Shiraishi, almost forgotten over the
years, still remains unsolved.

**$$$ / Rendezvous Lounge Daily 2pm-midnight, Justice
Sun-Thu 6am-11pm, Fri & Sat until midnight**
www.doubletreeladowntown.com
www.justicela.com

Fine Arts Building
10e Restaurant
Dublin's
811 West 7th Street
Los Angeles, CA 90017
Tel: 213 488 1096

Child Ghosts, Mobster Girls & Murder

The 1920s saw Los Angeles growing rapidly as a big city. Their motion pictures and movie stars were making money across the world, while their aviation industries were helping people fly across it – or at least parts of it.

Downtown Los Angeles was seeing "skyscrapers" changing the landscape, and in October 1925 the Fine Arts Building Company announced it was going to build as high as was allowed – 12 storeys.

They engaged the noted Walker & Eisen firm (already known for the James Oviatt Building) to design them something in the "Romanesque Revival" style.

Standing outside, the historical figures, dragons, birds and the two reclining men representing "sculpture" and "architecture' on the exterior of the third floor show that something special awaits inside. That trapezoidal shape to the first three floors is rather unusual too, and of course the penthouse at the top looks fit for a king or queen.

Once you step inside you'll realize that this is somewhere different: it's a hidden treasure of mosaics, arches and colorful tiles; a golden-tinted space that mixes a church with Moroccan luxury.

There's a gorgeous chandelier overhead, a balcony, marble floors, glittering pointed glass cases along each side that serve as art displays, and a stunning cross-barred roof – and this is just the lobby!

It's one of my favorite places in downtown – a real oasis of calm – and that sentiment was echoed by Tom (Joseph Gordon-Levitt), who also said it was his favorite building in *(500) Days of Summer*.

It also did duty as the New York office for Angelina Jolie in *Mr. and Mrs. Smith.*

Movies aside, part of the charm here is due to the bronze water sculpture in the lobby. Like the reclining figures on the exterior it was designed by Burt William Johnson, who used his daughter Cynthia Mae (3) and son Harvey (5) as models.

Johnson worked in a wheelchair – he had heart problems despite being only 37 years of age – and was even hoisted up into the air in it when he was working on the outside sculptures.

Other talented craftsmen who worked on the
interior included decorative tile maestro Ernest Batchelder
and painter/muralist Anthony Heinsbergen, who had
already been lauded for his work at movie theaters as well
as at the Roosevelt Hotel and City Hall.

The doors opened in December 1926, and it soon
became a center for society and the arts. Events of all kinds
were regularly held in the Artland Club's suite, while stores
selling luxury hats, furs and frocks located themselves here
alongside hairstylists and the more mundane offices.

Art exhibits were mounted in the lobby too – a
tradition that continues to this day.

But it didn't last. The Depression hit hard, and
began to rub away the glitz. The building was sold in 1930
and renamed the Signal Oil Building, and then again in
1933 when it became the Octane Petroleum Corporation.

Now more a center for oil than the arts, it mainly
housed attorneys, doctors and a bank, though the chain Pig
N' Whistle opened a café here in the space now taken by
the 10e Restaurant (though there have been many other
eateries on street level here over the years).

There was another name change – to the Havenstrite
Building – when oil man and Beverly Hills Polo Club
founder Russell Havenstrite took over the penthouse, and in
1970 it was bought and remodeled by Global Marine Inc.

More owners came and went, but in 1983 it was
rechristened the Fine Arts Building and restored by
Ratkovich, Bowers and Perez, the same firm who restored
the Oviatt Building.

The Fine Arts had finally come full circle when in
2012 it was sold to the owners of the famous Flatiron
Building in New York, and then in 2015 the 10e opened
here too.

While only the building's lobby is open to the
public, there have been some criminal activities going on
behind the doors here (and some odd things too).

SCRAMBLED IDENTITIES CAUSES GRID STAR GRIEF

On February 4, 1931 the *LA Times* reported that Guy W. "Tad" Davis had been forced to call a press conference in his office here when it was reported that he was "near death from a head injury."

Amusingly, he told reporters that "my only wife is the only one living with me at our home," and related how he had been the victim of mistaken identity three times in the last few years.

It seems that the error came about when a man who identified himself as "Guy W. Davis, Northwestern University football star" was admitted to hospital some time after signing over his property to his wife in El Paso, Texas, and then coming to L.A.

Davis (the real one) was indeed a Northwestern graduate but a "track and field star," not football, and his friends and family were "worried and confused."

Someone else taken in by the scam had also even attempted to wire money to "him."

Police were going to try and solve the mystery when the other "Davis" regained consciousness – if he ever did, as his condition was listed as critical.

Sadly, the report didn't mention whether that happened – nor about the other times Davis had been mistaken for someone else.

OPERATIONS GANG RAIDED

There were more serious allegations in June 1936 when it was reported that the then-Octane Petroleum Corp building had been one of three raided by the police in connection with an "illegal operation" ring (the term used in those days for abortions).

A large "well-furnished" doctor's office on the second floor was searched after an undercover female policeman had scheduled an then-illegal procedure, and a doctor and two nurses were arrested – though it seemed that quarters had been "hastily vacated," perhaps when word of the other raids had reached them.

Even so, a damning haul had been found, including "a truck load of medical instruments, medicines and operator's paraphernalia," and it was reckoned that they had been making thousands of dollars a month from this office and others in Hollywood and Long Beach.

All the offices were under the name of Dr. George E. Watts, and labeled envelopes containing diamond rings, bracelets and watches found in a safe indicated that these were pledges given in lieu of money by some unfortunate patients, friends or family.

Many years later in May 1958, artists Ruth Myers and her mother Barbara Larimer hung their paintings in the lobby in advance of an exhibition – and then later that day Myers was killed in a freeway accident.

That isn't the only sad story related to the lobby here. On a recent visit I spoke to the security guard Pat, who has worked there for five years.

She told me that the elevator doors regularly opened and closed on their own, and then recalled how a woman claiming to be a psychic came in one day and asked to "see the spookiest place in the building, so I took her to the basement!"

Once there the woman apparently "felt the presence of an older gentleman," and quickly departed.

She also mentioned that when new tenants recently came in – they had taken on five floors – some remodeling was necessary. "One of the contractors, working there alone, felt a tap on his shoulder – and heard the sound a little girl," said Pat.

The spirits of the fountain

As mentioned, the lobby fountain – which features a boy playing a flute in the middle and has two girls holding a fish at each end – was based around the children of architect Burt William Johnson, who died before the building was finished.

Is he the "older gentleman" sensed in the basement, and the "little girl" his daughter? Are they both roaming the building, trying to meet up so they can finally both look around the building that they helped bring to life?

Missing Securities Linked to Slaying of Two Secretaries

Later in 1967, there was something far darker borne here – a gruesome double murder that led police to Florida and an infamous criminal.

A story that you'd expect to see on "Dateline" or "20/20" if it happened today, it was reported in the *LA Times* in December that $7,200 had been linked to the "Slaying of Two Secretaries."

The report detailed how the bodies of secretaries Terry Kent Frank, 23, and Annelie Maria Mohn, 21, who both worked at a brokerage firm here, had been found in Florida.

They had both quit their jobs and taken a bus across the country a few weeks before, and were suspected of being in possession of securities that were missing.

What seemed like a possible Thelma and Louise-style escapade didn't last long though, and the money did them no good at all: their bodies – "clad only in bathing suits and jewelry" – had been found in a remote spot in Hollywood, Florida.

The bodies of the secretaries were found by fishermen in a remote section of the waterway reachable only by boat.

They had been bludgeoned and stabbed (Mohn had been shot too), and concrete blocks had been tied around their necks. Whoever killed them wanted them to stay lost.

While their sudden fleeing with money (only to meet their doom soon after) is reminiscent of the movie *Psycho* in a way, it's clear the pair ran into serious trouble – or perhaps already were, as Frank was the estranged wife of a man from Miami.

The Deadly "Beach Boys"?

Police hadn't named any suspects, though "unverified reports" said the women were friends of the infamous Florida "Beach Boys," a gang whose members including convicted thief Jack "Murph the Surf" Murphy.

He was already known to police for his part in the 1964 theft of the Star of India sapphire from the Museum of Natural History in New York, and was the subject of a cheesy 1975 movie.

Woman's Foot

After leaving L.A., the women had checked into a hotel in Miami Beach with little luggage, and the manager had got anonymous calls they were "deadbeats," so he threw them out – seemingly to their deaths, as a few days later a women's foot was seen sticking out of the water.

The friends had been dead 10 hours or so.

In 1969 a suspect was convicted, and it was indeed Murphy (with another man, Jack Griffith, convicted and sentenced to 45 years in prison a few years later).

Murphy however was granted parole after serving nearly 19 years of a life sentence in 1986, apparently because officials were impressed with his work as a born-again Christian and Lay minister.

Blood Money

Nevertheless, one of his parole conditions was that he had to pay money to a Meals on Wheels service due to a request from Kent's father Lewis, who said that it was blood money. "I couldn`t touch it," he said, adding that "in a few years he`ll be back (in prison) again. He`ll get what he deserves."

After staring at the ceilings and décor – and that fountain – in the Fine Arts, go next door to 10e, a restaurant that offers a wide-ranging menu of Armenian offerings, but in fact travels widely across the culinary Mediterranean.

Rather a rarity (in terms of the menu at least) in downtown, it's a smart, bright white restaurant with heavy glass doors, odd-shaped lights hanging randomly from the ceiling, an upstairs level, and a bar at the back – but don't let the rather corporate look fool you.

The menu range goes from *mezze* (starters), *bdzig* (small), *michag* (medium), and *medz* (large dishes) and while you might expect hummus or *jajuk* (yogurt with cucumber, dill, mint and olive oil) and a wide selection of beef, there's also vegan/vegetarian dishes, stylish kebabs, flatbreads and pastries.

A sweet tooth like mine tends to go for the brunch citrus and berry yogurt parfait (Greek yogurt, citrus, honey, berries and granola), and there's a long list of wines too, including many from Lebanon.

Prices are super-reasonable, and there's a daily social hour from 4-7pm – perhaps that's the best way to dip your toe into the Med.

Try a Black Sea cocktail (Jack Daniels, bitters, orange, cherry and soda), basturma (beef) and quail eggs, or, for a movie connection on the regular menu, spend some time with Sophia Loren (Rittenhouse rye, Italian Amaro liqueur and bitters).

Alternatively, on the left of the building is Dublin's sports bar, which reopened in 2016 after a long time closed – not the first bump in their road.

Originally they opened on Sunset Boulevard in West Hollywood well over a decade ago, and when they were due to replace a former Italian restaurant here at the Fine Arts, the transition took a year before the doors opened in 2011 – until the temporary closure.

Clearly the Dublin won't die – though this is no shamrock-heavy, farming equipment-lined old-style kind of Irish place (but do look out for the two severe sculptures on the wall).

It serves a range of bar snacks and has whiskeys and Scotch and lots of beers on tap, can and bottle, but the many large television screens and their beer-friendly daily happy hour (3-6pm) suggests their sports fans are indeed very loyal.

That said, cigar fan and magician Louis Lave performs here some evenings, and as a member of the Magic Castle he may have more ghost stories too.

$$ & $$$ / 10e Sun-Wed 11am-11.30pm, Thu, Fri & Sat 11am-11.30pm, Dublin's Daily 11am-2am
www.10erestaurant.com
www.dublins815.com

Bristol Hotel
Pellicola Pizzeria
423 West 8th Street
Los Angeles, CA 90014
Tel: 213 614 8000

Seven storeys high and almost unmissable today thanks to a huge billboard of fingers making a "w" sign on one side of the building, the Bristol Hotel has spent nearly 100 years staying largely on the quiet side, no matter if downtown was in its heyday, on the skids, or coming back to life.

The Woodward

Built in 1906 and named the Woodward Hotel after proprietor Guy Kerr Woodward, an Illinois businessman who later leased the Union Square Hotel in San Francisco, today it's a small building with just over 100 units – none of them with kitchens – for low-income housing.

It's had an interesting history nonetheless, including the years 2003 to 2010, when it was all-but abandoned after ambitious plans fell through and it became a sort of ghost hotel, away from the areas that were being gentrified.

The newest owners were looking to change that though, and funded a renovation that took it back to its roots – at a cost they were tight-lipped about revealing.

Their time seems to be here though, with late night Pellicola Pizzeria in one of the street level units, Club El Guacho in the basement, and the historic Golden Gopher bar next door.

The El Guacho is easy to miss – it has half a unit on the street level (the other side is a convenience store) but has been there for over 20 years – while on the other side is the pizzeria, a minimalist, split-level scrubbed wood floor place that's joined by a door to the Bristol's lobby.

Though the Woodward is almost forgotten now – in name, anyway – it certainly hit the headlines a few times, and not always in a good way.

ROBBERS BIND AND GAG CLERK IN WOODWARD HOTEL; ROB SAFE.

In December 1910, two robbers "evidently old hands at the business" said the *LA Times*, gagged and tied up the clerk H.A. Lee after he stepped out of the elevator, hid him so he couldn't be seen from the street, and then robbed the safe of $60.

After looking deeper into the archives, it seems that the Woodward was probably renamed the Bristol Hotel sometime after it was sold for $300,000 in October 1920 to what the *LA Times* called "Easterners" from Minneapolis.

The report said the owners were looking to refurbish the hotel and create a dining room; that was almost certainly the Italian Village, a restaurant noted for music and dancing, and which the *LA Times* said was celebrating its 15th anniversary in 1935.

That didn't stop the new owners from experiencing an early tragedy when, almost exactly two years after the sale, police were called in on October 17, 1922.

DEAD MAN ·
FOUND IN
HIS ROOM

It appeared W. O. Halley, 49, had died of natural causes after being in poor health for some time. Little was known of his past except that he was born in South Dakota in 1873, had travelled across the US, and that his exciting occupation was as a deep sea diver!

In March 1926 original owner Woodward died of a heart attack aged 60 in San Diego, where he and his sister had been running the Warner Hot Springs resort (which is seemingly still there, albeit renamed a little as the Warner Springs Ranch Resort).

Then in June 1929, the *LA Times* revealed news of the arrest of a resident here.

BURGLARY REIGN MAY
BE LINKED TO CRIPPLE

Billy Russell, a 28 year old man who (apparently) needed crutches to walk, was caught red-handed ransacking the apartment of E. A. Tupper, who wrestled Russell to the ground and held him until police arrived.

They held Russell until the chemical analysis of paint found on a pen knife he was carrying was complete; would it match the paint on the windows of houses recently burglarized? Sadly the archives don't tell us.

Then, just before Christmas 1931, there was the bloodiest incident in the history of the Bristol.

Shell-Shocked Veteran Slays Wife and Self

As reported in the *LA Times*, a room here was the scene of a "double tragedy" when veteran Oliver S. Heath, 38, shot and killed his wife Lillian Mae, and then turned the gun on himself.

They had been quarreling when Heath pumped five bullets into her, but despite "her lungs punctured and her body virtually riddled with bullets," Lillian managed to flee the room, summon the elevator and make it to the lobby before collapsing.

She died later in hospital after having "gasped out" the details to police, while Heath left a note saying:

"I have a good mind to kill you."

This threat was addressed to banker J.W. Lewis, who handled monthly payments made to him from a family trust – payments that were apparently under threat.

Heath wrote that any trial would be "framed-up," and that was why he had killed his wife, who had sought to gain control of these payments – and hinted that Heath "was addicted to the liquor habit."

Both bodies were taken to the county morgue.

In the many decades since – save for a fleeting appearance in *Fight Club* (1999) – the Bristol has stayed out of the headlines.

On a recent visit manager Yolanda said she didn't have any unusual or strange stories about the hotel, though she had only started working there recently.

She did however say that Dean, the owner of the basement Club El Gaucho would, though as dive bars go this might be one to avoid: I certainly did!

So, since the Bristol lobby is closed to non-residents (though you can see where Lillian Mae gasped her last through the window), why not grab a slice and carry on your search for stories – or order a whole pie and stay for their Tuesday and Wednesday night movie screenings?

$$ / Sun-Wed 5pm-1am, Thu-Sat until 3am
http://213dthospitality.com/project/pellicola-pizzeria/

King Eddy Saloon
King Edward Hotel
131 East 5th Street
Los Angeles, CA 90013
Tel: 213 629 2023

Tunnels and Suicides

In 1906 the *LA Times* noted that the new building planned for 5th Street was "such an American hotel, although with such a very English name, don't you know."

Designed by architects John Parkinson and G. Edwin Bergstrom, the fireproof six story King Edward hotel boasted a marble lobby, mosaic floors, "a telephone in every room," and all the materials used in construction were made right here in Los Angeles.

People are still staying at the King Edward (though it's very much a low-income residence these days), while Parkinson went on to make a huge mark on the skyline: he was also the man behind City Hall, Union Station, the Los Angeles Memorial Coliseum and many others.

Down on street level, the King Eddy Saloon has been here almost as long as the hotel itself, and that includes during the 1920s and 1930s, when it was store selling pianos (though what was really for sale could be bought by coming into through a separate entrance into the "speakeasy" in the basement).

This was the time of Prohibition, and the King Eddy was at the centre of it all. Corrupt local officials turned a blind eye, enjoying the secret drinking and some of the profits, while underneath the bar there was a 133 foot tunnel that was part of a network of service and utility tunnels across downtown – just perfect for deliveries of bootleg liquor.

After prohibition ended in 1933 the speakeasy disappeared and it went back to being a dive bar with what it says is the longest-standing liquor license in town.

As for the dusty tunnels, they have a few faded murals and are home to junk and old equipment – though occasionally tours are arranged.

Novelist Charles Bukowski drank here, and maybe it inspired John Fante to write his semi-autobiographical *Ask the Dust* (1939), a story about Arturo Bandini, who was a struggling writer living in downtown L.A.

Sadly, the hotel had some unhappy memories from its early days too.

Shortly after opening its doors, one of the guests committed suicide in his room following an apparent three-day drinking and gambling spree.

The *LA Times* of September 15, 1906 reported that Benjamin E. Smith, who had been left by his wife nine months before due to his "slavery" to liquor and gambling, drank laudanum before writing several suicide letters.

> "She sold my property illegally. She could be sent up for it.
> "Please give this to my wife.
> "If I have done harm to anyone, I hope they will forgive me.
> "I now lay down to die.
> "Minnie, you killed me.

In one he blamed his wife Minnie as the "cause of it all" noted the *Los Angeles Herald*, and in another letter he accused his aunt of illegally selling his property and hoped that "her soul would be in torment forever."

Virtually the last words he wrote before the poison took its fatal hold were:

"Minnie, you killed me."

The hotel changed hands for $50,000 in March 1909, and the new owners had to deal with a Christmas tragedy that same year.

As reported in the *LA Times*, in the early hours of Christmas Day, H.F. Windward shot himself in the head with a .38 caliber revolver while his friend S.F. Oliver sat just yards away.

MYSTERIOUS,

S ENDS BULLET THROUGH HEAD.

Registered under the name Brown, Windward was dictating some letters to Oliver – one of which was regarding a woman whom "he was ready to give up a thousand lives" – before he took his fateful decision, a cause of death that the *Los Angeles Evening Herald* called "self-destruction founded on shattered love."

A few months before that there had been a very melodramatic moment for the King Eddy when the *LA Times* headline thrilled in the story "Spurns Bride: She Turns" and reported how Michael W. Scanlon, the King Eddy's former bartender, was in jail in Yuma, Arizona.

Scorned Woman Has Man Draggcd Off, Train.

Bitter Tears Quench Love; Law's Vcngcancc.

He had been charged with "wife desertion" by his new bride, "whole-hearted Irish girl" Margaret.

They had been married in New York three months before and were now living in downtown, but then Scanlon suddenly left for Seattle in order to "obtain better wages," saying he would "soon be able to send for her."

The distraught Margaret found out in fact that he planned to return to New York, and rushed to the station to confront him.

There was a row, a struggle, and the poor woman was left abandoned on the platform as the train pulled off into the distance.

Undeterred, she went straight to the District Attorney's office to file papers, and the law said Scanlon needed to send her $100 to have the matter dismissed.

Aged Man Ends Life in Hotel by Poison Draught

Just over 15 years later in January 10, 1925, death came to the King Edward again when Albert Andrew Walker drank poison – cyanide – in his room here. There were no indicators to whether Walker had any relatives, though he did leave a note saying:

"Good-by, everybody."

Just over four years after that there was the bloodiest night in the history of the King Edward Hotel, as reported by the *LA Times* on January 29, 1929.

Bodies Discovered in Room at Hotel Here

Richard L. Boggs, a patrolman of the US Immigration Service, stabbed his wife through the heart and then shot himself in the head with a .45 Colt automatic, a murder-suicide that Boggs had written in advance to his father Richard about, only that father's phone call to police – tragically – was too late to save either of the victims.

COUPLE DEAD IN DUAL TRAGEDY

Boggs wrote in the letter that he was suffering from tuberculosis and was going to end his own life "and take his wife with him."

The unnamed wife had apparently put up "a terrific struggle" before being killed by the hunting knife; it also seemed a towel had been stuffed in her mouth "to stifle her cries."

In 1933 the King Edward Hotel was bought by C.F. Stillwell, former owner of the still-standing Stillwell Hotel and the long-gone El Rey, but a few years after he had made some room improvements, there was an attempted suicide here.

Wrist and Throat Slashed, Woman Found in Room

Clara P. Mohr, a 43 year old teacher from San Francisco, tried to end her days in September 1937, but then things seemed quiet – at least in terms of newspaper headlines – for decades.

There was however a story in the *LA Times* of September 29, 1970 that told of police officer Fred Kahl, who saved a potential leaper at the hotel.

She was sitting on her second floor window ledge in her blue nightgown when people going to work saw her and called 911 – the new emergency phone number that had come into use in early 1968.

While other police tried to break down her door, Kahl stood underneath and she shouted:

"Get out of the way. I want to kill myself, but I don't want to hurt you."

WOULDN'T GET OUT OF WAY

As the hotel door gave way, the woman moved along the window ledge and slipped – right into brave officer Kahl's arms. He only had minor bruises and she a broken ankle for all the melodrama.

Fugitive Sought in Son's Slaying Seized in L.A.

Early in 1983, the King Edward was in the news once again when Ronald Giedraitis was arrested here and charged with the murder of his four year old son the previous year.

Geidraitis, 33, was on the run from Canada and was on their Top 10 Most Wanted List. Unbelievably, he had apparently called the FBI to ask if he was still a wanted man, and of course they had traced the call.

Unless you're a resident or visiting someone you can't go into the hotel, but you can pop in and have a look at the bare lobby. The grand staircase is still here, as is the clock behind the front desk that's dedicated to Theodore Roosevelt, who stayed here on a visit to Los Angeles when he was President.

As for spooky stories, according to GHOULA (Ghost Hunters of Los Angeles), the King Eddy is said to the original home of one of greatest mythical ghost stories – that of the vanishing hitchhiker.

The King Eddy "version" is that a woman patron asked for a ride to the Belvedere Garden section of east L.A., and en route the driver offered her his coat.

However, when they passed the Evergreen Cemetery in Boyle Heights (one of the oldest in the city), she jumped out.

He gave chase, but it seemed she had disappeared, as he could see no sign of her – until he came across a grave with his coat draped over it…and her name etched in the stone!

Whether it's really inspired by something that happened here or even by the passage in *Ask The Dust* when Arturo talks about going to "the King Edward Cellar" and finding there "a girl with yellow hair and sickness in her smile," we'll never know.

At the time of writing the King Eddy is closed and going through a change of management, but it will reopen soon and so no matter how it turns out, this is one of L.A.'s most famous "skid row" bars – and is worth a visit.

For now though, here's a look at the new logo, which is bright gold:

www.kingeddysaloon.com

**Roosevelt Building
Salvage Bar
727 West 7th Street
Los Angeles, CA 90017
Tel: 213 226 1727**

Suicidal Women, Disappearances – and O.J. Simpson?

Opened in 1927 and designed by local architects Curlett
and Beelman, the Roosevelt Building was named after
President Theodore Roosevelt, and is an excellent example
of the Italian Renaissance Revival style.
   The exterior is pretty much the same as it was when
it opened its doors, and on entering you go under three 30
foot high arches and step onto an intricate lobby terrazzo
floor, with a gorgeous chandelier overhead.

   The building was financed by a group of L.A.
bankers and financiers called the Sun Realty Company,
whose president promised it "would be one of the finest
office buildings in the United States."

It was said to be the largest in California, and the *LA Times* of April 4, 1926 had included a sketch of what the building – which was due to cost $4m and run 250 foot along 7th Street and 137 along Flower – would look like; a mix of marble, terra cotta and walnut finishing and supplied with nine high speed elevators.

Unfortunately, one of the realities of construction in the days before strong safety regulations was the fact that new buildings often came with a human price, and that deadly account opened early at the Roosevelt.

In July 1926, the *LA Times* had trumpeted the grand scale of the project, noting that there had been a record concrete pour during construction: 1800 cubic yards over four 24 hour day work periods the previous week, with deliveries of 11,000 sacks of cement, 1800 tons of rock, and 1500 tons of sand.

LABORER KILLED IN SIX-STORY PLUNGE

Yet in the paper that same day – though getting far fewer column inches – was news of the first life taken by the building.

Worker Enrico Garcia, 35, had fallen from the sixth floor and suffered compound fractures of the skull, dying some time later in hospital.

Worker Killed in Plunge Down Eight Stories

Barely six months after that there was fatality number two: laborer R. Ponce, 45, had slipped into an empty elevator shaft, then fallen eight storeys to his death.

Over the years the building was home to businesses such as doctors, dentists, jewelers, travel agents, shoe stores, accountants and others, but the level of customers it was looking to attract was perhaps best reflected during the holiday season of 1927, when the Four Aces Mining Co. put six bars of gold bullion on display in their office.

Then, in December 1931 there was the first oddity at the Roosevelt Building when Adrienne Reeve went with her husband Raymond to his office here – and never saw him again.

MAN VANISHES IN MYSTERY

Reeve was supposed to go with a representative of Six Companies to the Boulder Dam (better known as the Hoover Dam) on the Nevada/Arizona border and negotiate a hefty deal regarding safety equipment, but he never arrived – and wasn't even expected there.

More chillingly, Six Companies had no employee with the "representative's" name.

Pledging forgiveness no matter what her husband might have done, Adrienne felt that "foul play has befallen him" at the hands of the imposter, and the *LA Times* reported she and her 3 year old son Morton, who was nicknamed "Buzz," were "prostrated with fear."

The *Los Angeles* Examiner relished this Christmas mystery, and printed a touching picture of the young boy, his hands clasped in prayer as he apparently said:

"Dear Santa Claus, bring daddy when you come here please."

Was Reeve a murder or kidnap victim? Had there been an accident? Or had he left his family for a lover or suffered a breakdown of some kind?

Despite an extensive, multi-state search by police, they were still searching for a single clue about what had happened to Reeve according to an update on December 26 – and after that the archives remain silent.

Some years later in 1940, the *LA Times* reported on the upcoming burial of long-time Salvation Army officer George Guirey, who had died of a heart attack here, and then June 1943 saw the first suicide at this building.

Woman's Fatal Leap Almost Hurts Another

Accompanied with a picture complete with dotted line showing Bessie Morris's fall from the ninth floor, the *LA Times* of June 4 explained that Morris, 71, had been in extremely poor health and had left her purse, gloves and hat on the fire escape before jumping to her death.

She almost landed on a passer-by on the sidewalk below, but her falling body only knocked the purse out of Nell Hendrick's hand, leaving her shocked but injured.

Morris was the first of five female suicides listed in the archives as taking place at the Roosevelt, with three male suicides on that list too.

Eight deaths of this kind are rather unusual for a non-residential building – at least within the locations featured in both *Gourmet Ghosts* books – and it's also unusual that the majority were women, and that they all jumped to their death.

For many decades poison was easily available, and most women (and some men too), seemed to take a fatal dose when they wanted to die.

Restrictions on deadly chemicals have seen them somewhat replaced by prescription drugs as a way to end lives, though suicide by gun has remained popular for men, and hanging is chosen by both sexes.

Later in 1943 there was perhaps the deadliest day in the history of the Roosevelt Building – and a crime that led to legal history.

DR. VERNE HUNT SLAIN AT DESK BY EX-PATIENT

Killer Commits Suicide After Shooting Prominent Surgeon; Illness Blamed for Tragedy

Nationally known physician Dr. Verne Carlton Hunt, 55, had treated the Mexican President, football pioneer George Halas and actress Mary Pickford in his office here in room 516.

On Monday December 13, a disgruntled patient named Ephrem Mounsey came to the office, pushed past Hunt's assistant, and confronted him.

"Why didn't you operate on me?" the *Los Angeles Evening Herald-Express* reported Mounsey, 69, said, not waiting for an answer before he pulled a gun and shot Hunt three times, then put the .32 revolver in his mouth and pulled the trigger.

The murder-suicide shocked the city (though the Coroner didn't order an inquest), but what came after had lasting implications.

Slaying Victim's Heirs May Sue, Court Decides

Mounsey's will hinted that he had planned the crime as well as leaving $35,000 to his sister, and in June 1946 it was reported in the *LA Times* that the California Supreme Court had made a final ruling that Hunt's widow, Mona, could sue her (i.e. the slayer's estate) for damages.

It's a legal occurrence that's extremely common these days, with perhaps the $40m suit brought against O.J. Simpson by the families of Nicole Brown and Ron Goldman, whom he had been cleared of murdering in October 1995, being the most famous example.

Man, 48, Leaps to His Death on Busy Street

A couple of years later in January 1948, Abe Steier, 48, threw himself from the 10th floor fire escape. He too almost killed an unwitting pedestrian below – Karl Bierly Jr. – but instead his body crashed through an awning before striking the sidewalk.

His widow told police Steier had had a nervous breakdown following the collapse of his business, and had been despondent for months.

Woman Plunges From 12th Floor Ledge to Death

A few months later in July, a "fashionably-dressed woman" jumped from the 12th floor fire escape, launching herself to her death just as two physicians who had been trying to persuade her to come back inside tried to pull her to safety.

She left her purse, hat, coat, dark glasses and a dime on the windowsill, and inside the purse was a $5 bill, two keys with a tag saying BBM, a gold wedding ring initialed EMM and other items.

The *LA Times* ran a picture of the keys, but two days later it was reported the "Plunge Victim" was still unidentified despite three people coming forward; now 30 more made appointments to view the body.

RING REVEALS IDENTITY OF DEATH LEAP VICTIM

By July 28, the victim had been claimed: she was Bessie M. Mumford, 65, who had been missing for a week – though police still had no idea why she had committed suicide.

In July 1950 there was another odd disappearance here. The *LA Times* reported that Captain Ernest Arthur Kollberg, a champion yacht racer, walked with his wife and a friend to the Roosevelt, then got into the elevator to go and see his doctor on the 10th floor.

CUP RACE SKIPPER DROPS FROM SIGHT

But he never arrived for his appointment.

Police put out an APB (all-points bulletin), but since Kollberg's health was poor and he had recently talked of suicide (to say nothing of insisting he visit the doctor alone), it seemed that his story probably had an unhappy ending somewhere else.

Anti-Communism in Los Angeles yesterday reached a new high.

There was another weird moment later that year, when the *LA Times* of December 14 reported that someone had called the paper to report the mustaches on the plaques of President Roosevelt here had been "touched up."

Now, apparently, they looked rather too much like representations of Soviet Union leader Joseph Stalin!

Unhappily, less than two weeks after this there was more serious news from the Roosevelt.

Hundreds See Woman Take Death Plunge

A few days before 1950 came to a close, an unidentified elderly woman leaped or fell to her death from the 12th floor, hitting the awning of a store before sliding to the sidewalk in full view of hundreds of shoppers.

She was DOA at hospital, and one passer-by fainted on witnessing the tragedy.

11-STORY FALL KILLS WOMAN

Another suicide occurred just a few months later in March 1951 when Mary M. Ahlskog jumped or fell from a window on the 11th floor, crashing through the skylight of Van De Grifts sports store before hitting the sidewalk.

Ahlskog, 50, who relatives said had been depressed and in ill health, arrived at a doctor's office on that floor and told the receptionist she was there to "meet her sister."

A few moments later the receptionist returned to see Ahlskog's coat and purse on the chair besides the open window, and the *Los Angeles Evening Herald-Express* reported that people saw her hanging from the window ledge before she finally fell.

Irma Bohnu, manager of Van De Grifts, said she heard what she thought was an explosion, and the room was splattered with glass.

Man Dies in Downtown Suicide Leap
Would-Be Rescuers Seconds Late in Reaching Scene

There was another suicide in February 1957, when Frederick Mittelstadt jumped from the 10th floor. The *LA Times* noted that two police officers called to the scene were barely a minute too late to save him.

One had taken the elevator, the other the stairs, in an attempt to reach the "leaper," but both arrived only to find his glasses case on the ledge.

Apparently Mittelstadt had been unemployed for two months, and a note later found in his hotel dresser drawer asked that his brother Louis be notified "in the event anything happens to me."

It seems the building was quiet – at least in terms of bad luck or bad news – for decades after that, and on March 31, 1987 the *LA Times* noted a $2m renovation which saw those famous archways redone in polished brass.

In the 1990s the 7th Street/Metro Center subway stop opened here (at some of the subway exits you come out right at the Roosevelt), while in 2007 the building was listed on the National Register of Historic Places.

Though today it's really more apartments than offices and stores, when I asked about any strange events or reported experiences here, the woman working at the foyer front desk said she hadn't experienced anything herself, but residents had spoken to her:

"They've mentioned strange noises, footsteps, the sound of things being moved around – but nothing specific, and not only any particular floor."

They're noises you might expect in a busy building perhaps, though there is a link to history of the Roosevelt in one of the many food and drink outlets at street level.

There's Marie's Coffee, Japanese fusion restaurant The Octopus, gourmet burger joint The Counter (love their "adult" spiked shakes!), and my preferred destination there, the Salvage Bar.

Though it's only a few years old, this bar has a direct connection to the past of the Roosevelt – and the clue's in the name.

Feeling a bit like a cross between a contemporary, smart lounge and a hidden Art Deco drinking den from back in the day, it was decorated using items actually found in the basement (panels, doors and the gorgeous windows), some of them dating back to the early days of the building.

Check out the hand-blown crystal glass above the ballroom-style main room and order a 7th Street Mule (Pinnacle vodka, lime juice and Fever Tree ginger beer).

There's a $5 happy hour from 4-8pm every weekday, but since this is a bar only – no food – maybe stop here for a drink and enjoy the regular music nights, before you move on to somewhere else.

Either way, examine the bar top when your beer, wine or cocktail arrives. They're made out of the building's original elevator doors, and seem glazed thanks to nearly 20 gallons of resin that they poured onto them.

They are the same doors that many people passed through before they went to their deaths or vanished into history…

$$$ / Mon-Fri 3pm-2am, Sat 8pm-2am, Sun 4pm-2am
www.salvagela.com

Stillwell Hotel
Hank's Bar
Gill's Indian
Uncle John's Café
838 South Grand Avenue
Los Angeles, CA 90017
Tel: 213 623 7718

Today the Stillwell stands alone, the only structure within a large area given over to parking, but at over 100 years old it has plenty of stories to tell – and oddly enough, the very first reference to the Stillwell in the archives is (kind of) related to death on a grand scale.

The October 27, 1912 edition of the *LA Times* noted the new fireproof hotel was funded by the Los Angeles Cemetery Association, and that architects Frederick Noonan and Charles H. Kysor had revised the building plans.

It was still going to be in the Spanish and Mission style, but now there were to be elaborate decorations on the ninth and 10th floor, and the iron fire escape was going to be deliberately placed at the front and center of the building.

Inside there were 235 rooms, a billiard room, ladies' parlors and a dozen rooms on each floor en suite. Charles H. Stillwell took the first lease, opening the doors in 1913 at $30 rates, and was known for personally driving the hotel bus – a seven-seater Studebaker – to collect guests; over the years he bought other downtown hotels including the El Rey and the King Edward too.

Just a few months after that opening, the Stillwell was the location for a very sad story – that of Mrs. George Crane, "whose mind had apparently been weakened by a great and mysterious sorrow."

Visitor Here in a Pathetic Plight.

The *LA Times* of May 14 explained that Crane had lost interest in her son George, stopped eating, and was wandering the corridors in "a boudoir gown with the sad eyes and meaningless words of Ophelia."

The pair had been at the hotel for several months and were seen as being of "wealth and culture," but after being found at 4am one morning she was taken back to her room – and then locked herself in, a crying George being found outside the door that night.

The lock was removed from the door, but now Mrs. Crane was asking how far it was to the ocean, and for some "strong medicine to make her sleep."

An alarmed Stillwell called authorities but would not charge that she was insane, deciding instead to send telegrams to her relatives.

George meanwhile was happy being showered with attention from fellow guests, though the wary Stillwell was quoted as saying that "it appeared there was danger of something happening."

Sadly, the archives offer no further clues about what happened to the unfortunate mother and her son.

Years later, South Grand was the location of a "terrific gun battle" in June 1921, when garage employee E. Ross and two police officers exchanged fire with two "bandits" who had held up Nathan Lowestein, the Stillwell night clerk, taking $101 from the cash register.

Prisoner Trapped in Cellar Confesses to Crime.

One injured thief escaped, while the other was found in the hotel's basement and arrested; it was the second time night clerk Lowenstein had been held up here.

SHERLOCK IS OUTCLASSED

Bellboy's Ready Ear at Hotel Keyhole Foils Asserted Bunko Plot; Two Are Jailed

Referring to the famous fictional British detective, the *LA Times* headline of May 1923 noted that Stillwell got a black eye after he and bellboy Ande Vacha confronted two "bunko men" Vacha had overheard demanding money from an unknown man in one of the rooms.

There was a struggle during which "the fist of one came in contact with Mr. Stillwell's eye," though both conmen were eventually arrested and charged.

In May 1926 Stillwell sold the lease for $1m to Ben Weingart and the Lincoln Company; they planned on a large remodel with new furniture and "a bright and cheerful atmosphere," according to the *LA Times*.

There wasn't much happiness in March 1928 when last rites were announced for Shella Leigh Hunt, a 53 year old student and author who had recently died in his apartment here after a long illness, nor that December, when petroleum engineer John B. Overstreet, 33, drank poison in his bathroom here.

ACCUSED MAN
DRINKS POISON

Suspect Tries Suicide as He Faces Jail Cell

Out of jail on a $2,500 bond for check fraud offences, Overstreet had been unable to get the money to pay it. A private detective had been watching him since his release too, and they were in Overstreet's room when he excused himself to the bathroom.

"Goodbye, I've just take poison," he said when he returned, before collapsing. His chances of surviving were "slight."

Girl in Death Leap Identified

On August 28, 1933 there was a small piece in the *LA Times* about Helen Millard, who had left her home in Long Beach the previous Wednesday and checked in, then jumped to her death on the Sunday night.

There was another redecoration in 1934 so the hotel would be "ready for prosperity" said manager Alex Nord, and in June 1936 there was certainly a glamorous and eye-catching story here – though not quite what he imagined.

"Infuriated Suitor Kills Dancer and Commits Suicide"

That was the June 5 *LA Examiner* headline above a picture of a smiling, curly-haired blond woman posing in a tutu – 26 year old Donna Park.

The report revealed that a few weeks previously, acrobatic dancer Irving La Zarr, 28, had been talking to a friend, agent Paul Savoy, in his room at the Stillwell Hotel and said:

"What good is my life without Donna's love? I'm either going to kill her and then myself or God knows what?"

That deadly threat came true, as he did indeed shoot exotic ballet dancer Park and then himself later – and now Savoy was unhappily recalling those words:

"He used to come to my room nearly every night and talk wild about Donna."

A dancing instructor named Theodore Kosloff also remembered what Donna had said to him just a few weeks before:

"I'm going to get married. I don't want to. I know this is coming to a tragic end. I want to go on dancing, not be a wife."

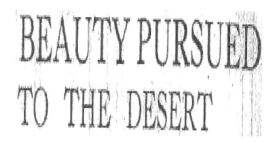

The *Examiner* really ran with the story, their opening line screaming:

"Love's misunderstanding – violent death!"

The report then went into more detail, explaining that La Zarr seemingly followed Park to Phoenix, Arizona, and rented the room next to her.

That night they sat in deckchairs on the veranda and talked until 4am, but when Park suggested they go back inside, La Zarr made his deadly decision.

The *Examiner* article also revealed that La Zarr had a steel plate in his skull – the result of a car crash in Chicago three years previously – and the fracture it covered had never really healed; was there a chance he was perhaps mentally ill as a result?

Either way their bodies were found "hands clasped in death," something the *Examiner* called a macabre "finis" to their broken engagement and their ended lives.

There was a very different – but still tragic – story in February 1939, when choral lecturer and conductor Alexander Stewart, 70, died of a heart attack in his room here at the Stillwell.

His wife Ethel suffered a nervous collapse when she heard the news, and had been in a sanatorium ever since, even missing his funeral, but then:

Mrs. Alexandar Stewart Succumbs Three Hours After Mate's Funeral

Barely two months later in April, Lilly O. Reichling Dyer, 74, also died of a heart attack in her room here. She was founder of the Native Daughters of the Golden West, a fraternal and religious society based around the values of the Pioneers – an organization that still does charitable work today.

In August 1941 there was another suicide here, though a note left behind gave details about where $1000 in twenty $50 bills could be found in a glass jar and given to someone who clearly meant a lot to the victim, Fred French of Glendale.

Glendale Man Leaves Note About $1000 Before Suicide

French's body was found after his (deliberately early) 2am alarm call went unanswered, and the note – apparently written at midnight – listed the two kinds of poison he had taken, even describing their effects:

"Here goes then, waiting for results. Working O.Kay, getting dizzy..."

In April 1944 Charles Stilwell himself died – though not at the hotel he had owned and bore his name.

He had been a pioneer in bringing the rental car business to California, and though he left the Stillwell for good in 1930, he later helped design Stillwell's Auto Hotel, a uniform grid of rooms with plenty of room for cars that we'd recognize today as a roadside motel.

Somehow the death of Stillwell seemed to bring a peace to the hotel, and it was criminally quiet for many years – until June 1976, when the *LA Times* reported that Mary C. Farrington, 82, had been found dead in her fourth floor room.

Coroner's deputies said preliminary tests showed that Mary C. Farrington, 82, died of a stab wound in the neck in her fourth floor room at the downtown Stillwell Hotel. Her room had been ransacked, police said.

It looked like a robbery that had turned violent, and a few months later in September, police thought there may be connection to the murder of another unidentified elderly woman at her apartment some five blocks away.

Elderly Woman Found Murdered in Her Apartment

There was a $2m renovation in 1987, but over the years it became a lower-budget residence, perhaps because it was a distance away from the main hotels in downtown and now stands alone. Nevertheless, it's close to the L.A. Live complex, the Convention Center and Staples Center.

In terms of food, drink and other delights here at the Stillwell, early plans included space for a grill room and café, and that has pretty much continued – though there was a beauty shop here at one time too.

Today, the Stillwell is home to Uncle John's Café. Their logo of a friendly cartoon chef doesn't mean this is a fast-action diner though; it's a very smart place that mixes Chinese and American staples in large portions (their most popular dish is pork chops and eggs), has televisions on the walls, and a door that opens right into the hotel's lobby.

They're doing something right too, as they've been here nearly 20 years, as their predecessor seemed to be Lily's Grill, whom I last found reference to in the *LA Times* in 1998.

Here for even longer (they opened in 1981) is Gill's Indian Restaurant, which is right at the back of the lobby (just follow your nose for the smell of curry!).

It's a small place with a dozen tables, a few booths, Bollywood videos on TV, and décor including elephants, Hindu gods and (strangely) a painting of the Eiffel Tower.

I recently popped in for the lunch buffet – potatoes and spinach, kidney beans, rice, chicken curry, naan bread and more – and though it wasn't as spicy as would have liked, it was still a bargain for under $11 including tax.

They also have a sense of humor, as a line in Gill's menu reads: "You've tried the cowboys now try the Indians."

On the way out I saw a door with Gill's Travel Service written on it, and on stepping inside the paper and file-filled room I learned from Raj, a lady sitting at one of the desks inside, that this was the office for the hotel.

She told me that the Gill family has owned the hotel since 1979 (hence the name of the restaurant) and that the grand older man with a beard and a turban nearby was her father, the current owner of the hotel.

Walking back into the lobby, I saw a makeshift lounge/library with red chairs and several shelves of books (many hotels have a bring-one-leave-one scheme).

Also connected to the hotel via a lobby door is one of downtown's most famous dives: Hank's.

Opened in 1959 by Hank Holzer, a former New York welterweight boxer, it's been a beacon for people of all types ever since – from shady guys to cops, construction workers to lawyers, and secretaries to serious drinkers.

One of their noted customers was philanthropist Ben Wiengart, who bought the Stillwell back in the late 1920s and who founded the Weingart Center, a large homeless organization on Skid Row.

Holzer and his wife Frances had originally moved to California for the warmer climate – she was suffering from diabetes – and he ran the bar until 1973 or so until he had to quit so he could take care of her.

A decade later, Frances told Hank to buy back the bar he so loved – a loving gesture from his wife of over 40 years, who died soon after.

Everyone had a scare when Hank's was suddenly closed in February 2015 (luckily for just a short period of time), but by then Hank himself had long gone to his grave, his lengthy 88 years put down to non-smoking and regular screwdriver cocktails!

In late December 2015 a visit to Hank's at opening time revealed an atmospheric, old-style place. The bar is long but narrow, with a few booths and dozen or so stools.

There's dark wood everywhere, a wooden bird cage on the wall, a (working, if slightly out of tune) piano at the back, mirrors, and a great old fashioned shiny push-button cash register.

It's dark and inviting – somewhere you could easily get very comfortable – and there's a plaque here that seems to know what you're thinking:

"Dedicated to those who are dedicated to delightful dining and drinking."

There are pictures of Hank and other memorabilia, including a sign he put up long before a certain TV show:

"Welcome to Hank's, where everyone knows your name, where everyone's glad you came."

I spoke to Sarah, a dark-haired, fast-talking bartender who said she was a "clairvoyant, pagan, actor, poet and musician," and she told me that there was a ghost here – a very cheeky one!

"It's grabbed my ass when I was behind the bar, facing away from the customers – about three times now!"

Tina, who had worked there for six years, added:

"When I close up at night, it feels like there's someone in here with me."

Sarah added that even some of the customers have mentioned an eerie feeling at the back of the bar, and then admitted that she doesn't like closing up by herself.

"The bar is very long, and when I close up I move from the front of the bar to the back – where the exit is. That means I have to turn off the lights at the front as I leave, so I end up half in the dark. If I ever realize I have left something behind, I won't go back in."

An *LA Times* article in January 1998 reported on the tearful get-together held here to celebrate Hank's life, and it mentioned a man who worked at the hotel and was wearing a black turban:

"Hank was a celebrity around here," he said. *"He was very nice to everyone. It didn't matter if you were from India or Pakistan or Bangladesh. In my religion, there is a saying that some people, when they die, they leave their goodness here. Hank was one of those people."*

$ & $$ / Hank's Daily 6pm-2am, Gill's Daily 11m-3pm and 5-10.30pm, closed Sunday, Uncle John's Mon-Fri 6.30am-3pm, Sat from 7am, closed Sunday
www.gillsrestaurant.com

Stowell Hotel (now El Dorado Lofts)
Le Petit Paris
418 South Spring Street
Los Angeles, CA 90013
Tel: 213 217 4445

Scandal Behind The Scenes

Over 100 years old, the 12 storey Stowell Hotel was the brainchild of financier N.W. Stowell and run in the early years by his nephew A.W., who had a scandalous, tabloid-friendly moment some years later – not the first time someone in charge here found themselves in the headlines.

Designed by architects Frederick Noonan and William Richards and opened in 1914 on what was being called "The Wall Street of the West," it cost somewhere close to $600,000 and had 264 rooms aimed at businessmen clients – though its grand looks soon attracted celebrities and movie stars too.

The hotel highlighted Southern Californian materials to the max – terra cotta, green-glazed brick on the outside, golden Batchelder tiles inside – and rates went from $1.50 - $5 a day.

There was also a kind of vending machine where you could buy toiletry essentials like a toothbrush, razor or cold cream for a quarter – quite a forward-looking idea in those days.

There was also apparently a policy where wives could stay for free – as long as they checked in with their husbands (or at least signed in as such) – and this was perhaps an innovation Stowell regretted when in June 1923 his nephew was paraded in the *LA Times*.

GIRL ACCUSES HOTEL MAN

"Ada Robinson sues A.W. Stowell for $125,000 Charging Breach of Promise and Betrayal" ran the sub headline along with a picture of a glum-looking lady in a big hat.

Poor Ida charged that A.W. had promised to marry her once his divorce was finalized, but then "betrayed her and later cast her off" – it seemed he had never even made the final application, and was in fact reconciled with his wife – the cad!

More seriously – for those times, anyway – she also
said that "improper relations" had existed between them,
and her consent to this was only because he had made that
marital offer.

Robinson – who had worked as a book-keeper at the
Stowell for several years until she'd been suddenly fired –
said she was "a nervous wreck," an outcome that makes
this seem like it could be a piece in today's *LA Times*, even
though it happened nearly 95 years ago.

But even before the scandal of Ida there had already
been a shocking love affair unearthed here.

FLEES WITH SODA CLERK.

That was the tantalizing headline of the January 10, 1920 edition of the *LA Times*, which reported that Estelle Masters, a 55 year old widow, and Fred Rehm, the 45 year old soda clerk, had registered here as man and wife after arriving from Boston.

They had been arrested on instructions sent from Massachusetts, and were charged with passing fake checks and violation of the Mann Act – crossing state borders for sexual purposes – something that today is associated with child abuse and sex trafficking, but in those more austere times was more related to non-marital sex.

Rehm had apparently left a wife and four young kids in Boston for this "midwinter romance" and – like Ida's heartbreak – it was a story you might well read about in the newspaper today.

Charlie Chaplin Really Stayed Here

Years before that – soon after the Stowell had opened its doors in fact – the hotel welcomed perhaps its most famous ever resident: Charlie Chaplin.

He referred specifically to "the Stoll" in his 1964 autobiography, and had taken up residence here to save money while working for Essenay Pictures.

He was hardly a "Little Tramp," though. He was earning over $1000 a week – a huge amount of money in those days – and during his year stay he even got an offer of $25,000 for two weeks work in New York!

HAND FEELS WAY TO DEADLY PILL

The Stowell almost had a tragedy soon after opening too, when a Mrs. E.S. Deering staggered out of bed and groped around for what she thought was a bottle of headache tablets.

But they weren't – and within hours she was suffering from stomach cramps:

"My God, I've taken poison!"

She survived her accidental poisoning, and the *LA Times* took it as an opportunity to call for protection from lethal tablets – an issue still relevant today.

Unidentified.

WOMAN HOTEL SUICIDE DEAD FOR SEVERAL DAYS.

Within a couple of years though, the first suicide at the Stowell had taken place.

The February 26, 1917 edition of the *LA Times* reported that Mrs. W. Taylor, 28, had shot herself with a "new automatic pistol of small caliber" in her room, but there was no suicide note to explain her desperate act.

Police Order Test of Would-be Suicide's Sanity After Hearing Story of Michigan Killing

Later in 1923 there was another attempt at suicide here, when Leonard Rogers slashed himself with a razor.

Arrested on charges of passing fake checks in Chicago, he said he was also involved in a murder there – though police said the real suspect was missing a few fingers, and Rogers had all his on both hands.

Just over two years later, the hotel was sold to H.J. Tremain in June 1925. He planned to spend $20,000 on improvements and – in a nod to the emerging presence of motor cars – to convert the basement into a garage.

Barely a few weeks after the change of ownership, there was another love story printed about the Stowell – though this time it was more heartwarming than salacious.

LOVE'S MESSENGER THWARTED

The *LA Times* of Jun 29, 1925 reported that Fred Carter had checked out, but had left something behind in his room; a carrier pigeon with a note attached to its leg:

"Dearest Louise, next time I come to Los Angeles I hope you will be with me and we will be on our honeymoon. With love, Fred."

Apparently the young man had left his sweetheart in New Mexico, and had promised to send her messages by carrier pigeon. What had actually happened, no one knew.

Had the pigeon failed to make it out of L.A? Or had "Don Cupid," as the *Los Angeles Herald* nicknamed him, forgotten to take his feathered friend along?

After some effort, the staff took the pigeon to the roof and it flew away "in that part of the empyrean lying towards New Mexico," the *Herald* hopefully concluded.

WIFE ESCAPES AS LEAD FLIES

Less than two years later, a week before Valentine's Day in 1927, another love story went awry when it was reported that Andrew Jankowski had tried to shoot his wife while they were playing on the golf course, but accidentally shot his friend, Cornelius J. Callahan, instead.

He then shot himself in the head with his .32 caliber revolver, dying instantly, while Callahan was in a critical condition.

The trio had checked in to the Stowell on vacation from Ohio, and Mrs. Jankowski later told police her husband had been "tortured into the sudden madness by hallucinations that his life was being plotted against."

Callahan had in fact bravely stood in front of her and taken the bullet, causing her to cry:

"You've shot the best friend I ever had."

Several years later in August 1931 there was a another behind-the-scenes story at the Stowell when the *LA Times* reported that David H. Clark, accused of the murders of Herbert F. Spencer and gangster Charles H. Crawford some months before, had stayed here following the killings.

CLARK TO FACE 'HIDEOUT' QUIZ

Clark claimed the two men had pulled a gun on him at an office on Sunset Boulevard, threatening him for his stance against the underworld and wanting him to be part of a plan to frame the Police Chief.

This was a big scandal, as Clark was a noted former deputy District Attorney – and quite the looker, too. Had he acted out of self-defense, killing at least one menace to Los Angeles, or was he mixed in with the bad guys?

Clark was tried twice – the first was deadlocked, the second saw him acquitted – but his later life was just as dramatic.

In 1937 he went missing and was found in France, apparently "insane," and was later convicted of murder: that of one of his friends after a drunken party argument.

He only served three weeks of his sentence though, dying in Chino Prison of a brain hemorrhage on February 20, 1954.

As for the late Crawford, his widow built him a memorial on the site where he was killed: the now-famous Crossroads of the World (see the entry in the **Hollywood & W. Hollywood** chapter).

Mother Writes Where to Find Body in Hotel

Almost exactly a year later in August 1932 there was another exotic drama: the suicide of Louise Hickman in her room, number 610.

She actually sent a letter to her daughter explaining her actions, though of course by the time police had been alerted, Hickman was long gone.

The 55 year old nurse had apparently tried suicide before due to financial troubles, though this time she had taken the Gothic romantic route, injecting a peach with poison before taking her final bite of life.

She was found in bed, her clothes neatly piled on the chair, but with the Olympics taking place in L.A. at the time there was little space for anything else in the papers, though the *Los Angeles Herald-Express* headline read:

"Woman Ends Her Life By Bite of 'Poison' Peach."

There was another change of ownership in early 1938 – the cost being around $400,000 – though it probably didn't mean much to employee Samuel J. Perron, who was found dead in his bathtub that October, a small pistol in his hand and a bullet in his head.

He had set his alarm clock for the fatal time, leaving a note reading:

"My execution has been set for 6 o'clock."

Improvements by the new owners probably suffered some damage three years later, when a fire broke out on the 12th floor. Six hundred guests fled onto the street, though there was only one smoke inhalation casualty – and it was in his room where the blaze started.

That didn't affect the sale price in 1944 though, when it went for $500,000.

A few months after that in March 1945, the war came to the Stowell – literally – when the key to room 611, still stained by the black volcanic ashes of Iwo Jima, was sent back here after being found on the Japanese battlefield.

Death, Shooting Laid to Jealousy

Later that year in August there was a murder-suicide here, the *LA Times* showing a woman, her head bandaged and attended by nurses, in a picture alongside their August 26th report.

BROKER SHOOTS L. A. WOMAN AND KILLS SELF IN LOVE ROW

The report explained that Albert Goldberg, 40, had beaten and shot Josephine Norman in a room on the 10th floor. The *Los Angeles Evening Herald-Express* was bolder, showing a picture of Goldman's body, the .38 caliber pistol close by.

Los Angeles Public Library

Shot in the abdomen and arm, Norman managed to stagger into the elevator and go down to the lobby, while Goldberg remained in the room and shot himself in the head. The pair had been together for a couple of years, but she was looking to end the affair:

"I was afraid of him.... He thought I was in love with someone else and was intensely jealous."

Apparently her plans to go on vacation without him were the final flashpoint.

Just over a year later the Stowell was sold to George S. Allen for $850,000, and then just a few weeks later in January 1947 there was good and bad news.

Monday Hutchinson, 76, had died of a heart attack in his room, but his will had left $2,300 to David Russell, an *LA Times* vendor outside the Biltmore Hotel.

BOY TO INHERIT $2300 LEFT BY DAD'S FRIEND

In the last five years Hutchinson had got to know Russell's family, and had left all his money to Hutchinson's son Edgar, 10, to spend on his education: it was a kind act from beyond the grave.

In August another guest died in her room – her name was Leonora Fairbank – and then in November 1949 there was trouble again for a Stowell owner; George Allen was facing tax evasion charges in the princely sum of nearly $71,000.

Allen said, after his arrest, that he didn't "know what the charge is all about." Bond was fixed by the indictment at $5000.

It may have been this financial affair that led to a name change at the Stowell, because the next time this address was in the *LA Times* it was as the El Dorado Hotel.

Two Newsmen Periled as Prisoner Grabs Policeman's Gun, Shoots Self

The date was May 14, 1956 and the story – and exciting pictures – showed the moment when Clarence E. Swetters, 24, who had been hanging from the Stowell's 13th floor ledge but was saved by police officers, was bought down in handcuffs. Suddenly he yelled:

"I'm going to kill you guys!"

Swetters then made a grab for one of the officer's guns and a bullet was fired, passing through Swetters' right foot and ricocheting off the corridor wall. Actually not a guest at the hotel, he was booked on suspicion of assault, and attempt to commit murder – but still vowed:

"I'll do it again when I get the chance."

Police Officer Thwarts Death Leap From Hotel

Another policeman played hero at the Stowell in May the next year, when officer L.J. Patterson saved William J. Weydt, 28, who had been about to leap from the third floor fire escape. Weydt had left a rambling note saying he was "despondent."

Six-Story Plunge Kills Man, 76

Unfortunately retired New York salesman Mark A. Klein, 76, wasn't saved in 1962, and he jumped to his death from the El Dorado's sixth floor just after midnight on September 10th.

In June 1970 there was another suicide here when Katheryn Sherrell, 20, left her 9 month old son with friends on the fourth floor, and then leaped to her death from a window on the 10th.

Unable to find a job after arriving in Los Angeles, she must have felt this was her only way out.

Thankfully, the El Dorado seemed not to bother journalists – or police – for the next decade or so, but by now it was a single residence hotel and on the long slide downhill, like many of its neighbors.

By the end of the 1980s it was almost completely abandoned, and for years after that it sat empty until it was bought in the early 2000s by a company who restored the building and converted it into condominiums – the El Dorado Lofts that you see today.

There were restaurants in the street-level spaces over the years (I found reference to at least one, Araceli, in the late 1980s and early 1990s), but things really took off in culinary terms with the opening of Petit Paris L.A. in 2015.

A huge eaterie with room for several hundred diners, it took over the hotel lobby and two mezzanine levels, then lined the walls with modern artworks that complimented the original etchings.

The mezzanines are reached by the very grandest of staircases – it's the same one that Charlie Chaplin used and is worth walking up and down, just for the thrill!

The developers and restorers did an amazing job here: huge candle lanterns, skylights, red chairs lining the bar, and everything lined with ornate gold trimmings.

It feels very much of the Old World-style, and is even bigger than Bottega Louie at the Brockman Building.

Do make sure you pop into the small store too; lots of delicious treats, fancy gifts and evocative smells.

The Ghost of Charlie?

I had breakfast here soon after it opened (a delicious Eggs Benedict and a mimosa), and of course the menu is very French – the owner's original restaurant is still in Cannes, France.

While I was there I was told by a staff member that when he was there alone, things have "just flown off the shelves" in the kitchen, and that among the staff generally, they say that anything unusual or strange is due to the ghost of Chaplin.

He's also said to haunt another restaurant, Musso & Frank in Hollywood, a place he regularly dined at and where his favorite booth (number 1) is still available for you to visit (full details in *Gourmet Ghosts – Los Angeles*).

$$$ / Mon-Wed 11am-11pm, Thu & Fri until midnight, Sat 10am-midnight, Sunday 10am-11pm
www.lepetitparisla.com

The Hoax Drowning

Though I couldn't find the restaurant that was linked to this story, it was just so unusual that I just had to include it – especially when I read this headline:

"Ghost" Reveals Weird Tale of "Inner Force"

On June 23, 1928 the *LA Times* reported that a smelter had been arrested for handling stolen gold and silver, including $270,700 worth stolen by a San Francisco-based gang including Ferdinand Albor, who had been operating in Los Angeles for the last year.

Nothing unusual about that you might think, but then four days later the *LA Times* reported that nearly four years after his clothes had been found abandoned on a beach in Venice, California.

K.L. Baumgartner had returned from the dead.

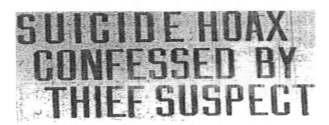

Amazingly, Ferdinand Albor, the burglar who had been arrested several days before, had admitted to police that he was in fact Baumgartner:

"I was not drowned in the ocean, but fled because of an inner force that keeps me moving whether I really want to stay or not."

Police confirmed Baumgartner's identity, but then it was realized that his wife had (unsurprisingly) remarried in the meantime, and now needed to obtain an annulment and then re-marry her new husband Robert Busby (a process that would take at least a year).

Arbor – as he called himself then – had been arrested for a San Pedro burglary the previous week (and doubtless linked to the smelter case), and in his "strange confession" he told detectives that he had received a head injury while working in the Seattle shipyards during WWI:

"Since then, I have not been wholly able to control my actions."

He said he had also worked as a cook in logging camps and "other out-of-the-way places" during that time, and pledged to help his wife "regain her freedom."

They had owned a restaurant on Main Street in downtown L.A., but one day he said he had "felt an irresistible urge to leave."

'Widow' Greets 'Dead' Husband in County Jail

The odd meeting between the Lazarus-like Baumgartner and his remarried wife took place in the County Jail, and the *LA Times*, understatedly, said it was a "strange reunion." Apparently Baumgartner whispered "How do you do?" and an awkward conversation followed.

Asked by reporters what she would do next, the shell-shocked wife-of-two said she and Busby were happy together; hopefully that continued to be so.

It was an amazing story for sure, but ironically (and tragically) one of the newspaper reports about it was placed next to this one:

POLICEMAN DROWNED AT BEACH

Heroic Efforts of Young Brother to Rescue Him Prove Ineffectual

Skeletons in the Closet
L.A. Country Dept. of Medical Examiner-Coroner
1104 North Mission Road
Los Angeles, CA 90033
Tel: 323 343 0760

Dying For Your Business

The L.A. County Dept. of Medical Examiner-Coroner is not usually somewhere you'd want to visit.

It's where people who have died in suspicious or unexplained circumstances are sent for an autopsy to try and determine the cause of death.

Over the years a number of celebrities including Whitney Houston, Michael Jackson, The Notorious BIG and River Phoenix, as well as many everyday Joes or Janes, have ended up on the slab here, all of them equal in death.

The coroner's department has existed in L.A. for over 100 years, but it's now located in the Administration Building, which used to be the old Los Angeles General Hospital in Boyle Heights.

When you walk in it's like you've stepped into a 1940s film noir. There's an ornate tiled floor, marble walls, a big black staircase, gorgeous wooden chairs with red leather cushions, a big chandelier and four frosted glass doors with gold writing on them.

You almost expect to see a grizzled Humphrey Bogart walking out of one of them holding the Maltese Falcon and pointing a gun at you.

Three of the doors are marked Identification (for tracing Jane and John Does), Notification (for contacting relatives and family) and Personal Property Release, where relatives can collect possessions of their dearly departed.

There's no viewings done here though; that's in another building altogether.

The fourth door leads into something very unique, though there's no sign – just the same lettering you see on the other doors, and maybe a small velvet rope.

The only one of its kind in the world, this room (officially number 208) is a place that many people would say could exist "only in America" – it's called Skeletons in the Closet, and is the official Coroner's gift shop.

Opened in 1993, it sells souvenirs like t-shirts, tote bags, baseball caps, toe-tag key chains, pins, buttons, boxer shorts called "undertakers," books about the history of the Coroners in L.A., "My First Skeleton," water bottles, crime scene tape that says "Warning! There's a party going on" and much, much more.

The idea for the gift shop came out of special coffee mugs and t-shirts created for the annual professional Coroner Conference, and all profits go to the Youthful Drunk Driving Visitation Program (YDDVP).

It was of course a media sensation from day one – they do a thriving mail order business too – and overall it's meant to try and look for some humor, to remind people that life is precious and you must enjoy every moment of it: no wonder their slogan is "We're dying for your business."

Inside there's a coffin converted into a black leather couch with "Law and Science Serving The Community" written on it, while their most popular item (believe it or not), is a large beach towel with the chalk body outline on it – so you can lie down and play dead in the sun.

Certainly an interesting place to visit, it's worth remembering that every victim in the City of Angels comes to this building, but you can walk out alive…

SS / Mon-Fri 8.30am-4pm, Closed Sat & Sun
www.lacoroner.com

Updates – Downtown

At the **Alexandria Hotel**, the noted "Ghost Wing" was purchased in late 2012, with $3m due to be spent on renovations and repairs to transform it into apartments called The Chelsea.

Developer Nick Hadim spoke on behalf of other investors to the media about his trip across a ladder into the deserted, dusty annex of rooms, which have no stairs and elevator and were sealed off in a dispute among the hotel's owners in 1934.

Inside he found a battered bowler hat, an antique typewriter and some claw-foot bathtubs.

That was creepy and interesting, but as of the writing of this book the windows were still gray with years of dust: who knows what is going on in there?

Also, at the **Bonaventure Hotel** it is in fact possible to stay in 2419, the room the *LA Times* called an "abattoir" where two murder victims were cut up with a cleaver in October 1979.

The body parts were stuffed into a garment bag and a suitcase, taken down to a car in the garage, and then dumped in trash bins in Van Nuys and Sherman Oaks.

Creepily, there are two luggage stores in the Bonaventure complex, and it's possible they were both visited by one of the killers as he searched for something to carry away the bloody body parts.

Staff here probably don't know about the story – or at least won't admit it – though the valets have reported hearing screams in the basement parking garage.

At the nearby **Checkers Hotel**, further research has revealed some stories from the days before the hotel opened its doors as the Mayflower Hotel in 1927.

Way back in 1897 when this site was a private home – or maybe a small rooming house – it was reported in the *LA Times* that former physician Alfred B. Gregory had taken poison here; he had been ill for some time.

By 1907 this location was certainly the 100 room Key West Hotel, and in December 1911 the *LA Times* reported on the mystery of Charles Clark, 9, who had disappeared after playing outside with "other lads about his own age."

Suspicions had fallen on one of them, Gilbert Johnson (whose age wasn't given), who was reported as having a probation record.

The father and mother of "Little Charlie" were not together, but were said to be "frantic" and "prostrated."

Sadly, the archives offered no further information about what had happened to him, but eyewitness reports from staff here over 100 years later (noted in *Gourmet Ghosts – Los Angeles*) say that the non-automatic front doors have opened on their own when there's no one there.

Mystified, they checked it out on CCTV, but couldn't find an explanation: maybe it was Charlie coming back to his mother after all these years.

380 Mile Drive To Death

Some years later in 1925, disabled war veteran Clifford R. Blair shot himself in his room here. He had arrived just a few hours ago by taxi from Arizona, and graciously left instructions in his will to make sure the driver was paid for the very long ride.

Then, barely a year before ground was broken on the Mayflower in 1927 (and the Key West destroyed), George K. Wallace also took poison here in his room.

POLICE HOLD MAN POSING AS DIPLOMAT

There was more mysterious scandal in March 1931, when Roy J. Angus was arrested for passing himself off as a representative of the British Foreign Office.

Angus, 35, had been taken on a tour of San Quentin island prison and even given lectures about the "penal, economic and social conditions in the British Isles," but apparently it had all been a sham – and he was arrested for embezzlement at the request of Oklahoma authorities.

In early 1932 the Mayflower changed hands for $1m and was renamed when they became part of the Hilton Hotel group, the *LA Times* taking a picture of female parachutist-turned-lumberjack Cherie May hanging high above the street replacing the hotel sign.

At the **Biltmore Hotel** right opposite, research has revealed another tourist-friendly ghostly tale.

Before "The Black Dahlia" Disappeared....

Apparently the last place Elizabeth Short – known as "The Black Dahlia" after her gruesome 1947 murder – was seen alive, the Biltmore is also said to be a place she haunts (she's been seen in the lobby, elevators and halls wearing – of course – a black dress).

Research and interviews for *Gourmet Ghosts – Los Angeles* actually had a kind of link to this; security guard Louie said that a maid called Lourdes had talked about a "black ghost" or "black spirit" that she'd seen here in a room off the Rendezvous Court.

More recently, scouring the *LA Times* archives bought a Biltmore suicide to light: that of Ruth K. Wilson, who had apparently been "despondent."

The *Los Angeles Herald-Examiner* of July 3, 1953, printed a picture taken from the ninth floor which showed an arrow leading down to her sheet-covered body on the street below.

Finally, the **Figueroa Hotel** is currently undergoing a major renovation – I attended the massive auction that saw the selling-off of almost all their Moroccan-style fixtures and fittings.

It links to a story I found in the archives: in July 1948 the owner-operator of the Figueroa, Ray L. Langer, 63, died of a heart attack in his room here. Hopefully he approves of the new look!

Chapter 4
Silver Lake to the SFV

El Cid
4212 Sunset Boulevard
Los Angeles, CA 90029
Tel: 323 668 0318

The Music Never Stops...

A century ago, where El Cid is now was merely empty and dusty ground right in the middle of a cornfield – but it was already famous.

One of cinema's early superstar directors, DW Griffith, had a studio nearby, and he used this area to film some scenes for his 1915 epic movie *The Birth of a Nation*.

More than that, he might have even had this original structure built as part of his plans.

Ten years later in September 1925, eaterie the Jail Café opened its doors here. Looking like it would have been great fun, pictures show that this themed environment had a watchtower, V.I.P. jail cells and waiters who wore prison uniforms.

Guests could honestly say "I was behind bars last night" without any fear of real jail time as they ordered from the simple fare on the menu.

Famous for their $1.25 dinners, the Jail Café was part of a trend that had started in France around 1900 and spread to the USA (e.g. Clifton's, the Pup Café (now at the rear of the barrel-shaped Idle Hour Bar), Randy's Donuts, the Jurassic Restaurant in City of Industry, and more).

The Jail Café didn't last though, and was converted into the theatre/stage you see today. It was known from 1932 as the Gateway Theatre, then from 1950 to 1961 or so as the Cabaret Concert Theatre.

The Cabaret had a pretty good run. It was a proving ground for shows that went all the way to Broadway and kick-started some careers, but the performers usually received little or no pay, so they supplemented their income by waiting on tables and taking tickets (a tradition that continues among actors to this day).

Judge Stops Singer From Warbling 'Born in a Bar'

The Cabaret occasionally hit the headlines outside the entertainment pages too. In 1955 the Judy Garland impersonator Barbara Heller was served with a Court Order and told to stop singing "Born in a Bar."

She was sued for $50K by fellow singer Muriel Landers, who said she had exclusive performance rights to the song from the composers, who had written the parody of "Born in a Trunk," a song the real Garland was famous for from the 1954 movie *A Star Is Born*.

Heller countered by saying that the composers had give her the song to sing in return for a loan – and "for love and affection."

When the Cabaret came to an end, El Cid took to the stage. The distinctive name was probably inspired by the 1961 hit movie that told the story of Castillian Knight Don Rodrigo Díaz de Vivar – nicknamed "El Cid" – who had fought the North African moors and contributed to the unification of Spain in the 11th century.

Charlton Heston starred as "El Cid" alongside Sophia Loren, and the rather gruesome story that made El Cid a legend was that after his death his corpse was put into his armor and mounted on his horse as if for battle – such was his fearsome reputation.

It's also possible that the name was chosen because it made for a cheap sign, but either way the Spanish theme was dominant when they opened in 1963 as a 16th Century-style tavern and an oasis for live Flamenco entertainment in Los Angeles.

New Flamenco Club Will Open

El Cid was the brainchild of Flamenco-mad Margarita Cordova, her husband singer/guitarist Clark Allen, and her dance partner Juan Talavera.

Cordova and Talavera studied in Granada, Spain, for more than a year before returning to Los Angeles, and El Cid was a home for Flamenco and Spanish cuisines and wine – though the food wasn't as big a draw as the energetic dancing.

But there were some difficult and dangerous times at El Cid over the years too.

Owner Shot, $780 Stolen. In Holdup

In early October 1972, a thief hid in the light control room and snuck out after customers had gone. Brandishing a gun he held up Margarita, Clark and the members of staff, took their wallets and purses and the money from the till, then said:

"If any of you look at me I'll kill you."

As he was leaving with his haul, the thief turned and fired – hitting Allen in the chest. It took him nearly a year to recover from the wound.

There was also a deadly event in 2007, when a teenaged homeless girl was strangled in a nearby hotel and her body, wrapped in a bed sheet, was dumped in the alley behind El Cid, where it was found the next morning.

Her killer – a convicted rapist and drug dealer – had just been released on parole; he's now serving life without the possibility for parole for her murder.

A few years after that El Cid was taken over by new owner Scott Milano. He revamped the menu and cocktails, replaced the sound system and red velvet curtains and re-landscaped the *al fresco* gorgeous back patio, which is the best place to hang out with a margarita and *patatas bravas* during $5 happy hour (Mon-Fri 4-6pm).

At the same time on a Saturday is "paella on the patio" – a big-plate treat that comes with tapas – while later that night is the time for La Verbena, a vegan-friendly street party-style pop up.

Foodie and organic jam-maker Laura Ann Masura was part of that revamping team, and, explaining that she had already worked here from 2004-2007, added some information for new guests:

"Everyone here has a ghost story. It's totally haunted. Without a doubt."

Just one example happened a few days before I gave a *Gourmet Ghosts* talk there as part of the Dearly Departed Tours Weekend in October 2014: she was closing up the bar at night and went on the stage to turn a light off.

No sooner had she done that and walked away when the light came on again. She went back and turned it off, but again it turned back on – and then it happened again.

Angry, she swore out loud and shouted "Quit doing that, I want to go home!" Sure enough, the light went off!

Another employee named Sam, who overheard our conversation, said that he saw a man with a ponytail walking by him at 3am a couple of weeks ago – when the bar was definitely empty – and other reports said that whoever the ghost or presence is, he (or she) certainly seems to be mischievous, smashing glasses, turning lights on and off, and locking the bathroom door.

Laura Ann also mentioned that she had:

"Seen a bottle float across the bar, three or four feet in the air, though we had no CCTV then to get it on film. Believe me, if we had I would have watched it again and again."

Guitar Ghosts

It seemed that strange goings-on are pretty common here, though perhaps the most interesting phenomenon is that people have heard guitar playing coming from the stage when there's no one performing, and the sound system is turned off.

courtesy El Cid

That might connect directly with the late Gino D'Auri, who died of cancer on January 26, 2007 aged 69 and was the resident guitarist here for many years.

He's still very much a part of El Cid though; you can see a picture of him above the ATM, and the dressing room is still known as "Gino's dressing room."

Born in Rome, Italy, he was the grandson of a gypsy and recorded a couple of albums, playing on several others too.

He toured with dance companies in Italy and Spain and moved to Los Angeles in the 1960s, performing at local restaurants and dance events until arriving at El Cid in the late 1970s.

There's another strong candidate for the person still haunting their old stomping ground – Clark Allen himself, the former owner.

He died aged 82 a year or so after D'Auri, and was a folk singer, an actor and an artist.

Horror legend Vincent Price actually began collecting Allen's paintings in the 1960s, and Clark provided musical accompaniment for Bette Davis and her husband Gary Merrill in the national theatrical poetry/prose show *The World of Carl Sandburg* in 1959-1960.

Clark Allen by Nathan Fowkes

Allen also showed musical skills on the small screen in episodes of "Peter Gunn" and notably in a *Twilight Zone* episode entitled "Five Characters in Search of an Exit," where he played a bagpiper stuck between ethereal planes in a netherworld.

As to which of these two El Cid legends are still here, staff member Jill thought it was probably Gino, though Laura Ann was sure it wasn't him:

"The ghost was here way before he died."

No matter who is here from the spirit world at El Cid, the last piece of evidence is a picture that was sent to me soon after the Dearly Departed Weekend, and was taken on one of the nights.

Better in color – see www.gourmetghosts.com – it looks like a large, white, bubble-like shape floating under the roof: is it a possible orb?

$$ / Mon-Thu 6pm-1am, Fri until 2am, Sat 3pm-2am, Sun 11am-midnight
www.elcidla.com

Tam O'Shanter
2980 Los Feliz Boulevard
Los Angeles, CA 90039
Tel: 323 664 0228

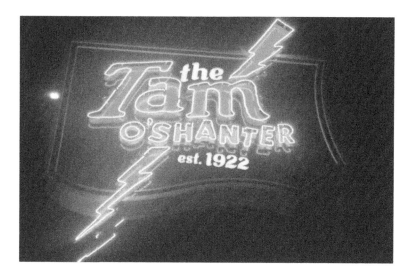

Disney and Ghosts at Dinner

The first thing you will notice about the distinct "Tam" is that it looks like a kind of English country home combined with a witch's castle – something that influenced certain future diners in a very big way (more about that later).

Back in the 1920s Los Feliz Boulevard was only a dirt path, yet Lawrence Frank and Walter Van de Kamp – of the famous Van de Kamp bakeries – formed the Lawry's Company and hired architect Henry Oliver to build a restaurant for them right at this very spot.

They initially wanted it to be in the style of a fairy-tale European house that Hansel and Gretel might have found irresistible, but soon after opening its doors as the Montgomery County Inn in 1922 – check out the cooking souvenir on the wall – it seemed the public didn't agree.

They decided to try something new, renaming their place Monteclair and then finally picking the little-known Scottish tale of Tam O'Shanter as their inspiration.

The restaurant was re-designed to give it a Scottish theme – staff uniforms, flags, kilts, bagpipes and all – and everyone hoped that Tam O'Shanter, whose tale sees him outsmart a coven of witches – would bring hungry diners to their doors.

They introduced an early form of the Drive-In restaurant too, but arguably their biggest contribution to the California way of life was through the inspiration that Walt Disney and his companions found inside these walls – and that others from the "Mouse House" still come here for.

Walt's Table

Lawry's

Disney was in the midst of creating his theme park at the time, and he regularly dined here; there's even the Walt Disney Table (number 31 – reservations required!), though he actually only occasionally ate there, preferring instead to sit in the bar.

Other staff – and celebrities – working at the then-nearby Disney and Fox studios came in too, including Fatty Arbuckle, Tom Mix, Mary Pickford and a young John Wayne, but it was Disney and his colleagues who took on The Tam, jokingly calling it their "studio commissary."

Even today, the Tam O'Shanter still has many pieces of signed artwork from noted (and often hungry but broke) Disney animators hanging on their walls.

As to whether it directly inspired anything, the original interior of Toad Hall in "Mr Toad's Wild Ride" does look similar to the main dining room…

By that time though, Frank and de Kamp had long since moved on to another project, and had opened their flagship Lawry's Prime Rib in Beverly Hills in 1937.

Explosion!

BLAST DAMAGE—Det. Sgts. Richard Hobson, pointing, and N. E. Finn examine damage caused by charge of dynamite in Tam O'Shanter cafe, Los Feliz Blvd. The structure was partially wrecked by the blast, and other buildings in vicinity were shaken.

It was no joke a few years later though, as the *LA Times* reported on April Fool's Day 1947. A dynamite explosion "partially wrecked" the Tam O'Shanter, though there was no other archive evidence about whether this was an accident or something more. Either way, no one was hurt in the blast.

In 1968 the restaurant had a major renovation, changing its name to "The Great Scot" and keeping the Scottish theme, though few of the original fixtures and fittings remained. In 1982 they again went back to the Tam O'Shanter name, and it has remained that way ever since.

Will you see Charlie?

There are some ghost stories associated with the Tam, and nearly all of them are based around the Bonnie Prince Charlie room at the far end of the restaurant.

The most famous apparition in this room is a small child who has been nicknamed "Charlie" because of his strong resemblance to Charles Edward Stuart, a "pretender" to the English royal throne in the 18th century, and whose portrait is on the wall in this room.

Phantom Diners

A group of phantom diners has been seen sitting at the corner table in the far end in this room too, and an old man has been seen sitting alone or walking past the private dining room door.

A one-time manager, before turning on the alarm and leaving for the night, would shut the door to this room and lean chairs up against it, as if to keep whatever was inside locked in.

Table 13?

Elsewhere in the restaurant an elderly woman who reportedly died during her meal has been seen at table 13 (of course it was table 13), though there's no archival evidence to support that this ever happened.

Finally, in June 2016 it was announced that the Tam was planning to build a 40 seat "English garden" outdoor patio complete with fireplace – ideal for the L.A. weather!

Until then, when I visit I usually take a leaf out of Walt's book and sit at the Ale & Sandwich Bar, or snag one of the comfy leather seats in the small snugs if I can.

To drink you can keep to the theme by having a draft Gone to Plaid Wee Heavy Scotch Ale or a Table 31 cocktail (Woodford reserve rye, jasmine and apple bitters), while the most popular dish in the main hall is the Tam O'Shanter cut of prime beef, which comes with Yorkshire pudding, mashed potatoes and gray, horseradish and creamed spinach or corn.

You can get cuts of them when you sit at the bar too, as well as burgers, sandwiches, entrées and salads, and the menu has other choices under the amusing headings Odds And Sods, God Save The Green, Spot-On Sides and others – you get the idea. And yes, there's even haggis (their version of it anyway), though I haven't been brave enough to try it yet…

$$$ / Ale & Sandwich Bar 11am-midnight, Dinner Mon-Thu 5-9pm, Fri to 10pm, Sat 4-10pm, Sun until 9pm, Weekend Brunch 10.30am-2.30pm
www.lawrysonline.com/tam-oshanter

Tonga Hut
12808 Victory Boulevard
North Hollywood, CA 91606
Tel: 818 769 0708

Dottie's Joint

Back in the 1950s and 1960s, tiki bars and restaurants were the hottest spots in town – and they were all over America. Borne out of travels in the South Pacific seas and driven by WWII adventures and "exotica" music, they offered a kitschy décor of wooden canoes, fountains, rattan furniture, sultry grass-skirted women and tall statues.

There's one of these "tikis" – a 10 foot high, grim-faced "Big Mo" – by the door on the way in to the Tonga Hut, but there's always a friendly welcome here, and it's all mixed up with lashings of fruity rum-based cocktails with names like Ginger Flame and Zombie.

The tiki craze began here in California when Ernest Gantt, fresh from his travels throughout the South Pacific, opened what would become his first Don the Beachcomber bar in Hollywood in 1934.

It was an instant success – and was instantly copied (Victor Bergeron's "Trader Vic's" opened in Oakland a few years later.)

The oldest surviving tiki bar in Los Angeles, the Tonga Hut was opened by brothers Ace and Ed Libby in 1958, with a sister bar opening in Palm Springs in 2013.

There are other tiki bars around L.A., and they're all kept going by a hard core of fans – though things weren't always they way they like it.

When tiki bar aficionado Jeff "Beachbum" Berry visited the Tonga Hut in the early 1990s, he loved the authenticity but found most people were drinking Budweiser, and that the bartender had no idea what a Mai Tai was.

Needless to say, it was one of the times when tiki was out of fashion – though that moment did inspire Berry to write the *Grog Log*, a guide to tropical tipples that has spawned many sequels and variations.

Perhaps the most unusual feature at the Tonga Hut is the chance to join the "Order of The Drooling Bastard" – a select group of men and women who take on the year-long challenge of drinking every one of the 78 cocktails in the aforementioned *Grog Log*.

The Order was established in 2009, and already has over 50 people in its ranks despite the fact that it probably costs close to $1,000 to complete.

Once they've downed the final drink they get their "tiki names" immortalized on the wall opposite the bar alongside Bora Bora Dog, Morticia Baddams, Swifty, Tiki TV, Dr. G and others, and the "honor" of wearing a wood-effect Buckoff pennant that gets $1 off any drink from that day onwards.

The Painkiller (a strong drink with orange juice, coconut, cinnamon and nutmeg) is a customer favorite, while almost no one has liked old "classic" the Beachcomber's Gold (French and Italian vermouth, bitters, Pernod and light rum), a drink that most have only for the challenge – and usually hold their nose while chugging it down in one go.

If you look at the names of the Bastards, you'll see there's a posthumously awarded one for Dottie, who was a fixture at the Tonga Hut six days a week for 49 years.

Her stool is marked "reserved" during Happy Hour (daily 4-8pm), and it pays tribute to a dedicated drinker who stuck rigidly to her order of Brandy Alexander for more than 20 years, and then switched to her husband's tipple – scotch and soda with a lemon twist and water back – after he passed away.

Tonga Hut manager and tiki genius Marie King knew Dottie well, and remembered the time that she was persuaded to try a cocktail. "She took one sip and went right back to the spirits," King laughs, adding that after Dottie's death it seemed she still regularly came to the bar:

"We had a crazy cleaner with us for a while, and she said she had conversations with Dottie's ghost all the time."

When you're in North Hollywood, you really should pop in to pay respect to Dottie and to meet some really fun people (Hawaiian shirts or not).

Don't be limited by what's on that menu either. I've visited both Tonga Huts several times and can confirm that their talented bartenders can easily whip up a concoction if you're ready to be brave or simply ask for the tastes that you like; you never know what you might get!

$$ / Daily 4pm-2am
www.tongahut.com

Sportsmen's Lodge
River Rock Bar
12825 Ventura Boulevard
Studio City, CA 91604
Tel: 818 769 4700

As you might guess from the old school name, the Sportsmen's Lodge has been around for a long time – and really was a place you could go to try and catch a few fish, a sport that was way bigger than we might think back in the day.

Opening its doors in the 1880s (and named the rather less glamorous Hollywood Trout Farm and Trout Lakes), it flourished due to its close proximity to the San Fernando Valley's river, canyons and watering holes, and was kind of an oasis for many.

In those days there were manmade ponds here, and you could take your fresh catch right up to the restaurant and have them fry it up for dinner!

As Studio City came into being, the Lodge became a hangout for actors and crews alike.

It's said that Clark Gable, Humphrey Bogart and John Wayne taught their children to fish here, while Tallulah Bankhead, Bette Davis, Spencer Tracy, Katharine Hepburn, Lauren Bacall and others hung out around the ponds and pier, picnicking and drinking cocktails.

Towards the end of WWII it was renamed the Sportsmen's Lodge, and a restaurant and cocktail lounge were added to the attractions – though you could still catch your own dinner if you wanted. Rooms cost around $9 for a single, and $25 for a suite.

As the San Fernando Valley grew rapidly, a modern Sportsmen's Lodge Hotel was built adjacent to the original lodge in 1962, and continued the tradition of being the place Hollywood legends came to relax and dine.

Woman, Accused of Trying to Kill Husband Last Year, Found Dead

In late May 1968 though, the Lodge was touched by tragedy when former actress Mildred J. Beebe, 68, was found dead in her bed here after taking 14 capsules of barbiturates.

"Please bury me in this dress"

Laid out on the bed opposite her was a three piece white dress reported the *LA Times*, noting that she had only checked in the day before.

Further investigation revealed that she had been jailed the year before for trying to kill her husband Hugh, 36, when they had met to discuss the end of their two month marriage.

Beebe, who had already been married three times, accused him of "bilking her" out of $45,000 and wildly opened fire with a small caliber pistol, causing no injuries but assuring herself of a jail cell.

She had planned everything for her swan song too; she left behind a mortician's business card about her reserved funeral plot, and keys to a safety deposit box.

RFK's Last Night

It was certainly a potentially scandalous story, but it was overshadowed by a bigger tragedy just a week later, when a very important guest checked in here – presidential candidate Robert Kennedy. He stayed here overnight, and the next day he was assassinated at the Ambassador Hotel.

That didn't stop the famous visitors though: former Beach Boy Brian Wilson loved to lounge by the pool, and other celebrities including Marlon Brando, Doris Day, David Lee Roth, Billy Bob Thornton and others have taken time out here. It's also still a popular choice for rock stars and bands when they're on tour.

Man's Body Found in Car Parked at Hotel

There were no deadly reports from the Sportsmen's Lodge for nearly 20 years after the suicide, but then in September 1986 there came the disturbing news that the body of Rouben Mekhitarian, 25, had been found in the front seat of a Mercedes parked here.

It appeared he had been shot to death, though his wallet was not missing – which perhaps ruled out robbery as a motive – and investigators were stumped.

The *LA Times* reported that Mekhitarian had left home saying he was going to meet someone on the corner at Coldwater Canyon Avenue, and would be back in 10 minutes. He was never seen alive again.

Double Brother Murder?

Amazingly, almost exactly 10 years later his older brother, Nshan, now the owner of Rouben's grocery store, was shot when he answered the doorbell of his home in North Hollywood.

Police issued a sketch of a suspect, but again could find no motive for the murder – were the killings somehow connected?

The Lodge is often used in movies and television programs – what with its oasis-style vibe – and in 2007 it was sold for $50m to a developer who wanted to try and bring back some of the golden days, and to introduce more retail on the site.

More recently, in 2013 the 190 rooms got a serious upgrade and their Olympic-sized swimming pool was said to be the largest in Los Angeles.

Night Ghosts – and Mildred?

As for ghosts, there have been some reports listed by guests on the website Weird California.

In 2011 and 2012 "Susan," who said she was a regular here, wrote that she was woken by her screaming husband, who said that he felt a force pushing him down into the mattress – he apparently had red marks on his neck for several days afterward.

Unsurprisingly, they asked to move to another room, and the maintenance man who helped them said that the hotel was haunted – especially the fifth floor.

The next night Susan's young granddaughter was frightened when something pulled her hair while she was bathing, and after they again moved rooms they were again told by other employees that the hotel was home to ghosts.

"Roxanna" from Yuma, Arizona reported a similar experience of being choked, or something pressing down on her throat in July 2013, and also mentioned seeing an elderly lady with short, blond hair pointing at her.

Something very similar to this was mentioned by "Kathleen" of Bel Air, Maryland, in July 2013 – only this time she said that an elderly woman had tapped on the shoulder and said:

"Kathleen, it's time to get up."

She thought it was the ghost of her late mother waking her, and though all these experiences could have rational explanations, the sad story of Mildred Beebe's suicide does seem to connect with them in a way.

Nevertheless, Kathleen wrote:

"I am glad we only stayed one night."

In March 2012 there was a violent death here when a woman was shot in the head by her estranged partner, but we won't go into further details as we prefer to stop our investigations around 1985 or so.

There's a pool bar and a patio café here (the latter with funky orange furniture and movie posters signed by Hollywood cowboys like Roy Rogers and Gene Autry), but you can still relive the trout farm days.

There are fish over the fireplace at the River Rock, a joint where the décor is smart and modern and there's a daily happy hour with some great $5 bites from 5-8pm.

The menu is bar snack fare, though in keeping with that rock star vibe the Sunday brunch menu includes something that, as a Brit, I couldn't resist: baked beans on toast (though there's a British omelette too; diced ham onions, cheddar cheese and hash browns).

Also, the dinner menu offers a Make Your Own S'Mores Kit, which, while having a British sweet tooth (but a pretty decent set of gnashers), I couldn't say no to either.

$$ / River Rock Bar Monday closed, Tue-Thu 5-11pm, Fri until 2am, Sat 11am-2am, Sun until 9pm, Patio Café daily 7am-2pm
www.sportsmenslodge.com
www.riverrockbarla.com

Sheraton Universal
333 Universal Hollywood Drive
Universal City, CA 91608
Tel: 818 980 1212

"One of the longer-lasting mysteries of Los Angeles"
Harry Bosch creator/former journalist Michael Connelly

Part of the huge Sheraton chain, this location was christened the "Hotel of the Stars" due to its connection to Universal Studios, one of L.A.'s top tourist attractions – and of course the home of many television shows and movies for over 50 years.

The hotel was funded by MCA – the Music Corp of America – who also owned Universal, so it's not surprising that this well-located hotel has been chosen by politicians, celebrities and other notable names since it was reported in the *LA Times* in October 1964.

Touted as the largest hotel west of Chicago and "overlooking the Hollywood freeway," it was announced to the world at a press conference held on their helicopter pad.

Designed by architect William B. Tabler and due to feature around 500 rooms, the 20 storey hotel – and the surrounding City – has gotten bigger since then, with the Universal CityWalk opening alongside in 1993.

The Walk is worth a stroll as it has restaurants, bars, stores, indoor sky diving, a large movie theater and lots of loud music and neon lights, and they regularly film the TV show "Extra" here too.

Construction of the Sheraton Universal complex took several years, with the doors finally opening in 1969.

Over the years the archives seem to show that while the hotel had good and bad times, it had been struggling for a while when it went up for sale in 2010.

It had been sold for $122m in 2007 and the new owner spent $25m on improvements, but the worldwide recession hit home and it was now valued at around $90m.

That was indeed the price that Chinese developer Shenzhen New World Group paid in 2011, upping their investment in 2012 with a further $30m renovation.

In 2016 the hotel again started a major renovation – "pardon our stardust" was how they announced it – which means that their Californias restaurant and In The Mix bar may (or may not) be different when you read this.

With the CityWalk so near, coming to the hotel for a drink or a meal might not be the first choice, but at the time of writing In the Mix has a 50% off weekday happy hour (5-7pm), and my recommendation would be the chicken pot stickers with a Bloody Belvedere (Belvedere vodka, tomato and lemon juices, a dash of Worcestershire sauce and Tabasco, and of course a stick of celery).

The archives are fairly quiet about the dark side of the hotel, but there have been some deadly moments…

Sharpshooter and Severed Fingers

On January 14, 1970 a hawk-eyed LAPD officer prevented a possible behind-the-scenes tragedy here. At around 2am electrician Larry Jones had arrived at the hotel and begun arguing with his ex-wife Shirley, who worked as the night auditor.

The pair struggled and she received a small head wound, reported the *LA Times*, but then Jones drew a small-caliber pistol and opened fire. The police were called, and officer Gerd Konieczny arrived to see Jones, his gun still drawn, through the office window.

Pulling off an amazing shot, Konieczny shot the gun out of Jones's hand – severing two of the man's fingers in the process – and ensured no further injuries.

Luckily the late hour meant there were only a couple of people in the lobby; who knows what might have happened if this had taken place in the middle of the day?

Sports Figure's Body Found in Car Trunk

Less than a decade later, there was a very nasty discovery in an abandoned Rolls-Royce on the second level of the car park here.

In the trunk was the badly-decomposed body of Victor J. Weiss, a businessman and sports agent who had been missing for several days after leaving a meeting with Jerry Buss, new owner of the Los Angeles Lakers, and another promoter.

He had been carrying nearly $40,000 in cash – that was gone – and he had been wrapped in a yellow blanket with his hands tied behind his back.

He had been shot twice in the head according to the *LA Times*, and though the car was parked in front of a security camera, it seemed to have been tampered with.

Weiss was a regular at the hotel, and was said (at the time) to have no known criminal connections – though the *LA Times* recalled the still-unsolved murder of boxing gym owner Howie Steindler, whose battered body was found in his car on the shoulder of the Ventura Freeway, just a few miles from the Sheraton Universal in 1977: could there be a connection?

There was a strange death related to Weiss though. The wife of his business partner had been killed when her car apparently went out of control, smashed through a wall and plunged down a cliff – though police found everything in working order. That case had now been reopened in the light of Weiss's killing,

Probe Mystery Slaying

That was the *Los Angeles Herald-Examiner* headline about the killing, which saw investigations move to Las Vegas and, bizarrely, officers listening to tapes made by a famous British spiritualist/clairaudient Doris Stokes, who said she had "talked" to Weiss after his death.

She had apparently been sitting at the Beverly Hills Hotel when a man named "Vic" talked to her, saying he had been taken into some trees by a group of men and shot:

"It blew my head... I was already tied. They made me kneel down."

She also claimed that Weiss said: "Why Louie, why?" and asked his business partner to look for something in his desk, adding that when she drove to the Sheraton Universal, he then "told" her the word "Luger."

Police Seeking Three in Sports Promoter's Death

In June 1980, the *LA Times* reported that there were suspects in the case – three men out of Las Vegas who were involved in "bookmaking and/or narcotics" – and that they had a witness to Weiss's abduction.

But one of the Valley's most notorious murders remained unsolved, the *LA Times* running a long piece about the mystery in 1989.

The journalist was none other than Michael Connelly, who went on to write the Harry Bosch and Lincoln Lawyer books and even made the Weiss murder the basis of his 1997 novel *Trunk Music*.

It reported that police still believed organized crime was behind the killing: Weiss apparently had gambling debts and, agreeing to deliver laundered money to Vegas to pay them off, had unwisely begun skimming off the top.

Three other criminals investigated over the years in connection to the case died violently too, and, tragically, Vic's son Wolf (who had vowed to find his father's killer), died in Iraq in 2004, where he was working as a contractor.

The Weiss story came to an end of sorts in 2008, when Vic's widow Rose was murdered at home by their troubled daughter Lauren, who was living as a transient and had faced many mental health problems.

As for Vic's death, it's now a cold case.

$$$ / Californias Mon-Fri 6.30am-12pm and 5-9pm, Sat & Sun 7am-12pm and 5-10pm (Sat) and to 9pm (Sun) In the Mix Sun-Thu 2pm-midnight, Fri until 1am, Sun until 2am
www.sheratonuniversal.com

Chapter 5
Beaches & Further Afield

Sofia Hotel (formerly the Pickwick Hotel)
Currant Brasserie
150 West Broadway
San Diego, CA 92101
Tel: 619 702 6309

The Sofia Hotel

At over 100 miles from Los Angeles it's perhaps a stretch to include this in the **Beaches & Further Afield** chapter, but the two interviews I did with people about the hotel were so revealing that I had to include them.

I first heard about the Sofia Hotel when I was in the Frolic Room in Hollywood. The person next to me at the bar had overheard me asking about ghosts, and introduced himself as Cody.

He said that he had worked the nightshift on the front desk at the Sofia, and though the lobby restaurant Currant Brasserie was locked after it closed, every night between midnight and 3am there was a knocking on one of restaurant's walls that came from the men's restroom on the other side.

The knocking would get louder and faster "almost like it was a child playing," he said, until you knocked on the wall in return. The knocking would then stop – for a while.

Cody said he was determined to work out where the noise was coming from. "People thought I was crazy," he laughed, but the plumber he called in could find no obvious explanation for the noises in the building's pipes.

The Cold Room & The Man

He also mentioned when his colleague Kenny took a call from an upstairs room. A garbled voice had said that "the room was really cold," and, thinking it must be the air conditioning malfunctioning, Cody was sent up to the room to check.

He knocked once – no reply – and after trying again and getting no response he called Kenny to confirm he'd definitely got the right room; he had.

Cody knocked again, and then said out loud that he was using a master key to come in. However, the room was empty and the bed freshly made and unused – but the room was indeed "deathly cold."

They also both knew another staff member – "an elderly guy from Venezuela" – who had once run down the stairs, "his face red, breathing as if he was about to have a stroke," but would say nothing about what had happened.

"He would never, ever talk about it," said Cody, "but then at the annual work party Kenny decided to get him drunk, to see if he would talk, and it only took one beer before it all came out." Apparently he had been at the dead end of a hallway when he turned round to see a huge man standing there and looking at him...

Going back in time, the hotel was actually called The Pickwick Hotel when it opened nearly 90 years ago.

It was one of many so named by the Pickwick Corporation, which also had interests in coaches, airlines, radio and hotels.

The first Pickwick was in Union Square in San Francisco (and is still there today), while in May 1927 this Neo Gothic, two-tower "motor hotel" opened for business.

It was luxurious for its time, with all rooms en suite: their slogan was "A Room and a Bath for Two and a Half."

Two more towers were added to this seven storey hotel the next year, bringing the number of rooms to 230, and a radio station the company owned, KGB, was based on the first two floors.

The hotel was a popular spot until the late 1950s, when the expanding city saw downtown lose its shine as the entertainment center and it began a slow decline that ran into the mid 1980s.

The hotel was sold for $6.8m in late 1986, but it wasn't until the new millennium that downtown bounced back, and in 2005 the new owners announced a $16m renovation and a new name, The Sofia Hotel, which was revealed to the public on the grand re-opening in 2006.

I contacted the Currant Brasserie, a stylish and often-busy place that opened in 2007 (and that Cody had mentioned), and received an enthusiastic email from their events manager, Lindsay Sudul.

Talking on the phone later, it was clear that stories of ghosts and strange events weren't just something that had happened to night staff:

"There were numerous deaths here, but even though the hotel has signs of spirits, they are actually calm and nice visitors!"

She very kindly said she would gather the stories from the hotel together, and send them to me.

A couple of them were perhaps easy to explain, but some were too strange not to pass on:

Walking The Floors...

"There is a very short little man that runs around on the seventh floor. He's been seen by guests and is always seen by our housekeepers. There is also a cat that roams a room on the sixth floor, you can feel him (or her) sit on the bed and then scurry away."

I asked if it was perhaps a real not supernatural cat, but she was certain:

"No, it's a ghost cat!"

Lindsay then told me about an elderly long-term resident who became ill and died in his room here. "He is seen walking to the elevator, but then always takes the stairs. He seems confused."

Then she mentioned something that seemed like it would have made the newspapers:

"A "lady of the night" left her two kids in the car in the garage, and they suffocated. You can hear kids playing, laughing and crying in that particular area of the garage."

A tragic tale for sure, though there was no evidence of it in the *LA Times* – but then she told me about a gruesome murder that happened here:

"A man took apart his wife limb by limb and he disposed of the body in the linen chute, where he would go to the parking garage and get the parts to put them in his car so he could dump the remains."

Apparently the killer was arrested, but the spirit of the victim seems to have remained:

"There are many sightings and cold feelings when the housekeepers are doing the laundry. They hear a woman crying too, and they feel her spirit."

The Jane Doe Murder

After accessing the microfiches of the *San Diego Union-Tribune*, I found evidence that a dreadful murder like this had indeed happened at the Pickwick, and that in some ways (allowing for misunderstandings over time), could well be the source of the story.

Man sought for questioning in the death of companion

In May 1997 police were searching for Matthew Wanser in connection with the discovery of a female corpse wrapped in a bloody blanket and stuffed into bag, and then thrown into a shopping cart.

The body of "Jane Doe" had been found near San Diego City Hall, and, after hearing from witnesses at the Pickwick about a man pushing a shopping cart, detectives followed the trial of blood from the cart back to the hotel, where they believed the suspect had been living with a woman for the last few weeks.

After the net was thrown as far as Las Vegas to capture Wanser, he was returned to San Diego and charged with the murder of "Jane Doe" in September 1998 – only now her identity had been established: it was his girlfriend Jacqueline Antar, who Wanser had drowned in the bathtub.

The row had had probably started while Ansar and Wanser were in the bathroom, and she had confessed that Wanser was not the father of her child.

She was six months pregnant, and this emotional bombshell seemingly caused an argument, a struggle and death – and another charge for Wanser.

Jurors find man guilty of killing his girlfriend, unborn child

Searching further through the newspaper archives of the *San Diego Reader*, another odd story jumped out from March 1980.

Grave Sins

Visitors at the Mount Hope Cemetery had been shocked to see a decayed corpse spread on the grass near a crypt. Worse than that, the corpse's head was missing and, barely a day later, San Diego police got a call informing them that a guest at the Pickwick Hotel could see a skull resting on a ledge outside.

Going further back in time, in August 1932 there was perhaps the first published story in the newspapers about deadly events at the Pickwick – or right outside.

San Diego Taxi Driver Shot Dead

Taxi driver Harry Gregory, 52, was reading a newspaper in his cab when he was shot five times in the head – apparently by his brother-in-law Luis Jauregur, who was said to have been unhappy with the way Gregory treated his wife and stepdaughter.

Much later in September 1978, the *LA Times* reported that Thomas O. Jenkins, 66, had jumped to his death from a sixth floor window.

Passers-by saw him on the ledge and called police, but they arrived too late. Jenkins was a local man, and had been at the hotel for three days.

On April 16, 1983, there was another suicide here – though it seemed to be utterly spontaneous.

Man, 31, Leaps to Death From Hotel Window

Glenn Michael Young, 31, another local, had run a red light and hit a car parked by the Pickwick.

There were no injuries and little damage, but Young ran from his car, went up to the fifth floor and, without any hesitation, jumped. He landed on a roof extension and was rushed to hospital, but died soon after.

Police found a psychiatrist's name in Young's wallet and apparently he was "low on money," but they were still baffled by his deadly decision.

Clairemont Man Is Slain in Home

A few years after that in May 1988 police arrested a guest here, Michael Burgess, on suspicion of the beating and stabbing murder of John W. Pickens, 41, who had been found dead at his home.

I couldn't find out the number of the room that Antar murder was committed in, so if you're staying here I guess you're taking a chance in some ways – though the odds are well over 200-1 against you getting that room (and there is a yoga studio here if you need to relax).

As for the Currant Brasserie, they serve French cuisine with an American twist. I haven't visited myself, and apparently many might like it to stay that way: it's seems to be rather a hidden treasure for the locals.

But I do know I'd try their powdered beignets for breakfast, or perhaps for dinner I'd try their potato gnocchi with white wine-lemon cream, black truffle and parmesan (gnocchi's my favorite pasta).

Failing that, during the daily happy hour (4-7pm) the grilled sausage and some moules frites would be great, and if you don't even have time for that, the "popcorn of the moment" is selected daily; and it's not just caramel or butter – it might be duck confit and gruyere cheese!

$$ / Breakfast Mon-Fri 7-10am, Lunch 11.30am-2.30pm Dinner 5-10pm, Weekend Brunch 9am-2.30pm
www.thesofiahotel.com
www.currantrestaurant.com

The Orchid Poisoner?
(and the Deadly World of Mortuaries)

Ex-Mortician Charged in Oleander Poisoning

The February 10, 1990 edition of the *LA Times* reported that – for the first time in American history – someone had been charged with murder using the weapon of oleander, a toxic plant that's nonetheless very common in gardens.

David Wayne Sconce was the accused, and it was alleged that back in 1985 he had killed a rival mortician, Timothy R. Waters, to stop him exposing some dark and illegal activities at the Lamb Funeral Home, the family business where Sconce worked.

A Mortuary Tangled in the Macabre

By that time Sconce was already in jail for those illegal acts – mingling human remains, stealing body parts and removing gold teeth from cadavers.

Though "mingling" sounds rather innocuous, in the most notorious incident it saw 38 bodies stuffed into two furnaces, an employee later admitting that breaking one of the corpse's legs to make it fit perhaps led to a chimney blockage and the Altadena mortuary burning to the ground.

Grotesque Cremation Discovery

Incredibly, Sconce's parents Laurieanne and Jerry were also awaiting trial on similar charges, but it was earlier in 1985 that rival mortician Waters had been assaulted in his office by hired thug Danny Gambalos, who said that Sconce had paid him to carry out the crime.

A few weeks later in April, Waters died after becoming unexpectedly ill while baby-sitting for his sister in Malibu.

After two days of agony his death was thought possibly to be linked to heart problems, but it later emerged that a witness said he saw Sconce slipping something into Waters' drink at the (now long-gone) Reuben's Plankhouse restaurant in Simi Valley.

Sconce – whose car license plate once read "I BRN 4U" – was also said to have bragged about it to a cellmate and others.

He was also accused of making murderous threats against other people, and the shocking story – which seemed ideal for a Hollywood movie – tore back the lid on what a highly lucrative but competitive (and seemingly dangerous) business it is to be involved with the dead.

The Sconces' empire stretched from Pasadena to beyond, and Sconce was alleged to have said that he made $5,000 - 6,000 a month from the purloined gold teeth alone.

The oleander poisoning however could never be comprehensively proved scientifically – nor was it certain where it might have been administered or ingested – so those charges were eventually dismissed, but even then that wasn't the end of the story.

Jailed For Life

Sconce's name appeared again in the *LA Times* in July 2013, and again it was under strange circumstances. This time he had been sentenced to 25 years to life after violating his probation from a 1997 case in which he'd been charged conspiracy to murder a former district attorney who had been assigned to him.

At the conclusion of that case he'd been given the unusual sentence of lifetime probation, but when Sconce – now 56 – was convicted in Montana of stealing a rifle from a neighbor and trying to sell it in a pawn shop, he violated that probation.

Sconce argued that the neighbor had merely given him the rifle and he was going to use it to "protect his pets from wolves," but now he felt the force of the law.

That said, with so much time already served, it was reckoned he might be out of jail within 10 years.

Don The Beachcomber
16278 Pacific Coast Highway
Huntington Beach, CA 92649
Tel: 562 592 1321

For obvious reasons, California has always been a center for the tiki craze – it was invented here after all.

The popularity of Polynesian-influenced décor, countless rum drinks and crazy shirts has waxed and waned over the years since it really became popular in the 1940s and 1950s, but doubtless many were thrilled when Sam's Seafood was "tiki-fied" in 1960/1961.

Though the tiki's faces were often garishly colored at Sam's, it was a popular joint for years – at least until its closure in June 2006, when it was then renamed Kona, and then a few years later after that the owner struck a deal to re-brand it as Don the Beachcomber.

As you can read in the entry about the Tonga Hut in the **Silver Lake to the SFV** chapter, the first Don the Beachcomber bar opened in Hollywood in 1934, but over the decades the chain got smaller and smaller as other imitators joined the market.

A rarity then, this Don's installed new signs, added many of the original drinks to the menu (including the Mai Tai), and bought in branded tiki mugs. There's a great blue neon swordfish sign outside, and inside it's pretty much everything you'd want from a tiki bar.

As for the best food and drink choices here, I defer to my foodie friend Dog Davis, who is one of the Drooling Bastards at the Tonga Hut. He recommends the chicken and waffle for lunch, and the panko fish (Baso sole) and chips for dinner.

As for drinks, take a seat in the Dagger Bar and select something that Don created himself, like the Zombie (lime juice, falernum, gold Puerto Rican or Jamaican rum, Lemon Hart Demerara rum, grenadine, Pernod, a dash of Angostura bitters, grapefruit juice and cinnamon-infused sugar syrup).

Beware though – they really have a kick, and they won't serve you more than two!

You can also fly the flag with Navy Grog (fresh lime juice, white grapefruit juice, club soda, gold Demerara rum, dark Jamaican rum, white Cuban or Puerto Rican rum and honey mix).

Tonga Hut manager and tiki expert Marie King worked here from February 2009 to November 2010 – just in that period when they were opening their doors – and she had some very interesting stories about her time here.

She said that the original location opened in the 1920s and was in fact a seafood market as well as a bar. It was situated right on the beach, which meant that during Prohibition rum runners could bring their boats right up to the doors – and to the thirsty guests.

That location was destroyed by a fire though, and it moved to its current location in the 1930s, the owners shrewdly building a large basement just in case Prohibition ever came back (and of course they already knew that the waterways were good for quick boat drop-offs).

Strange Noises – and a suicide?

As for strange stories, King did hear a rumor that a manager committed suicide in the office sometime in the 1980s (though it wasn't in the newspaper archives), and that there were odd noises and unexplained footsteps in the banquet room.

In 2009 Don's was owned by disgraced former councilman Art Snyder and his third wife Delia, a young Taiwanese lady, and, perhaps being aware of these rumors, they bought in a family from Taiwan to perform *feng shui*.

Feng shui relates to the arrangement and positing of spaces in relation to the flow of energy (*qi*), and is often used when designing or even siting buildings.

This family – led by a teenage "seer" who King recalled had a striking, androgynous look – quickly ordered that one of the offices was sealed off, as it still is today.

King also recalled how she regularly took people down into the basement (there were lots of old 1960s menus and other ephemera to see):

"You'd go down 20 steps and there were several rooms – all around 30 foot by 30 foot – full of old stuff. One was locked and used by the handyman to store his equipment and tools, and another had a grand piano, tortoiseshell lamps, fishing floats and other things in it – many of which are now in the Dagger Bar upstairs."

Opposite that room was a small nook or cupboard "about the size of a phone booth," which she speculated might have once been the location of a safe.

It could also have been a dumb waiter that moved between the basement and the upper floors (and perhaps once transported illegal booze?)

Bricked-in Forever

Anyway, the seers wanted that nook sealed off as well, and said that a new main entrance door should be built as well.

After the seers left and the building work was done there were no more reports of strange noises – until more construction was done a year later on the rooms above the sealed-off nook, when they started up again.

Snyder died in 2012 aged 79, and today, according to King, the owners and staff "want nothing to do" with any talk about the basement or the sealed-off areas.

$$ / Mon-Thu 3-10pm, Fri & Sat 11am-1.30am, Sun 11am-10pm, Happy Hour all day Monday, Tue-Thu until 7pm, Friday 3-6pm, Fri & Sat 11pm-close
www.donthebeachcomber.com

**The Warehouse
4499 Admiralty Way
Marina Del Rey, CA 90292
Tel: 310 823 5451**

Investigating Linda's Murder

Though this murder investigation is related to a (different) restaurant that no longer exists, I included it here because in researching it I talked to two journalists and even a private eye in an attempt to get all the facts straight.

Overlooking one of Marina Del Rey's swanky yacht clubs, The Warehouse could be Robinson Crusoe's dream desert island hangout.

It's constructed of real wharf posts, while around you the décor is a pirate's paradise of old wine and whiskey barrels, crates, ship's rigging and fishing nets – all of which were shipped in from some abandoned marine yards in San Pedro.

The original fittings and furniture were constructed of Malaysian bamboo and Hawaiian cane, and the vintage photos that decorate the walls are souvenirs from the many countries visited by Burt Hixson, the original owner and a professional cameraman, who opened up for business here in 1969.

Today the owner is Lee Spencer – who also owns the SmokeHouse in Burbank (great cheesy garlic bread!) – and it was him who told me about a murder that took place "right next door" to The Warehouse at what was then the Hungry Tiger restaurant.

Apparently, one night one of their cocktail waitresses had gone home with one of the customers – and her strangled, half-naked body was found the next day.

It was "just three blocks away," said Spencer, adding that it was "quite a sensation" in the neighborhood.

Not The Warehouse – but where?

Initial research failed to find any mention of the murder, but then I found a *LA Times* article from November 1978 about Gary Dean Smiddy. In October 1973 he had left a "Marina Del Rey restaurant" with 21 year old cocktail waitress Linda Caroline Miller, and was the last person to see her alive.

Her strangled body was found on a construction site the next day, and a few weeks later he was charged with first degree murder.

Man Wins Suit Against Police

However, this article also noted that the charges against him had been dismissed, and he had been awarded $250,000 for violation of his civil rights.

The LAPD had allegedly failed to fully question other suspects – including Miller's violent ex-boyfriend – and his lawyer had argued that Smiddy also had an alibi for Miller's death.

Moreover, the article then named the restaurant they had left together: it was called The Parasol, not the Hungry Tiger.

After more research – including examining a map and talking to Robert Rawitch, the *LA Times* reporter who wrote the article, and Colman Andrews, the restaurant columnist for *Gourmet* magazine – things became clearer.

Andrews, who had helped me with the very first story I looked into for Gourmet *Ghosts – Los Angeles*, told me that one of his ex-wives used to work at the Parasol.

Also, his ex-wife's stepmother, who had a tennis shop on Lincoln Boulevard and "spent lots of time in the Marina" definitely recalled the Hungry Tiger ("good food and good jazz," apparently).

It seemed that perhaps Spencer had simply confused the Hungry Tiger and The Parasol, but as for the murder itself, private investigator Larry Larsen, who worked on a Channel 7 television program called "Who Killed Linda Caroline Miller?" confirmed the Smiddy connection in an email:

"The police were convinced they had the right man, so they did no further investigation that I know of."

Larsen added that he'd never heard of any hauntings around the crime scene, but since the murder is officially still unsolved, perhaps Miller's ghost is still walking the sea front and hoping to find the man who killed her...

FBI and The Spy

Something unusual that did happen at The Warehouse was reported in the *LA Times* in May 1985.

The world was at the height of the Cold War in those days, and it emerged that FBI counterintelligence agent John Hunt met the young and glamorous Russian Svetlana Ogorodnikova – an informant and potential double agent codenamed "Marie" – numerous times here in 1982 and early 1983.

However, Svetlana became too attached to the married Hunt, and any possible plans fizzled away.

Hunt resigned from the FBI soon after, but a couple of years later Ogorodnikova and her husband Nikolai were arrested on charges of espionage and conspiring with another FBI agent to pass information to the Soviet Union.

Aside from stories of spying, the menu here is understandably heavy on the seafood, with steaks, pastas and salads if you're not one for the *fruits de la mer*.

Grab a table on one of the outdoor decks and try house specialty the Split Cargo – bacon-wrapped filet mignon with Malaysian prawns – but be sure to keep an eye on any secretive-looking people you see, because you never know…

$$$ / Mon-Thu 11.30am-10pm, Fri & Sat until 11pm, Sun 10am-10pm, Bar/Lounge open until 2am
www.mdrwarehouse.com

Updates –
Beaches & Further Afield

Firstly, further news about **The Victorian** (a vintage Santa Monica building with the trendy **Basement Bar** that's in, as you might have guessed, the basement).

As noted in *Gourmet Ghosts – Los Angeles*, in 1973 the building – originally the home of the Kyte family – was moved from its previous location to be a luxury eatery at the Heritage Square museum, and after legal wrangles it did indeed open as The Chronicle Restaurant.

Two Haunted Restaurants – and a Murder

The Chronicle hit the headlines in December 1986 when it was revealed that it had hired John Sweeney as their Head Chef.

He had only been out of prison several months, having served less than four years for the October 1982 killing of his ex-girlfriend Dominique Dunne, an actress and the daughter of noted novelist, journalist and producer Dominick Dunne.

The murder and trial were a sensation, especially when Sweeney was convicted of the lesser charge of voluntary manslaughter. The trial also revealed that he and Dunne had first met at Ma Maison, where Sweeney was training to be a chef, in 1981.

Strangely, Ma Maison (now the **Sweet Lady Jane Bakery**) was also in *Gourmet Ghosts – Los Angeles*; it's said that the smell of former Ma Maison regular Orson Welles's brandy and cigars still lingers there, and that he can sometimes be seen sitting at his old table in back.

Sweeney didn't last long at The Chronicle, which closed around 1987, and apparently he then changed his name and moved out-of-state.

After being re-named The Victorian, the building became a venue for weddings and events, and in 2010 the bar opened up – and it soon became clear that something supernatural had been awakened at the old Kyte House.

Delia's Home

A lady called "Delia" was said to be a former owner of the building, and *Gourmet Ghosts – Los Angeles* noted that Ashia – the manager of The Victorian – told me two of Delia's nieces (one who lived in Italy, the other in San Diego) had visited and walked round the house.

Ashia added that lights turned on and off in The Victorian and that she felt "someone was there," and when she mentioned the idea that Delia might still be in the building to the nieces, "they both replied that 'we would not doubt that whatsoever.'"

The manager of The Basement, TJ Williams, related his own experiences of hearing noises:

"I've heard it three or four times: running footsteps, the sound of opening drawers and opening doors. It wasn't clanking pipes or house noises, and we've gone upstairs with a flashlight and looked around, but all the doors are locked and no-one is there. One night it happened a couple of times and we were all thinking 'let's get out of here.'"

Perhaps wisely, the bar created "Delia's Elixir" – a special cocktail of bourbon, agave, raspberries and lemon – to honor her, and even though there's no archival evidence of Delia, why not raise a glass to her anyway?

The *Grey Ghost*

The *RMS Queen Mary* in Long Beach – which celebrated the 80th anniversary of her maiden voyage in 2016 – is well worth a visit, and alongside a fascinating history, it has many fun ghost tours you can take.

That said, many people really have died on board this ocean liner, especially during her years of service as a prisoner ship and troop carrier during WWII, when she was nicknamed *The Grey Ghost*.

It was also during her wartime service that, as part of a convoy, she accidentally collided with British cruiser *HMS Curacao*.

Under orders not to stop for any reason, the damaged *Grey Ghost* had to leave hundreds of men struggling in the water. Over 300 perished, a tragedy that was kept secret until the war was over.

Other deaths have been officially associated with the ship – including that of shipyard construction workers and a crewman crushed by a closing engine room door in 1966 – but after 1967, when she docked forever at Long Beach and became a museum and hotel, fatalities have been limited to people jumping off the deck as a deadly prank.

There are plenty of ghost reports about the *Queen Mary* in *Gourmet Ghosts – Los Angeles*, but for this update it's again worth mentioning that a vortex – a spiraling area of energy, maybe even a portal to the spirit world – has been sensed by visitors, psychics and investigators alike behind the rear facing wall of the former first class swimming pool.

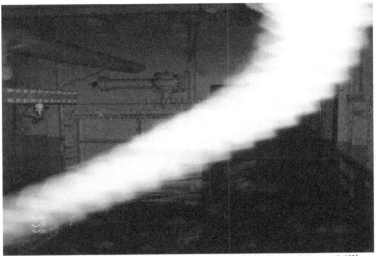

Karen and Jason Miller

Ceca Basilio

Exclusive to *Gourmet Ghosts – Los Angeles*, the first picture was taken by the door where that engineer died during a 1999 visit by Karen and Jason Miller; it shows what might be a kind of spiraling, vortex shape.

The second picture – also previously unpublished – was taken onboard in August 2013 by Cesca Basilio. Maybe it's flash or a reflection, but it certainly grabs the attention too.

In August 2016, a $15m "boutique" makeover of the historic liner was announced by new lease-owners Urban Commons.

The hotel will get new soft furnishings, larger TVs and better wifi, but there was also talk of perhaps a club or speakeasy in the boiler room, a cinema, and an update to the classy Observation Bar.

Work is due to be completed by the end of 2017, and is part of a $250m plan to develop 45 acres of the surrounding area.

Chapter 6
Take Out / Off The Menu

Take Out:

Off The Menu:

Take Out:

Little Nashville (now The Drunken Crab)
13350 Sherman Way
North Hollywood, CA 91605
Tel: 818 982 9000

Trial for Suspected Slayer of 6 Ordered

Today it's an all-you-can-eat crab chain restaurant, which is why I listed it as a take-out place more than a distinctive restaurant, but before that it was a Mexican hangout called La Cascada, and over the years it's had many other names.

But *Gourmet Ghosts 2* is most interested about the time it was known as Little Nashville…

As you might guess, Little Nashville was a cowboy bar where you could line dance to country disco, wear blue denim, and see some crackin' good bands.

Rockabilly fans had their own night here too, and while country music isn't as popular now as it was back in the 1980s and 1990s, for many years Little Nashville was a jumpin' joint where people came for a good time.

People like nurse Carol Bundy and Douglas Daniel Clark, who met here one night back in the 1980s: it was the beginning of a twisted and bloody relationship that saw the gruesome murder of several women (mainly runaways or working girls) and more horror besides.

The "Sunset Strip Killers"

Christened with this pseudo-glamorous nickname, their deadly nighttime activities were a huge scandal – and the August 15, 1980 edition of the *LA Times* gave a sense of his crimes, and her role in the affair.

The article noted how Clark now had four more charges added to his long rap sheet; sexual offences against a minor and aiding and abetting a murder suspect.

The writing was already on the wall for Clark, who was charged with the murders of five women aged 15-24 who had been shot in the head with a small caliber gun.

One of them was also decapitated, and Clark had sex with some of the dead bodies.

Clark's aiding and abetting charge was related to Bundy, who he lived with in an apartment in Burbank and who shared his dark sexual tastes.

She herself had been charged in the murder of John R. Murray, who had also been decapitated and whose head had also never been found.

She had shot and killed Murray, her former lover, with a 9mm Beretta after confessing Clark's crimes to him and panicking that he might go to the police.

Ironically she had almost called them once herself, though apparently she was happier for Clark to keep one of his victim's heads in the fridge, even putting make-up on it before he "made use" of it.

Eventually Murray's van (which was parked behind the Nashville) began to smell so badly that the authorities were called, and the gruesome discovery was made.

Soon after that, Bundy finally confessed her crimes to a co-worker, and the floodgates opened.

By October that year the number of Clark's victims had been raised to six, and the legal process eventually saw Clark sentenced to die in the gas chamber in 1983.

Sunset Strip Slayer's Girlfriend Pleads Guilty in 2 of the Murders

Despite her insistence that Clark was a "maniac" who "overwhelmed" her with his dominance and charm, Bundy was found guilty of two murders.

She had also been changed with involvement in the death of one of Clark's victims – an as-yet-identified Jane Doe – by handing him the gun, and it seemed she often accompanied him on his drives along the Strip to hunt for prostitutes, some of which they both had sex with.

Their diabolical actions had some parallels with perhaps the most infamous murderers in British legal history, "Moors Murderers" Myra Hindley and Ian Brady.

'Moors Murders' Pair Given Life Sentences

They were also two obsessive, violent lovers who lured several children to torture and death at the hands of Brady in the mid 1960s, burying their victims on the vast Yorkshire Moors (one of them has still never been found).

Bundy argued that she suffered from temporary insanity, but a haunting comment she made said otherwise:

"I don't know if you guys have ever in your life shot anybody, but it's really fun to do. It sounds terrible, but it is…"

Clark, who of course blamed Bundy for everything, still sits on Death Row, while she was sentenced to life in prison, dying there of heart failure in 2003 aged 61.

Another of Clark's possible victims, a woman whose skeletonized remains were found in Newhall, California in August 1980, still remains unidentified.

\$\$ / Sun-Thu 12-10pm, Fri & Sat until 11pm

www.drunkencrab.com

Off The Menu:

Gershwin Apts (was the Gershwin/St. Francis Hotel)
5533 Hollywood Boulevard
Los Angeles, CA 90028

MLK's Assassin in Room 403

Located at the far east of Hollywood, the smart-looking Gershwin Apartments are designed to attract young, creative – and edgy – types to this part of town, one of the selling points being that they're a stone's throw from the Hollywood and Western stop on the Metro Red line.

The city is building several more subway lines at this very moment, and so anywhere near a stop has become a real hot property in a town where accommodation is already at a premium – sometimes regardless of its past history.

This five storey building has been here for many years, initially opening its doors in 1928 as the St. Francis Hotel, which was what it was called right up until 2000. Soon after that subway station opened, and it became the Gershwin Hotel for a decade or so.

HOSTELRY NETS
$850,000 IN DEAL

The St. Francis was actually snapped up soon after it first opened, the *LA Times* reporting that it had a writing room, a music room, and a ladies' parlor – as well as a café and barber shop on the street level – alongside the 104 rooms.

It was noted even then that the Hollywood/Western location was becoming a center for offices and casting bureaus of the "principal motion picture concerns."

As the later Gershwin Hotel it was a lively, often-dangerous place populated by addicts, artists, musicians and all other aspirational types.

An *LA Weekly* article from 2005 mentions one of the residents was filmmaker Kenneth Anger, while others were drag queens, meth heads, or roamed the corridors dressed in a full pirate costume.

It seemed to be the definition of somewhere that many might find exciting, and others might studiously avoid; a community of friendly eccentrics with the odd dash of violence thrown into the mix.

In summary, let's just say that the most famous resident listed in that article was the "Crypt Keeper," a man with one ear who lived with a seven foot tall giant with a long beard and uncut toenails.

The Dead Zone

Whether these residents are still here is unknown – and whether the back wing of the building, abandoned for years after an earthquake and long-known as "The Dead Zone" – is a past history or not, this isn't a hotel you can stay at anymore.

There is a fast food and a healthy-eating outlet on the street level spaces, but to say they're unique or even "gourmet" is too much of a stretch – even the Sultan Room, the old hotel bar at the back – is now a yoga/martial arts studio (which tells you how far the area has come).

However, the Gershwin Apartments make it into this book not only because of the dark deeds that happened here – well, at least the ones that made the newspapers – but also because of its most infamous resident, one that was a surprise to me to learn about.

MLK's Killer

In November 1967 a man calling himself Eric Galt checked in. He had recently escaped from the Missouri State Penitentiary, which was doubtless why he chose a fake name – but it was his real name, James Earl Ray, that would go down in history.

Yes, the assassin who shot and killed Martin Luther King, Jr. in Memphis on April 4, 1968 stayed here at what was then the St. Francis, and certainly starting making plans for his hideous assault on history during that time.

Besides working for the presidential campaign of notorious segregationist George Wallace, court records revealed that Ray also took dancing lessons, graduated from bartending school, and, shortly before he started his cross-country journey to kill King, got a nose job from a plastic surgeon.

He also spent plenty of time in the hotel bar and watching television in his room, on the back of which investigators apparently found a racial slur about King.

After four months living in room 403, Ray set off for Atlanta, King's hometown. En route he bought a Remington 760 Gamemaster .30-06 calibre rifle in Birmingham, Alabama, and then a few days after that he fired the fatal bullet.

Ray was caught two months after the assassination having made it to England by airplane from Canada, and was in jail for the rest of his life, dying in 1998.

Of course, there's more to the story than this, but one thing is certain: one of the most famous assassins in history stayed – and planned out his killing – right here.

Ex-Commander
of D.A.V. Dies

As for deaths in situ, the first one noted in the *LA Times* is from August 1942 and was of Frank J. Irwin, a former war hero and founder of the Disabled American Veterans, who died after a long illness.

Rites Set Today for TV Actor John Deering

The next person to pass away here was former television actor John Deering, 54.

The cause of death wasn't listed in the *LA Times* for February 1, 1959, but it also seemed to be natural causes (his IMDB entry says it was a cerebral hemorrhage).

The Strangler?

It wasn't until December 1977 that the St. Francis was in the papers again, this time when a resident made a hoax call to the LAPD claiming that he was the "Hillside Strangler."

The actual killers were a pair of men, Kenneth A. Bianchi and Angelo Buono Jr, who were convicted of kidnapping, raping, torturing, and killing ten females during 1977/1978 (see the entry for the Hollywood Plaza Hotel in the **Hollywood & W. Hollywood** chapter).

Police Question Couple After Call on Strangler

Police traced the 20 minute call to a phone on the third floor, and arrested a man and woman. Both had long arrest records, but after being extensively interviewed they were released without charge.

Shootings

In June 1982 there was the first violent death here (at least that I found in the *LA Times* archives), when a 34 year old resident was shot several times and, running to the fire escape, then fell the three storeys to the ground.

His name was not released, and police said they had no motive for the shooting.

Just over a year later in September 1983, tenant J. Anthony Scott, 44, was found stabbed to death in his room; fellow tenant Luis Felipe Ruiz was immediately arrested and booked on suspicion of murder.

Amazingly, the police had been called to the hotel an hour before when Sifa P. Ngungutau had been shot and injured; his condition was stable, and detectives felt the two incidents could be related.

The *LA Weekly* article mentioned that a former manager said the hotel had been the location for suicides (something very common in all hotels), and that:

"The Gershwin is very haunted. Everyone there knows it."

A former resident and employee also said that another resident – a prostitute – had been beaten to death with a VCR.

The smell of her undiscovered dead body soon started to bother other tenants apparently, so they put a 24 hour notice under her door.

She added that the owners apparently then said:

"So, should we keep the mattress?"

None of these incidents could be found in the *LA Times*, but since Hollywood was known as dangerous place in the 1970s, 1980s and even into the 1990s – especially on the fringes, and perhaps even more so in a, shall we say, "energetic" hotel like the Gershwin – it's possible that they all might have happened...

www.gershwinapartments.com

Off The Menu:

Holland Hotel (& MacArthur Park)
1404 West 7th Street
Los Angeles, CA 90017

The Holland Hotel is now a seemingly empty and totally forgotten building.

The first reference to it – or at least to this address – was in November 1902, when the *LA Times* reported that notorious "Wagon Load Thief" Clarence D. Jackson had been arrested here in his "fine two story flat," which was furnished with the ill-gotten gains from around 60 robberies – and probably many more – that he and accomplices had committed in 18 months.

"WAGON-LOAD" THIEF FOUND.

They'd run the police ragged, deliberately targeting furnished apartments for rent, with Jackson then using what he'd stolen to furnish other apartments and even his own flats, which he rented out at "fancy prices" while he and his wife and young baby lived in a small part of it.

More than that, apparently they were about to move into a building with twenty rooms!

A SHES OF THE DEAD STOLEN BY JACKSON.

---◆---

"WAGONLOAD" THIEF DIDN'T STOP AT FUNERAL URNS.

Robbery victims came to Jackson's flats and other buildings in a steady stream over the next few days to look for their possessions, and among them there was a "grewsome" find: two urns containing human ashes.

Luckily, the ashes were traced back to their owner – a Mrs. Bliesner – who was glad to have her parents back home again, along with the other things Jackson had stolen. It's thought he didn't know the urns were more than a cute mantel decoration.

The only other reference in the *LA Times* archives to the Holland Hotel was in February 1936, when it was listed among other hotels as recently changing hands, so it's unclear when the hotel was actually built.

The Rose Murder

That said, in its day it was also the home of a wild spree killer and a man who committed what was called "The Rose Murder."

At first glance it seemed that the note attached to several bouquets of roses Otis W. Hall had sent to his wife Barbara were a last romantic gesture, as he had attempted suicide soon after, his note reading in part:

"Good-by, my darling, see you in heaven . . ."

But Hall was found by his landlady and rushed to hospital. There he confessed all to his brother James, and it emerged that his seemingly sad story was far more deadly.

As reported in the *LA Times* of May 30, 1942, it seemed the newlyweds had quarreled recently and separated, and when a jealous Hall suspected she was having an affair, he strangled her.

Man Admits Killing Wife and Sending Her Roses

Hall told his brother to go to her room (number 307) and there he did indeed find the body and a note that read:

"God forgive me, I loved her too much."

Though they were former high school sweethearts, Barbara had married another man – and had a daughter aged 7 – before she and Otis were married barely nine months before.

Things had been tempestuous though, and Hall had been arrested several times for being drunk in public.

On the day of the murder, Hall said he had seen his wife walking with a soldier who had his arm around her.

She accused him of being "too jealous," but after they had gone back to her room, he saw a towel on the doorknob when he was leaving – something he knew was a "keep away" signal to others.

He returned to the room, there was another row, and he choked her. "I knew she was dead," he said, but he had to "make sure":

"I pulled the cord out of her red bathrobe and drew it tight around her neck..."

He then went back to his room at the Holland Hotel and spent $3 on sending three dozen "Roses of Death," as the *Los Angeles Evening Herald-Express* called them, to her room.

Of course, the bellboy got no answer when he knocked on the door of room – as Hall knew he wouldn't.

But by then he was elsewhere, reaching for a razor and hoping to end the tragic story that he had started...

Pictures published in the *Los Angeles Evening Herald* the very next day showed Hall alongside the carton with the roses inside, and the *LA Times* one was even more chilling.

Though he's partly covering his face with his hand when the roses are placed alongside him, the horror of what they represent – and what he had done – is clear in his eyes, even in the black and white of the faded newspaper page. A guilty verdict was a foregone conclusion...

Wife-Strangler Found Guilty

Lake Drowning

Another striking picture in the *LA Times* of July 24, 1951 showed a large group of photographers, their bulky cameras in their hands, at the side of MacArthur Park Lake as firemen were using grappling hooks to remove the dead body of a Holland Hotel resident, John Ray Thompson.

Death in MacArthur Park Lake Ends Man's Flight From Police

After propositioning an undercover vice officer he had been arrested on a morals charge, but he broke free and jumped into the lake, perhaps hitting his head as he did so.

The water was only three foot deep, but tragically it seems that either panic, the prospect of a trial, or perhaps being suspected of being gay, saw Thompson fighting off all efforts to save him before he finally drowned.

"Berserk Stabber"

Then in August 1968 came an orgy of violence that it's hard to believe wasn't a much bigger story at the time.

Armed with an eight inch butcher knife, Eugene V. Velasco, 27, left the Holland Hotel and went across the street to ask Garland Richardson for a drink. When the unknowing Richardson said he had none, Velasco stabbed him in the stomach.

6 Stabbed; 'Wild Man' Is Captured

It was the beginning of a "berserk, drink-crazed rampage" said the *Los Angeles Herald-Examiner*, noting that 'Wild Man' Velasco then visited three of his drinking friends and, after there was a row, he stabbed them all.

He then returned to the Holland and asked another resident and his friend who were emptying trash in the backyard for a drink – the "no" response again resulting in more slashes of the knife.

Police had already been called, and there was a chase through some backyards before Velasco, a laborer recently arrived from Colorado and with a record of burglaries, was arrested.

In barely a couple of hours he had killed three people and injured three more.

The Burning of the Black Dahlia's Killer?

Finally, there's a (slightly possible) connection between the Holland and the brutal 1947 murder of Elizabeth Short, better known as the "Black Dahlia."

One of the few online references to the Holland is on a Yahoo site dated in March 2011, when "Margaret" wrote about her father living at the Holland in 1953.

She says that it was a retirement hotel at that time, and that "old men wearing hats and smoking cigars would sit in the lobby and put quarters in the pay TV set to watch boxing."

She said some of the rooms had private bathrooms and that there were no kitchens, but then she mentions:

"I read that a couple of years after we left there, there was a fire and the man killed by the fire was a suspect in the black dahlia and one other notorious murder."

As you can imagine, this sent me diving into the newspaper archives, but despite other online sources also quoting that unlikely suspect Jack Anderson Wilson (AKA Arnold Smith) did indeed die in a fire, if it was at the Holland Hotel I couldn't find any evidence of it.

Wilson, a lifelong petty criminal and alcoholic, said he knew Short – or certainly the man who killed her, a man he referred to as "Mr. Jones."

Nonetheless, it's probably true to say that the Black Dahlia murder is like the killing spree of Jack the Ripper in 1888 London; events that will never be fully explained, but will still come up in the news every now and then.

As for the fire, maybe it was at another hotel called the Holland, or this Holland had a different name then.

Either way, we have to mark this possible Holland Hotel/Black Dahlia story down as extremely doubtful.

The Holland is a 10 minute walk from MacArthur Park, whose spouting fountain you'll know well from pop videos, television shows and movies like *Volcano* (1997), *Training Day* (2001) and *Kiss Kiss Bang Bang* (2005), or maybe even the Richard Harris hit song of 1968.

Built in the 1880s and originally known as Westlake Park in honor of Henricus Westlake, a Canadian physician who donated the land to the city, by the early 20th century it was surrounded by luxury hotels and the neighborhood was known as the Champs Élysées of Los Angeles.

The Park Plaza Hotel was one of them, and though today it's empty and mainly used for filming and events, this neo-gothic 1925 building is worth a look – try and find the elk antlers on the exterior!

In 1942 the park was renamed in honor of General Douglas MacArthur, but for many years in the 1980s and 1990s it had a reputation for prostitution, drug dealing, and as the dumping ground for gang shoot-out victims.

But the lake had long been a place for death; in fact I randomly found a story about a suicide from 1901 during my research:

BODY IS FOUND

IN PARK LAKE

Grewsome Catch Made by Small Boys

Who Is This Man?

"Who is this man?" the caption asked. Aged around 55, the victim seemed to be a miner who had jumped from the roof of a summer house alongside the lake.

A derby hat was found nearby, and, strangely, a paper bag of "peaches in a well preserved condition" was in his pocket.

Today the park is very much moving away from its checkered past. Bodies are rarely found in the lake, and sure the bustling streets are a place where you can buy counterfeit DVDs, false IDs and all sorts of junk, but art projects like in the picture below are looking forward.

The lake side of the park is home to a few gritty characters alongside the joggers and people hanging out, but there are friendly ducks and swans too, while on the family-friendly side of Wilshire Boulevard there's an amphitheatre, music pavilion, soccer fields, a children's playground and a recreation center.

Take a trip there one Saturday, and, though the Holland Hotel isn't open to you, visit the nearby Langer's Deli (www.langersdeli.com) which has been there since 1947; anything with pastrami is perfect!

Bibliography

Chapter 1 – Hollywood & W. Hollywood

Picture Failure Death leap – *Los Angeles Times*, Sep 20, 1932, p.A1

Suicide Laid To Film Jinx – *Los Angeles Times*, Sep 20, 1932, p.A1

Decorator Commits Suicide On Hollywood Bowl Stage – *Los Angeles Times*, Mar 26, 1938, p. A1

Death Under the Stars at Hollywood Bowl – *Los Angeles Examiner*, Vol. XXXV, No. 105, Part Two, Mar 26, 1938

Death Before 'Ghosts,' 'Under the Stars' – *Los Angeles Evening Herald-Express*, Vol. LXVII, No. 312, Mar 25, 1938, p. A-2

Teen-Ager Dies From Fall – *Los Angeles Times*, Mar 3, 1988, p. WS2

Is the Hollywood Sign Haunted? – Valerie Tejeda, *Vanity Fair*, Oct 31, 2014

Officer Kills Wife And Self – *Los Angeles Times*, Dec 16, 1933, p. A5

Trio Taken In Raid On Apartment – *Los Angeles Times*, Sep 22, 1934, p. A3

Sleeping Tablets Held Death Cause – *Los Angeles Times*, Apr 27, 1945 p. 4

One Man Found Slain; 2nd Wounded – *Los Angeles Times*, Mar 21, 1974, p. 3

Hemingway and Hollywood – Rick Setlowe, *Los Angeles Times*, Oct 14, 1979, p. O3

King Of Swat Drives Golf Ball Through Hotel – *Los Angeles Times*, Feb 11, 1927, p. B4

Ex-Bell Boy Back Home – *Los Angeles Times*, Aug 27, 1934, P. A1

Death Mates Chess Player – *Los Angeles Times*, Jan 18, 1928, p. A1

Autopsy Ordered in Visitor's Death – *Los Angeles Times*, Feb 4, 1940, p. A1

Pool Drowning May Be Traced to Heart Attack – *Los Angeles Times*, Mar 23, 1958, p. A2

150 Flee Second Fire at Hollywood's Plaza Hotel – *Los Angeles Times*, Oct 24, 1984, p. A1

Hotel's Completion Near – *Los Angeles Times*, Sep 20, 1925, p. F1

Wife Accused of Murdering Wealthy Husband Kills Self – *Los Angeles Times*, Mar 10, 1954, p.2

Beauty's Suicide May Have Been 'Too Soon" – *Los Angeles Herald-Express*, March 10, 1954

Hollywood-Plaza Hotel Completes $400,000 Modernization – *Los Angeles Times*, May 27, 1952, p.13

Hollywood Plaza Hotel Leased For $2,000,000 – *Los Angeles Times*, May 17, 1956, p. E2

Buono Tied to Another Slaying Victim – Bill Hazlett, *Los Angeles Times*, Mar 25, 1982, p. E8

School For Flyers Urged – *Los Angeles Times*, Dec 6, 1926, p. A18

Restaurant to Locate Store in Vine Street – *Los Angeles Times*, Jul 8, 1928, p. E1

Amundsen To Lecture On Exploits At Pole – *Los Angeles Times*, Feb 11, 1927, p. A6

Hotel Builder Christie Dies – *Los Angeles Times*, Mar 17, 1941, p. IA

Article 13 – No Title – *Los Angeles Times*, Sep 30, 1956, p. F1

Erin Count Is Held On Old Charge – *Los Angeles Times*, May 31, 1924, p. A5

Hotel Opens New Units – *Los Angeles Times*, Jan 12, 1958, p. F17

Sale of Christie Hotel in Hollywood – *Los Angeles Times*, Jun 21, 1931, p. D2

Christie Hotel, Hollywood, to Change Hands – *Los Angeles Times*, Dec 7, 1944, p. 12

Former Oilman Ends Life in Eight-Story Plunge at Hotel – *Los Angeles Times*, Feb 25, 1941, p. A3

Jobless Girl, 19, Plunges Eight Floors To Death – *Los Angeles Times*, May 19, 1948, p. A1

Elevator Death Scene – *Los Angeles Herald-Express*, Vol. LXXIII, No. 136, Sep 1, 1943, p. A-4

Girl Follows Friend in Death – *Los Angeles Times*, May 22, 1924, p. A1

Girl, 20, Finds Life 'Futile' – *Los Angeles Examiner*, Vol. XXI, No. 163, May 22, 1924, Section 1, p. 8

History marker mistakenly indentifies Hollywood hotel – Bob Pool, *Los Angeles Times*, Jun 20, 2011

'Bugsy' Siegel Jailed in Raid as Bookmaker – *Los Angeles Times*, May 26, 1944, p. 9

'Bugsy' Told to Face Trial – *Los Angeles Times*, Jul 21, 1944, p. A1

Hunt for Blonde Centers on Taxi Driver – *Los Angeles Times*, Apr 12, 1948, p. 9

Maria Gatica Tells Why She Works as Domestic – *Los Angeles Times*, Apr 14, 1948, p. A1

$1,000,000 Remodeling Program Furthered – *Los Angeles Times*, Dec 4, 1955, p. F1

Blonde Slashes Wrists, Attempts Suicide Leap – *Los Angeles Times*, Nov 20, 1953, p. 2

Woman Visitor Tries Suicide, Deputies Say – *Los Angeles Times*, Jun 14, 1954, p. 22

Suspect Admits $25,000 Cocktail Fete Robbery – *Los Angeles Times*, Feb 19, 1944, p. 3

Actor to Face Theft Trial Despite Plea for Dismissal – *Los Angeles Times*, Mar 9, 1944, p. 2

Business Owner Reported Suicide – *Los Angeles Times*, Dec 24, 1944, p. 4

Tawdry Tales of the Sunset Tower – Laurie Ochoa, *Los Angeles Times*, Jun 19, 1988, p. L98

Clark Left While Spencer Dying, Witness Swears – *Los Angeles Examiner*, Vol. XXVII, No. 243, Aug 11, 1931, p.1

Events at Murder Scene Described – *Los Angeles Times*, Aug 11, 1931, p. A1

Nurse Sentenced to 8-Year Term in Slaying of Actor – *Los Angeles Times*, Jan 29, 1980, p. B20

Developed Many Sleights of Hand – Burt A. Folkart, *Los Angeles Times*, Feb 25, 1984, p. A25

Maj. John Gaston Discovered Dead in Hotel Room – *Los Angeles Times*, Dec 14, 1949, p. 2

Baylies Funeral Will Be Today – *Los Angeles Times*, Sep 3, 1932, p. A1

Chapter 2 – Mid-City & Beverly Hills

Movie Director Dies 17 Hours After Wedding – *Los Angeles Times*, Dec 20, 1965, p. B14

Murder Indictment of Ex-Howard Hughes Aide Told – Bill Farr/Bill Hazlett, *Los Angeles Times*, Feb 10, 1981, p. C5

Nola Hahn, Onetime Pal of Gamblers, Ends Life – *Los Angeles Times*, Mar 31, 1957, p. 2

Time Capsule Placed in Beverly Hilton Hotel – *Los Angeles Times*, Jul 15, 1954, p. 29

Psychic Medium Thomas John Channels the Five Most Haunted Spots in and Around L.A. – Rakhee Bhatt, *Angeleno*, Mar 1, 2013

Horrified patrons witness murder-suicide at May Co. – Don Rosen, *Los Angeles Herald-Examiner*, Jun 22, 1989, p. 1

Pocket-Sized Crime Story Told in Shaft – Bettina Boxall, *Los Angeles Times*, Jun 27, 1988, p. C1

Man, 87, Kills Wife, Self at Fairfax Store – Paul Feldman/Mathis Chazanov, *Los Angeles Times*, Jun 22, 1989, p. 39

A Great Day for the Irish at Tom Bergin's – Patrick Mott, *Los Angeles Times*, Mar 14, 1987, p. D3

Two End Lives At Pasadena – *Los Angeles Times*, Jun 13, 1932, p. A8
Rug Importer Critically Ill After Suicide Attempt – *Los Angeles Times*, Sep 29, 1936, p. A3
Electric Shock Beheads Worker – *Los Angeles Examiner*, May 26, 1945, p. 1-4

Chapter 3 – Downtown

A Mysterious Leg – *Los Angeles Times*, Mar 3, 1895, p.11
Finding Of A Human Leg – *Los Angeles Examiner*, Mar 3, 1896
Ten More Raid Shelters Listed – *Los Angeles Times*, Sep 19, 1942, p. A9
Removal – *Los Angeles Times*, Aug 15, 1896, p. 9
Man Kills Self as Superior Shot – *Los Angeles Times*, Sep 26, 1942, p. 14
In Social Spheres – *Los Angeles Times*, May 22, 1901, p. 3
Hatchet Attacker Indicated in L.A. Slasher Murders – Bill Hazlett/Bill Farr, *Los Angeles Times*, Jan 24, 1976, p. A1
Speedy justice Promised for Confessed Slayer – *Los Angeles Times*, Nov 17, 1944, p. 2
'Ripper' Says Lust to Kill Made Him Hack Pair to Death – *Los Angeles Examiner*, Vol. XLI, No. 342, Nov 17, 1944
Romeo Slasher Waits Court Move In L.A. Murders – *Los Angeles Evening Herald-Express*, Vol. LXXIV, Nov 17, 1944, p.1
Van Nuys Changes Hands – *Los Angeles Times*, Mar 14, 1929, p. A1
Fell Three Stories – *Los Angeles Times*, Mar 4, 1897, p. 9
The Van Nuys Opened – *Los Angeles Times*, Jan 20, 1897, p.8
Visitor Falls to her Death– *Los Angeles Times*, Feb 29, 1944, p. 14
Amnesia Case Clew Found – *Los Angeles Times*, Oct 22, 1937, p. A2
The Southland – *Los Angeles Times*, Mar 3, 1981, p. B2

Southland – *Los Angeles Times*, Nov 14, 1979, p. 2

Suspect Dies – *Los Angeles Times*, Jan 5, 1984, p. A12

DA Won't Prosecute Man Who Said He Started Hotel Blaze – *Los Angeles Times*, Mar 18, 1972, Part II

Woman Killed in Barclay Hotel Fire Identified – *Los Angeles Times*, Mar 21, 1972, p. C4

Alarm System, Fire Doors Save Lives in Hotel Blaze, Official Says – Jack Jones, *Los Angeles Times*, Sep 12, 1974, p. 3

Effort To Prove Sanity Opens – *Los Angeles Times*, Jun 23, 1945, p. 3

Grand Jury Will Get Data on L.A. Slasher Murders – Bill Farr/Bill Hazlett, *Los Angeles Times*, Dec 9, 1975, p. C1

Downtown Lease Made – *Los Angeles Times*, Jul 13, 1935, p. A1

H. Lee Borden Dead – *Los Angeles Times*, Nov 23, 1902, p. C1

Bullard's Body Sent Home – *Los Angeles Times*, Jul 26, 1924, p. A6

Woman Dying As Result Of Slugging In Hotel – *Los Angeles Times*, Feb 4, 1937, p. 3

Bell Boy Killed – *Los Angeles Times*, Jan 3, 1900, p. 19

Recluse With Millions Dies – *Los Angeles Times*, Aug 3, 1911, p. II1

Curiosity Killed Him – *Los Angeles Times*, Sep 21, 1901, p.7

Carved With Bread Knife – *Los Angeles Times*, Aug 1, 1902, p. 5

Youth Takes Cyanide– *Los Angeles Times*, Jun 12, 1909, p. II2

Wife Is Blamed in Suicide Note – *Los Angeles Times*, Jan 29, 1924, p. A12

Secret Agent Or Dead Man? – *Los Angeles Times*, Jul 21, 1915, p. II1

Moore, J.M. *The History Of The Barclay Hotel* – 433 Publishing; Colton, California 2016

Surgeon Steals Handsome Wife? – *Los Angeles Times*, Aug 11,1920, p. II1
Police After Cave Man Now – *Los Angeles Times*, Sep 29, 1920, p. II1
Sudden End To Peppers Fight – *Los Angeles Times*, Dec 10, 1920, p.II6
Woman Tells Acid Threats – *Los Angeles Times*, May 9, 1925, p. A6
Human Fly Performs – *Los Angeles Times*, Jul 27, 1923, p. II20
"Human Fly" Dares Fate For Veterans – *Los Angeles Times*, Dec 18, 1923, p. II23
Human Fly To Scale Hotel – *Los Angeles Times*, Dec 17, 1923, p. II2
Crowd Watches Leap To Death – *Los Angeles Times*, Sep 3, 1919, p. III1
Brockman Funeral Friday – *Los Angeles Times*, May 31, 1925, p. A2
Convicted Arsonist Held in Hotel Fire Fatal to 3 – David Shaw, *Los Angeles Times*, Mar 16, 1972, p. E1
Incognito Shaken – *Los Angeles Times*, Jul 27, 1934, p. A10
Custer Aide Tells How Lack of Cavalry Horse Saved Him – *Los Angeles Times*, Feb 10, 1941, p. A2
Hotel Prowler Kills 2nd Woman – *Los Angeles Evening Herald Examiner*, Vol. XCIV, No. 71, Jun 5, 1964, p. 1.
New Year's Toll Heavy – *Los Angeles Times*, Jan 2, 1935, p. 16
A Chronology of the Night Stalker's Spree – Bob Baker, *Los Angeles Times*, Sep 1, 1985, p. A30
Woman Takes Death Plunge – *Los Angeles Times*, Mar 15, 1937, p. A3
Trail of Killings – Eric Malnic, *Los Angeles Times*, Mar 13, 1992, p. OCA3
Two Women Take Poison – *Los Angeles Times*, Apr 3, 1929, p. A9

Fraud Suspect Denies Knowing Credit Man He's Accused of Having Impersonated – *Los Angeles Times*, Dec 7, 1931, p. A2

Grandma Bandit Admits 2 Jobs – *Long Island Star-Journal*, Dec 26, 1952, p. 2

Robber Suspect, 60, Not Grandma, Police Decide – *Los Angeles Times*, Dec 5, 1952, p. 2

Café Manager Killed in Fight – *Los Angeles Times*, Sep 20, 1943, p. A3

Suspect In Burglaries Captured – *Los Angeles Times*, Feb 1, 1927, p. A8

Cecil Hotel Lease Closed – *Los Angeles Times*, May 11, 1941, p. E1

Veteran Mine Man Buried At Old Home – *Los Angeles Times*, Jun 19, 1926, p. A6

Officers Seize $10,000 Opium – *Los Angeles Times*, Aug 23, 1931, p. A2

Plane Passenger Killed – *Los Angeles Times*, Sep 4, 1927, p. B1

Security Guard Held in Shooting – *Los Angeles Times*, Dec 25, 1970, p. B1

Man Held in Huntington Beach Slaying – *Los Angeles Times*, Sep 8, 1988, p. AOC14

Ship Fireman In Suicide Leap – *Los Angeles Times*, Jan 10, 1938, p. 2

Matoon Aide Dies Of Poison – *Los Angeles Times*, Sep 19, 1932, p. A1

Bird Lover Slain, But Friends Remember – Eric Malnic, *Los Angeles Times*, Jun 6, 1964, p. 15

Ex-Mental Patient Seized in Rooftop Sniping Spree – Ken Hansen, *Los Angeles Times*, Dec 2, 1976, p. A3

Suspect Stalker Arraigned; Also Charged in S.F. – Robert W. Stewart, *Los Angeles Times*, Sep 4, 1985, p. A1

Teacher Near Death – *Los Angeles Times*, Jan 11, 1940, p. A3

Sailor Ends Life by Taking Poison – *Los Angeles Times*, May 29, 1939, p. 4

Woman Killed in Seven-Floor Hotel Plunge – *Los Angeles Times*, Oct 23, 1954, p. A6

Search for Man Ends in Finding Body at Hotel – *Los Angeles Times*, Nov 19, 1931, p. A2

Body Identified in Hotel Room Fall – *Los Angeles Times*, Nov 1, 1947, p. A1

Woman's Death Leap Kills Man on Street – *Los Angeles Times*, Oct 13, 1962, p. I1

Woman Leaps to Death From Hotel Window – *Los Angeles Times*, Feb 12, 1962, p. 26

Young Mother Freed in Baby Death Plunge – *Los Angeles Times*, Jan 6, 1945, p. A8

Mother Held After Baby Found Thrown To Death – *Los Angeles Times*, Sep 8, 1944, p. A3

Mother Held In Baby Death – *Los Angeles Examiner*, Sep 7, 1944, Part 1-3

'Thought He Was Dead' She Tells Police – *Los Angeles Herald-Express Times*, Vol. XXIV, Section A

Miura Named as Sole Suspect in 2 Slayings – Jerry Belcher/Sam Jameson, *Los Angeles Times*, Oct 4, 1985, p. B1

Japanese Police Arrest Mate of Woman Attacked in Hotel, Then Shot on Street – Jerry Belcher, *Los Angeles Times*, Sep 12, 1985, p. OCA6

Bled To Death – *Los Angeles Times*, Aug 6, 1986, p. 12

Otani Hotel Topped Out in Little Tokyo – *Los Angeles Times*, Feb 6, 1977, p. I2

Leaper Victim Identified – *Los Angeles Times*, Apr 8, 1979, p. B3

Operations Gang Raided – *Los Angeles Times*, Jun 6, 1936, p. A1

Scrambled Identities Cause Grid Star Grief – *Los Angeles Times*, Feb 4, 1931, p. A10

Charges Due in Slaying of 2 Secretaries – *Los Angeles Times*, Dec 29, 1967, p. 20

Missing Securities Linked to Slaying of Two Secretaries – *Los Angeles Times*, Dec 20, 1967, p. A1

News Of The Art World – *Los Angeles Times*, May 11, 1958, p. E7

News Of the Cafes – *Los Angeles Times*, May 24, 1935, p. A19

Shell-Shocked Veteran Slays Wife and Self in Downtown Hotel – *Los Angeles Times*, Dec 21, 1931, p. A2

Burglary Reign May Be Linked To Cripple – *Los Angeles Times*, Jun 25, 1929, p. A2

Guy K. Woodward Passes – *Los Angeles Times*, Mar 6, 1926, p. A8

Dead Man Found In His Room – *Los Angeles Times*, Oct 17, 1922, p. II12

Robbers Bind And Gag Clerk In Woodward Hotel: Rob Safe – *Los Angeles Times*, Dec 8, 1910, p. I13

Big Hotels Bought By Easterners – *Los Angeles Times*, Oct 10, 1920, p. V4

Curses Aunt As Life Ebbs – *Los Angeles Times*, Sep 15, 1906, p. I12

Sends Bullet Through Head – *Los Angeles Times*, Dec 25, 1909, p. I4

Spurns Bride; She Turns – *Los Angeles Times*, Sep 1, 1910, p. III1

Persistent Policeman Saves Woman Leaper – *Los Angeles Times*, Sep 29, 1970, p. A2

Couple Dead In Dual Tragedy – *Los Angeles Times*, Jan 29, 1929, p. A9

Fugitive Sought in Son's Slaying Seized in L.A. – *Los Angeles Times*, Jan 11, 1983, p. C6

Aged Man Ends Life in Hotel by Poison Draught – *Los Angeles Times*, Jan 10, 1925, p. A5

Wrist and Throat Slashes, Woman Found in Room – *Los Angeles Times*, Sep 13, 1937, p. A10

The King Edward Hotel – *Los Angeles Times*, Feb 18, 1906, p. V24
Disappointed In Love, He Commits Suicide – *Los Angeles Evening Herald*, Vol. XXXVII, Number 83, Dec 25, 1909, p. 6
Wife Fears Mate Victim Of Foul Play / 'Bring Him Back Santa' – *Los Angeles Examiner*, Dec 25, 1931
Worker Killed in Plunge Down Eight Stories – *Los Angeles Times*, Jan 7, 1927, p. A1
Four Aces And Six Bricks – *Los Angeles Times*, Dec 5, 1927, p. I5
Slaying Victim's Heirs May Sue, Court Decides – *Los Angeles Times*, Jun 8, 1946, p. 3
Salvation Army Officer's Burial Set – *Los Angeles Times*, May 5, 1940, p. A20
Man, 48, Leaps to His Death on Busy Street – *Los Angeles Times*, Jan 15, 1948, p. 2
Search Opens For Clubman – *Los Angeles Times*, Dec 25, 1931, p. A1
Sister Bequeathed Suicide's $35,000 – *Los Angeles Times*, Dec 22, 1943, p. A14
Inquest to Be Omitted in Slaying of Doctor – *Los Angeles Times*, Dec 15, 1943, p. A10
T.R.'s Mustache Mistaken For Joseph Stalin's – *Los Angeles Times*, Dec 14, 1950, p. A17
Roosevelt Job May Be Record – *Los Angeles Times*, Jul 18, 1926, p. E2
Woman Leaps to Death From Office Building – *Los Angeles Times*, Mar 17, 1951, p. I6
Hundreds See Woman Take Death Plunge – *Los Angeles Times*, Dec 29, 1950, p. 2
Dr. Verne Hunt Slain At Desk By Ex-Patient – *Los Angeles Examiner*, Vol. LXI, No. 3, Dec 14, 1943, p. III1
Women's Fatal Leap Almost Hurts Another – *Los Angeles Times*, Jun 4, 1953, p. 3

Woman Plunges From 12th Floor Ledge to Death – *Los Angeles Times*, Jul 22, 1948, p. 2

Ring Reveals Identity Of Death Leap Victim – *Los Angeles Times*, Jul 28, 1948, p. 6

Laborer Killed In Six-Story Plunge – *Los Angeles Times*, Jul 18, 1926, p. I7

Cup Race Skipper Drops From Sight – *Los Angeles Times*, Jul 28, 1950, P. A8

Roosevelt undergoes restoration – *Los Angeles Times*, Mar 31, 1987, p. F22

Fine Store and Office Addition Under Way in Downtown District – *Los Angeles Times*, Apr 4, 1926, p. E1

11-Story Fall Kills Woman – *Los Angeles Examiner*, Vol. XLVIII, No. 96, Mar 17, 1951, Sec 1-5

Man Dies in Downtown Suicide Leap – *Los Angeles Times*, Feb 26, 1957, p. 2

Woman Plunge Victim Still Not Identified – *Los Angeles Times*, Jul 24, 1948, p. 8

Elderly Woman Found Murdered in Her Apartment – *Los Angeles Times*, Sep 3, 1976, p. B26

Infuriated Suitor Kills Dancer and Commits Suicide – *Los Angeles Examiner*, Jun 5, 1936, Part Two

2 Women Found Slain in Rooms – *Los Angeles Times*, Jun 9, 1976, p. 26

S.C. Choral Professor Succumbs To Heart Attack – *Los Angeles Times*, Feb 18, 1939, p. A16

Choral Leader's Widow Dies – *Los Angeles Times*, Feb 26, 1939, p. A8

Accused Man Drinks Poison – *Los Angeles Times*, Dec 11, 1928, p. A3

Bandit Caught In Gun Battle – *Los Angeles Times*, Jun 13, 1921, p. II1

Hunt Rites Will be On Wednesday – *Los Angeles Times*, Mar 12, 1928, p. A1

Sherlock Is Outclassed – *Los Angeles Times*, May 9, 1923, p.II8

Stillwell Hotel To Be Remodeled – *Los Angeles Times*, May 2, 1926, p. E2

Girl in Death Leap Identified – *Los Angeles Times*, Aug 28, 1933, p. 6

Accepted Design for New Downtown Hostelry – *Los Angeles Times*, Oct 27, 1912, p. V1

Los Angeles Dancer Slain – *Los Angeles Times*, Jun 5, 1936, p. 3

Glendale Man Leaves Note About $1000 Before Suicide – *Los Angeles Times*, Aug 17, 1941, p. I9

Mind Confused, Son Forgotten – *Los Angeles Times*, May 14, 1914, p. II3

Pioneer Group Founder Dies – *Los Angeles Times*, Apr 29, 1939, p. A3

C.H. Stillwell, Hotel Builder, Taken by Death – *Los Angeles Times*, Apr 2, 1944, p. I5

A Slice of Runyon – Michael Krikorian, *Los Angeles Times*, Feb 11, 1997

Here's to Hank, Say Sad Friends of a Very Special Saloonkeeper – Michael Krikorian, *Los Angeles Times*, Jan 11, 1998

Broker Shoots L.A. Woman And Kills Self In Love Row – *Los Angeles Evening Herald-Express*, Vol. LXXV, No. 131, Aug 25, 1945

Auto Dealer Wounds Friend and Kills Self on Golf Course – *Los Angeles Times*, Feb 8, 1927, p. A2

Flees With Soda Clerk – *Los Angeles Times*, Jan 10, 1920, p. I4

Hand Feels Way To Deadly Pill – *Los Angeles Times*, Oct 4, 1915, p. II5

Doubt Murder Confession – *Los Angeles Times*, Oct 13, 1923, p. II5

Two Newsmen Periled as Prisoner Grabs Policeman's Gun, Shoots Self – *Los Angeles Times*, May 14, 1956, p. 2

Police Officer Thwarts Death Leap From Hotel – *Los Angeles Times*, Jul 20, 1957, p. 1

Love's Messenger Thwarted – *Los Angeles Times*, Jul 29, 1925, p. A3

Mrs. Leonora Fairbank – *Los Angeles Times*, Aug 12, 1947, p. A7

Boy To Inherit $2300 Left By Dad's Friend – *Los Angeles Times*, Jan 10, 1947, p. 9

Clark To Face 'Hideout' Quiz – *Los Angeles Times*, Aug 16, 1931, p. A1

Six Hundred Evacuate Hotel When 12th-Floor Fire Starts – *Los Angeles Times*, Jan 3, 1941, p. A5

Los Angeles Hotel key Found On Iwo Jima – *Los Angeles Times*, Mar 26, 1945, p. 1

Death, Shooting Laid to Jealousy – *Los Angeles Times*, Aug 26, 1945, p. 12

Girl Accuses Hotel Man – *Los Angeles Times*, Jun 27, 1923, p. II1

Tax Evasion Charges Faced By Hotel Man – *Los Angeles Times*, Nov 4, 1949, p. 2

Hotel Stowell Changes Hands – *Los Angeles Times*, Jan 28, 1938, p. A1

Stowell Hotel Business Sold to H.J. Tremain – *Los Angeles Times*, Jun 30, 1925, p. A2

Long Beach 16-Story Hotel Changes Hands – *Los Angeles Times*, Nov 27, 1946, p. A2

Stowell Hotel Building Sold – *Los Angeles Times*, Oct 28, 1944, p. A3

Woman Hotel Suicide Dead For Several Days – *Los Angeles Times*, Feb 26, 1917, p. I3

Six-Story Plunge Kills Man, 76 – *Los Angeles Times*, Sep 10, 1962, p. A1

Metropolitan – *Los Angeles Times*, Jun 18, 1970, p. 2

Mother Writes Where to Find Body in Hotel – *Los Angeles Times*, Aug 4, 1932, p. A7

Hotel Employee Ends Life With Gun – *Los Angeles Times*, Oct 1, 1938, p. A3

Smelter Arrested As 'Fence' – *Los Angeles Times*, Jun 23, 1928, p. A3

Man's Drowning Hoax Revealed – *Los Angeles Times*, Jun 27, 1928, p. B7

Conjugal Skein In Awful Mess – *Los Angeles Times*, Jul 3, 1928, p. A5

'Widow' Greets 'Dead' Husband in County Jail – *Los Angeles Examiner*, Jul 3, 1928

Suicide Hoax Confessed By Thief Suspect – *Los Angeles Examiner*, Jun 24, 1928, p. 1

Marital Mixup Is Caused by Death Hoax – *Los Angeles Evening Herald*, Vol. LIII, No. 205, Jun 27, 1928, p. A-7

Death Hoax Confession Found True – *Los Angeles Times*, Jul 1, 1928, p. B5

Tenth Story Plunge Fatal – *Los Angeles Examiner*, Vol. L, No. 205, Jul 4, 1953, Sec. 1-5

Woman Dives to Death – *Los Angeles Times*, Jul 4, 1953, p. 2

Mystery Man Sought in Grisly Slayings – Norman B. Chandler/John Kendall, *Los Angeles Times*, Oct 18, 1979, p. SDA8

Ray L. Langer, 63, Dies; Headed Group of Hotels – *Los Angeles Times*, Jul 7, 1948, p. A3

New Hotel Formally Dedicated – *Los Angeles Times*, Aug 15, 1926, p. I8

Mystery of Little Boy – *Los Angeles Times*, Dec 9, 1911, p. II1

Man Dies In Hospital From Dose Of Poison – *Los Angeles Times*, Mar 16, 1926, p. A12

Ends Life After Taxi Drive Here – *Los Angeles Times*, Jul 12, 1925, p. 22

Probably Suicide – *Los Angeles Times*, Feb 10, 1897, p. 8

Old Hotel to Begin a New Life – Evelyn De Wolfe, *Los Angeles Times*, Feb 19, 1989, p. H1

The Mayflower, New Downtown Hostelry, Opens – *Los Angeles Times*, Dec 25, 1927, p. B2

Police Hold Man Posing As Diplomat – *Los Angeles Times*, Mar 24, 1931, p. A12
Work Keeps Her Living High – *Los Angeles Times*, May 28, 1932, p. A2

Chapter 4 – Silver Lake to the SFV

News Of The Cafes – *Los Angeles Times*, Sep 25, 1925, p. A5
Night Life – Wally Guenther, *Los Angeles Times*, Jan 6, 1963, p. L11
Judge Stops Singer From Warbling 'Born in a Bar' – *Los Angeles Times*, Aug 23, 1955, p.11
Blast Damage – *Los Angeles Times*, Apr 1, 1947, p. 3
Man's Body Found in Car Parked at Hotel – *Los Angeles Times*, Sep 25, 1986, p. VA12
Woman, Accused of Trying Husband Last Year, Found Dead – *Los Angeles Times*, May 31, 1968, p. SF8
Huge Hotel Complex to Rise in Universal City – *Los Angeles Times*, Oct 28, 1964, p. A1
Police Seeking Three in Sports Promoter's Death – Nieson Himmel, *Los Angeles Times*, Jun 18, 1980, p. B22
Sports Figure's Body Found in Car Trunk – Tom Paegel/ Kris Lindgren, *Los Angeles Times*, Jun 19, 1979, p. C1
Weiss Dead 48 Hours Before Being Found – Richard West/Kris Lindgren, *Los Angeles Times*, Jun 20, 1979, p. B17
Probe Mystery Slaying –Darrell Walker, *Los Angeles Herald Examiner*, Vol. CIX, No. 79, Jun 19, 1979
Who Shot Vic Weiss? A Trail Gone Cold – Michael Connelly, *Los Angeles Times*, Jun 11, 1989, P.VY6
Officer Shoots Gun From Hand Of Man – Kenneth Hansen, *Los Angeles Times*, Jan 15, 1970, p. SF1

Chapter 5 – Beaches & Further Afield

Murder Laid to Merchant – *Los Angeles Times*, Aug 2, 1932, p. 7
San Diego Taxi Driver Shot Dead – *Los Angeles Examiner*, Aug 1, 1932, Section1, p. 5
San Diego – *Los Angeles Times*, Sep 4, 1978, p. SD2
Man, 31, Leaps to Death From Hotel Window – *Los Angeles Times*, Apr 16, 1983, p. SDA3
Clairemont Man Is Slain in Home – *Los Angeles Times*, May 15, 1988, p. ASD4
Man sought for questioning in death of companion – Joe Hughes, *San Diego Union-Tribune*, May 30, 1997, p. B-4
Jurors find man guilty of killing his girlfriend, unborn child – Bill Callahan, *San Diego Union-Tribune*, Sep 11, 1998, p. B-2
Grotesque Cremation Discovery – John Johnson, *Los Angeles Times*, Jan 3, 1989, p. N4
A Mortuary Tangled in the Macabre – John Johnson, *Los Angeles Times*, Dec 30, 1988, p. C1
Ex-Mortician Charged in Oleander Poisoning – John Johnson, *Los Angeles Times*, Feb 10, 1990, p. B1
Braidhill, Kathy. *Chop Shop – The Grisly True Story of the Lamb Funeral Home Scandal in Southern California* – Pinnacle Books; New York, 1993
Man Wins Suit Against Police – Robert Rawitch, *Los Angeles Times*, Nov 10, 1978, p. B3
Ex-FBI Man Tells of Intrigue With Alleged Spy – William Overend, *Los Angeles Times*, May 5, 1985, p. SDA10

Chapter 6 – Take Out/Off The Menu

Police Question Couple After Call on Strangler – *Los Angeles Times*, Dec 24, 1977, p. 6
Ex-Commander of D.A.V. Dies – *Los Angeles Times*, Aug 4, 1942, p. A8

Hostelry Nets $850,000 In Deal – *Los Angeles Times*, Jul 29, 1928, p. E3

Rites Set Today for TV Actor John Deering – *Los Angeles Times*, Feb 1, 1959, p. A3

The Southland – *Los Angeles Times*, June 21, 1982, p. B2

Desert Manhunt Begun After Officer Shot – Richard West, *Los Angeles Times*, Sep 12, 1983, p. OCA2

Pirates, Pimps, Artists and Anarchy – Dan Kapelovitz, *LA Weekly*, Apr 28, 2005

Man Kills Self in Lake Leap to Evade Arrest – *Los Angeles Times*, Jul 24, 1951, p. I2

Death in MacArthur Park Lake Ends Man's Flight From Police – *Los Angeles Examiner*, Jul 24, 1951, p.1

Gilmore, John. *Severed: The True Story of the Black Dahlia* – Amok Books; 1994

Suspect Held in Stabbing Deaths of 3 – *Los Angeles Times*, Aug 15, 1968, p. B2

6 Stabbed; 'Wild Man' Is Captured – *Los Angeles Examiner*, Vol. XCVIII, No. 141, Aug 14, 1968

"Wagon-Load" Thief Found – *Los Angeles Times*, Nov 22, 1902, p. A1

Would Kiss Detectives – *Los Angeles Times*, Nov 23, 1902, p. B9

Ashes Of The Dead Stolen By Jackson – *Los Angeles Times*, Nov 25, 1902, p. A1

Man Admits Killing Wife and Sending Her Roses – *Los Angeles Times*, Jun 1, 1942, p. 8

Strangles Wife, Slashes Wrists As Love Thwarted – *Los Angeles Examiner*, Vol. XXXIX, No. 172, Jun 1, 1942, Section 1-3

Jealousy Over Wife's Soldier Friend Told In Rose Killing – *Los Angeles Evening Herald-Express*, Vol. LXXII, No. 57, Jun 1, 1942, p. A-2

Article 3 – No Title – *Los Angeles Times*, Jun 1, 1942, p. 8

Wife Killing Case Testimony Begins – *Los Angeles Times*, Jul 30, 1942, p. A2

Wife-Strangler Found Guilty – *Los Angeles Times*, Aug 4, 1942, p. 10
Little Bit of Nashville in North Hollywood – Michael Arkush, *Los Angeles Times*, Jan 20, 1989, p. VYA22
Trial for Suspected Slayer of 6 Ordered – Bill Hazlett, *Los Angeles Times*, Oct 30, 1980, p. D4
Murder Suspect Arraigned on New Counts – Henry Mendoza, *Los Angeles Times*, Aug 15, 1980, p. C4
Sunset Strip Slayer's Girlfriend Pleads Guilty in 2 of the Murders – Ted Rohrlich, *Los Angeles Times*, May 3, 1983, p. B21
'Moors Murders' Pair Given Life Sentences – Robert C. Toth, *Los Angeles Times*, May 7, 1966, p. 9
Lloyd, Georgina. *The Part and Parcel Murders* – Bantam Books; New York, 1994, p.143-153

About The Author

Originally from London, James T. Bartlett has been living in Los Angeles since 2004 and has been a freelance writer since 1999. He has been published in over 100 magazines and newspapers including *Los Angeles Times, LA Weekly, American Way, The Guardian, Hemispheres, Delta Sky, The Telegraph, Variety, The Historian* and *Fortean Times*. He is also a contributor to BBC Radio, BBCAmerica.com and BBC.com. Email him at jbartlett2000@gmail.com

Gourmet Ghosts – Los Angeles, the first book in this series, is available online at Amazon and iTunes, plus at many bookstores and gift shops in L.A. and across California. ISBN 978-0-9849730-0-2 or see www.gourmetghosts.com

Made in the USA
Middletown, DE
19 September 2024